ZAGATSURVEY

2001/2002

WASHINGTON, D.C. BALTIMORE RESTAURANTS

Editors: Shirley Lawrence with Hal Farr

Local Editors: Olga Boikess and Marty Katz

Local Coordinator: Olga Boikess

Published and distributed by
ZAGAT SURVEY, LLC
4 Columbus Circle
New York, New York 10019
Web site: www.zagat.com

ZAGATSURVEY®

2001/2002

WASHINGTON, D.C.
BALTIMORE
RESTAURANTS

Editors: Sinting Lai with Gail Hall Zarr

**Local Editors: Olga Boikess
and Marty Katz**

Local Coordinator: Olga Boikess

Published and distributed by
ZAGAT SURVEY, LLC
4 Columbus Circle
New York, New York 10019
Tel: 212 977 6000
E-mail: washbalt@zagat.com
Web site: www.zagat.com

Acknowledgments

Besides thanking the nearly 3,900 Washington, D.C./ Baltimore restaurant-goers who shared their dining experiences with us, we are especially grateful to Alicia Ault, Darcy Bacon, Richard K. Bank, Cameron Barry, Nicolas Brown, Mary Ann Brownlow, Tom Bryant, Al and Ellen Butts, Karen Cathey, Fred Deutsch, Elaine Eff, Lorraine Fitzsimmons, the Justin Franks, Mark Freeland, Phyllis Frucht, Joanna Golden, Alexandra Greeley, Sue and Sandy Greenberg, Henry Hopkins III, Rochelle Jaffe, Barbara Johnson, Michael J. Kaplan, Jane and Danny Katz, Bill Kopit, Judy Levenson, Sue Ellen Malone, Mike McHale, Angie Miller, Suwanee Nivasabutr, Anne Nix, Richard Pine, David Richardson, Alan Schlaifer, Judy Seidman, Robert Singleton, Sol Snyder, George D. Stewart, Bob and Bonnie Temple and Juliet Zucker for their support. Our special thanks go to Pamela Horvath for her assistance.

This guide would not have been possible without the hard work of our staff: Deirdre Bourdet, Phil Cardone, Reni Chin, Anne Cole, Erica Curtis, Liz Daleske, Jessica Fields, Jeff Freier, Shelley Gallagher, Jessica Gonzalez, Diane Karlin, Natalie Lebert, Mike Liao, Dave Makulec, Jefferson Martin, Lorraine Mead, Andrew O'Neill, Doug Ornstein, Rob Poole, Brooke Rein, Jason Roth, Robert Seixas, Zamira Skalkottas, LaShana Smith and Kyle Zolner.

Contents

What's New

Shifting political sands and economic indicators haven't slaked Washington, D.C. and Baltimore area appetites, judging by their thriving dining scenes. Among significant trends:

• **Meat Mania Hits D.C.:** The nation's steakhouse boom resounds in its capital city, reflecting the area's prosperity and this dining genre's time-honored cachet. High-on-the-hoof chains like Nick & Stef's (brainchild of LA wunderkind Joachim Splichal), NYC's Angelo and Maxie's, and Shula's Steak House (coached by football legend Don Shula) opened sites in prime Downtown, Reston and Dupont Circle South locations respectively. And Capital Grille and Morton's court Tysons Corner and Reston dot-coms at additional sites. Meanwhile, hometown red-meat-and-greet specialists from Sam & Harry's joined big name investors to host the political and business elite at the ultra-clubby Caucus Room, and Blackie's multimillion-dollar upgrade turned a local institution into a happening address.

• **Top Toques Take Over:** Several of the city's most talented chefs are now cooking in their own restaurants. White House alumnus Frank Ruta's French- and Italian-influenced main dishes and Ann Amernick's desserts pack Palena in Cleveland Park. Susan Lindeborg's (ex Morrison-Clark Inn) modern Chesapeake and American classics fit perfectly her recast of Old Town Alexandria's Majestic Cafe, while Cesare Lanfranconi (ex Galileo) earns applause Downtown for Tosca, his svelte, contemporary Northern Italian.

• **Coming Attractions:** Star chef Bob Kinkead (Kinkead's) is slated to open Colvin Run Tavern in Primi Piatti's former Tysons Corner space, Peter Pastan's (Obelisk) Neapolitan-inspired pizzeria will soon fire up in Northwest D.C., and Northern VA techies await NYC-based Cello, whose deluxe digs and French seafood have Big Apple high rollers enthralled.

• **Bigger Is Better in Baltimore:** Despite economic worries and the passing of old-food stalwart Peerce's, Baltimore restaurants like Black Olive, Helen's Garden, Samos and San Sushi have all expanded next door, and Szechuan House is poised to do the same. Charleston, the Helmand and Ruth's Chris each have new siblings, Petit Louis, Tapas Teatro and Eurasian Harbor respectively. Both Bo Brooks Crab House and ESPN Zone have added dining barges. And in Easton, a bubbling pot of new talents – General Tanuki's, Inn at Easton, Mason's and Out of the Fire – joined Stephen Mangasarian (Columbia) in redefining Shore dining out.

• **Tabs Stay Trim:** Despite the continuing influx of world-class eateries, it's good news that the average cost to dine out in Washington, D.C. is a reasonable $28.77, and in Baltimore, an even better deal at $25.89.

Washington, D.C.   Olga Boikess
Baltimore, MD   Marty Katz
July 17, 2001

About This Survey

This *2001/2002 Survey* is an update reflecting significant developments since our last *Washington, D.C./Baltimore Restaurant Survey* was published. To bring this guide up to the minute, we have included 70 places that were not in the previous edition, as well as made changes throughout to indicate new addresses, branches and phone numbers, plus decor and chef changes and other new developments.

As a whole, this *Survey* covers 1,055 restaurants in the Washington, Baltimore and Annapolis areas, with input from nearly 3,900 people. We want to thank each of our participants. They are a widely diverse group in every respect but one – they are food lovers all. This book is really "theirs." Our reviews are designed to synopsize our surveyors' opinions, with exact comments shown in "quotes."

Of course, we are especially grateful to our editors, Olga Boikess, a Washington lawyer and avid restaurant-goer who has organized, edited and updated this *Survey* since it was first published in the fall of 1986, and Marty Katz, a photographer and writer who provided his insights on the Baltimore and Annapolis-area food scenes. Over the years, both Olga and Marty have gone beyond our expectations in putting their hearts, as well as their time, into producing this book. In the process, they have become two of our most valued friends.

To help guide our readers to the area's best meals and best buys, we have prepared a number of lists. See, for example, Washington's Most Popular restaurants (page 9), Top Ratings (pages 10–14) and Best Buys (page 15) and Baltimore's Most Popular restaurants (page 161), Top Ratings (pages 162–165) and Best Buys (page 166). To assist the user in finding just the right restaurant for any occasion, we have also provided handy indexes.

As companions to this guide, we also publish *America's Best Meal Deals*, *America's Top Restaurants* and *Top U.S. Hotels, Resorts & Spas*. To check out these or any of our other *Zagat Surveys* to more than 40 major markets, including London, Paris and Tokyo, see our Web site, zagat.com, where you can also vote or shop.

Your comments, suggestions and even criticisms of this *Survey* are also solicited. There is always room for improvement with your help. Contact us at washbalt@zagat.com, or write us at Zagat Survey, 4 Columbus Circle, New York, NY 10019.

New York, NY
July 17, 2001

Nina and Tim

Nina and Tim Zagat

Key to Ratings/Symbols

Name, Address & Phone Number

Zagat Ratings

Hours & Credit Cards

F	D	S	C
▽ 23	9	13	$15

Tim & Nina's ◑ 🅂 ⊅

4 Columbus Circle (8th Ave.), 212-977-6000

☑ Open 24/7, this "crowded", "overpopular" joint started the "Swedish-Mexican craze" (i.e. herring or lox on tiny tacos with mole or chimichurri sauce); though it looks like a "garage" and T & N "never heard of credit cards or reservations" – yours in particular – "dirt cheap" tabs for *"muy bien eats"* draw demented "debit-account" diners to this "deep dive."

Review, with surveyors' comments in quotes

Restaurants with the highest overall ratings and greatest popularity and importance are printed in CAPITAL LETTERS.

Before each review a symbol indicates whether responses were uniform ■ or mixed ☑.

Hours: ◑ serves after 11 PM
🅂 open on Sunday

Credit Cards: ⊅ no credit cards accepted

Ratings: Food, Decor and Service are rated on a scale of **0** to **30**. The Cost (C) column reflects our surveyors' estimate of the price of dinner including one drink and tip.

F Food	D Decor	S Service	C Cost
23	9	13	$15

0–9 poor to fair	**20–25** very good to excellent
10–15 fair to good	**26–30** extraordinary to perfection
16–19 good to very good	▽ low response/less reliable

A place listed without ratings is either an important **newcomer** or a popular **write-in**. For such places, the estimated cost is indicated by the following symbols.

I	$15 and below	E	$31 to $50
M	$16 to $30	VE	$51 or more

Washington, D.C.'s Most Popular

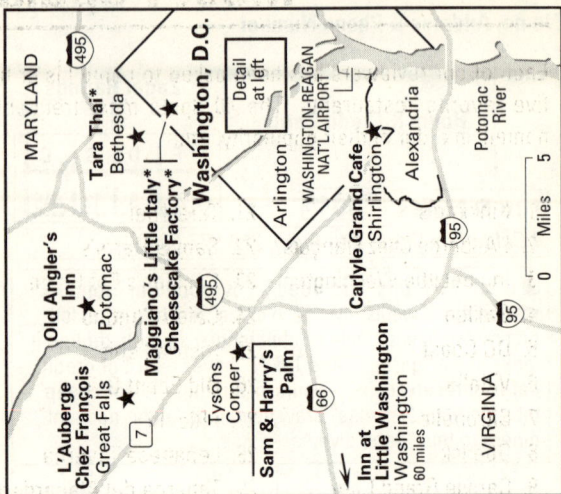

MARYLAND

495

Tara Thai*
Bethesda

Old Angler's
Inn
Potomac

L'Auberge
Chez François
Great Falls

Maggiano's Little Italy*
Cheesecake Factory*

Washington, D.C.

Detail
at left

WASHINGTON-REAGAN
NAT'L AIRPORT

Arlington

Alexandria

Potomac
River

Carlyle Grand Cafe
Shirlington

95

0   5
Miles

495

7

Tysons
Corner

Sam & Harry's Palm

66

Inn at
Little Washington
Washington
60 miles

Little Washington

VIRGINIA

95

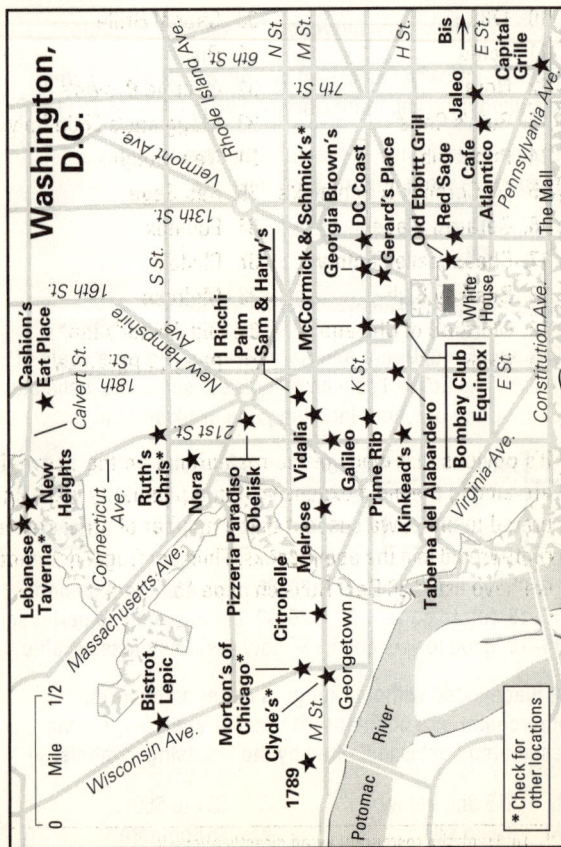

Washington,
D.C.

N St.

M St.

6th St.

Rhode Island Ave.

7th St.

H St.

E St.

Bis

Capital
Grille

Jaleo

Atlantico

Cafe

Red Sage

Vermont Ave.

13th St.

Old Ebbitt Grill

DC Coast

Gerard's Place

Georgia Brown's

McCormick & Schmick's*

S St.

16th St.

I Ricchi
Palm
Sam & Harry's

Pennsylvania Ave.

The Mall

White
House

New Hampshire Ave.

Cashion's
Eat Place

Calvert St.

18th St.

Bombay Club
Equinox

Constitution Ave.

E St.

New Heights

Ruth's Chris*

Nora

21st St.

Vidalia

Galileo

K St.

Prime Rib

Kinkead's

Taberna del Alabardero

Virginia Ave.

Lebanese Taverna*

Connecticut Ave.

Massachusetts Ave.

Pizzeria Paradiso

Obelisk

Melrose

Citronelle

Bistrot
Lepic

Morton's of
Chicago*

Clyde's*

Georgetown

M St.

Wisconsin Ave.

1789

0   1/2
Mile

River

Potomac
River

* Check for
other locations

8

www.zagat.com

Washington, D.C.'s Most Popular

Each of our reviewers has been asked to name his or her five favorite restaurants. The 40 spots most frequently named, in order of their popularity, are:

1. Kinkead's
2. L'Auberge Chez François
3. Inn at Little Washington
4. Galileo
5. DC Coast
6. Vidalia
7. Citronelle
8. Obelisk
9. Carlyle Grand Cafe
10. 1789
11. Jaleo
12. Nora
13. Ruth's Chris
14. Prime Rib
15. McCormick & Schmick's
16. Gerard's Place
17. Cheesecake Factory
18. Bombay Club
19. Morton's of Chicago
20. Palm
21. Tara Thai
22. Sam & Harry's
23. Cashion's Eat Place
24. Cafe Atlantico
25. Bistrot Lepic
26. Old Ebbitt Grill
27. I Ricchi
28. Lebanese Taverna
29. Taberna del Alabardero
30. Capital Grille
31. Bis
32. Georgia Brown's
33. Maggiano's Little Italy
34. New Heights
35. Red Sage
36. Equinox
37. Clyde's
38. Melrose
39. Old Angler's Inn*
40. Pizzeria Paradiso

It's obvious that many of the restaurants on the above list are among the most expensive, but if popularity were calibrated to price, we suspect that a number of other restaurants would join the above ranks. Thus, for frugal gourmets, we have listed 80 Best Buys on page 15.

---

* Tied with the restaurant listed directly above it

Top Ratings

Top lists exclude restaurants with low voting.

Top Food Ranking

29 Inn at Little Washington
28 Makoto
27 Kinkead's
   Citronelle
   Gerard's Place
   Obelisk
   L'Auberge Chez François
   Melrose
   L'Auberge Provencale
   Marcel's*
26 Galileo
   Vidalia
   Prime Rib
   Prince Michel
   1789
   Seasons
   Nora
25 Kaz Sushi Bistro
   Morton's of Chicago
   Rabieng

Persimmon
DC Coast
Ashby Inn
I Ricchi*
Pizzeria Paradiso*
La Bergerie
Taberna del Alabardero
Pasta Mia
Morrison-Clark Inn
Ruth's Chris
Sushi-Ko*
Bistrot Lepic
Four & Twenty Blackbirds
Duangrat's
Jerry Seafood*
Five Guys
Bombay Club
Jefferson Restaurant
Bis
24 Peking Gourmet Inn

Top Food by Cuisine

American (New)
27 Kinkead's
   Melrose
26 Vidalia
   1789
   Seasons

Asian
24 Yanyu
23 Asia Nora
20 Oodles Noodles
   Zuki Moon
18 Teaism

Barbecue
22 Rockland's
20 Red Hot & Blue
   Old Glory BBQ
19 Old Hickory Grill
18 King St. Blues

Cajun/Creole/New Orleans
22 R.T.'s
   Black's Bar & Kitchen
21 Cafe Marianna
20 Cajun Bangkok
   Louisiana Express Co.

Chinese
24 Peking Gourmet Inn
   Mr. K's
22 Mark's Duck House
   Hollywood East
   Taipei/Tokyo Cafe

Continental
24 Ritz-Carlton/Grill
22 Village Bistro
21 Tivoli
19 Serbian Crown

French (Bistro)
25 Bistrot Lepic
   Bis
23 La Cote d'Or Cafe
   La Chaumiere
   Le Refuge

French (Classic)
27 L'Auberge Chez François
25 La Bergerie
23 Jean-Michel
22 La Colline
   La Miche

* Tied with the restaurant listed directly above it

French (New)
- **27** Citronelle
  - Gerard's Place
  - Marcel's
- **24** Willard Room
- **22** Saveur

Hamburgers
- **25** Five Guys
- **24** Carlyle Grand Cafe
- **23** Addie's
- **21** Mike's American Grill
  - Occidental

Indian
- **25** Bombay Club
- **24** Udupi Palace
- **23** Heritage India
  - Haandi
  - Bombay Palace

Italian
- **27** Obelisk
- **26** Galileo
- **25** I Ricchi
  - Pasta Mia
- **24** Teatro Goldoni

Japanese
- **28** Makoto
- **25** Kaz Sushi Bistro
  - Sushi-Ko
- **24** Sushi Taro
  - Tachibana

Latin/South American
- **23** El Pollo Rico
  - Cafe Atlantico
- **22** Crisp & Juicy
- **21** Lauriol Plaza
- **20** Grill from Ipanema

Mediterranean
- **23** Mezza 9
- **22** Mediterranee
- **21** Cafe Promenade
- **20** Skewer's/Cafe Luna
  - Palomino Euro Bistro

Mexican/Tex-Mex
- **21** Lauriol Plaza
  - California Tortilla
  - Rio Grande Cafe
- **18** Cactus Cantina
  - Mi Rancho

Middle Eastern
- **23** Lebanese Taverna
- **22** Le Tarbouche
  - Kazan
  - Faryab Afghan
- **21** Bacchus

Pizza
- **25** Pizzeria Paradiso
- **23** Pasta Plus
  - Dolce Vita
- **20** Faccia Luna
- **19** Coppi's

Seafood
- **27** Kinkead's
- **25** DC Coast
  - Jerry Seafood
- **24** Pesce
  - Johnny's Half Shell

Southern
- **26** Vidalia
- **23** Georgia Brown's
- **21** Florida Ave. Grill
- **20** B. Smith's
- **19** Heart In Hand

Southwestern
- **23** Gabriel
- **21** Sweetwater Tavern
  - Red Sage
- **20** Silverado
- **19** Cottonwood Cafe

Spanish
- **25** Taberna del Alabardero
- **23** Jaleo
- **21** Lauriol Plaza
  - Andalucia
- **16** Toro Tapas

Steakhouse
- **26** Prime Rib
- **25** Morton's
  - Ruth's Chris
- **24** Palm
  - Sam & Harry's

Thai
- **25** Rabieng
  - Duangrat's
- **23** T.H.A.I.
- **22** Tara Thai
  - Crystal Thai

Top Food

Vegetarian Friendly
26 Nora
24 New Heights
   Udupi Palace
20 Vegetable Garden
19 Thyme Square

Vietnamese
24 Taste of Saigon
22 Pho 75
   Nam Viet
21 Queen Bee
   Saigonnais

Top Food by Special Feature

Breakfast*
23 Patisserie Poupon
22 La Colline
21 Bread Line
20 Old Ebbitt Grill
19 Original Pancake Hse.

Brunch
27 Kinkead's
   Melrose
26 Seasons
25 Morrison-Clark Inn
– Maestro

Business Lunch
27 Kinkead's
   Citronelle
   Gerard's Place
   Melrose
26 Galileo

Family Dining
23 Lebanese Taverna
22 Matuba
21 Rio Grande Cafe
   P.F. Chang's
20 Red Hot & Blue

Hotel Dining
27 Citronelle
   Latham Hotel
   Melrose
   Park Hyatt
26 Seasons
   Four Seasons
25 Morrison-Clark Inn
   Morrison-Clark Inn
   Jefferson Restaurant
   Jefferson Hotel

Newcomers/Unrated
   Caucus Room
   Majestic Cafe
   Nick & Stef's Steakhouse
   Palena
   Tosca

Saturday Lunch
27 Melrose
25 Bistrot Lepic
   Duangrat's
24 Pesce
– Majestic Cafe

Top of the Hill
25 Bis
22 La Colline
21 Two Quail
   Barolo
   La Brasserie

Worth a Trip
29 Inn at Little Washington
   Washington, VA
27 L'Auberge Provencale
   Boyce, VA
26 Prince Michel
   Leon, VA
25 Ashby Inn
   Paris, VA
   Four & Twenty Blackbirds
   Flint Hill, VA

---

* Other than hotels

Top Decor Ranking

29	Inn at Little Washington	Bis
28	Willard Room	Marcel's
27	Lafayette	Ashby Inn
	L'Auberge Chez François	DC Coast
	Ritz-Carlton/Grill	Le Tarbouche
26	L'Auberge Provencale	Red Sage
	Jefferson Restaurant	Dante
	1789	Galileo
	Teatro Goldoni	Kinkead's
	Seasons	Nora
	Bombay Club	23 Sequoia
25	Morrison-Clark Inn	La Ferme
	Taberna del Alabardero	Two Quail
	Citronelle	Matisse
	Melrose	La Bergerie
	Prime Rib	Mr. K's
	Palomino Euro Bistro	Makoto
	Coeur De Lion	701
	Yanyu	Occidental
24	Old Angler's Inn	Capital Grille

Outdoor

Gerard's Place	Old Angler's Inn
Hermitage Inn	Perry's
La Brasserie	Sequoia
L'Auberge Chez François	Tahoga

Rooms

Bis	Maestro
Bombay Club	Morrison-Clark Inn
Citronelle	Red Sage
DC Coast	Ritz-Carlton/Grill
Galileo	Seasons
Inn at Little Washington	1789
Jefferson Restaurant	Teatro Goldoni
Lafayette	Ten Pehn
Le Tarbouche	Willard Room

Views

Bleu Rock Inn	Potowmack Landing
Le Rivage	Roof Terrace Kennedy Ctr.
New Heights	Ruth's Chris (Crystal City)
Perry's	Sequoia

Top Service Ranking

29 Inn at Little Washington
27 L'Auberge Chez François
26 Prince Michel
 Obelisk
 Seasons
 Willard Room
 Melrose
 L'Auberge Provencale
 Makoto
25 Gerard's Place
 Prime Rib
 1789
 Coeur De Lion
 Kinkead's
 Citronelle
 Bombay Club
 Jefferson Restaurant
24 Ashby Inn
 Marcel's
 Morrison-Clark Inn

 Ritz-Carlton/Grill
 Taberna del Alabardero
 Vidalia
 Lafayette
 Nora
 Galileo
 La Bergerie
 Palm
 Fairmont Bar & Dining
 Mr. K's*
 Sam & Harry's
23 Morton's of Chicago
 Four & Twenty Blackbirds
 Rupperts
 Ruth's Chris
 701
 Bleu Rock Inn
 Dante
 Capital Grille
 Persimmon

---

* Tied with the restaurant listed directly above it

Best Buys

Top Bangs for the Buck

List derived by dividing the cost of a meal into its ratings.

1. Five Guys
2. Ben's Chili Bowl
3. California Tortilla
4. Panera Bread
5. El Pollo Rico
6. Burro
7. Firehook Bakery
8. Bob & Edith's Diner
9. Tryst
10. Così Sandwich Bar
11. Crisp & Juicy
12. Burrito Brothers
13. Bread Line
14. Wrap Works
15. C.F. Folks
16. A&J Restaurant
17. Florida Ave. Grill
18. Patisserie Poupon
19. Joe's Place
20. Original Pancake Hse.
21. Hard Times Cafe
22. Udupi Palace
23. Food Factory
24. Samadi Sweets
25. Moby Dick
26. Pho 75
27. Havana Breeze
28. Teaism
29. Haad Thai
30. Generous George's
31. Mexicali Blues
32. La Madeleine
33. Taipei/Tokyo Cafe
34. Parkway Deli
35. T.H.A.I.
36. Faccia Luna Pizzeria
37. Simply Grill
38. Ruan Thai
39. Cafe Parisien Express
40. Bombay Curry Co.

Additional Good Values

Bangkok Garden
Bombay Club
Cafe Marianna
Cafe Midi Cuisine
Cafe New Delhi
Cajun Bangkok
Carlyle Grand Cafe
El Gavilan
Fairmont Bar & Dining
Full Kee
Greenfield Churrascaria
Hope Key
Horace & Dickie's
Houston's
Il Radicchio
Iota
Johnny's Half Shell
Kabul Caravan
Lauriol Plaza
Lebanese Taverna
Levante's
Los Chorros
Lotte Plaza Market
Malibu Grill Brazilian
Martin's Tavern
Medaterra
Mehak
Neisha Thai
Old Hickory Grill
Pasta Mia
Raaga
Ricciuti's
Rockland's
Rocky's Cafe
Savory
Thai Basil
Thai Derm
Tony Cheng's
White Tiger
Zuki Moon

Washington, D.C.
Restaurant Directory

Washington, D.C.

F | D | S | C

A&J Restaurant 🅂 ⊅　　　　　20 | 6 | 16 | $11
*Little River Ctr., 4316B Markham St. (Little River Tpke.),
Annandale, VA, 703-813-8181*
*Woodmont Ctr., 1319C Rockville Pike (bet. Talbott St. &
Templeton Pl.), Rockville, MD, 301-251-7878*
■ The dim sum and noodle soups at this "no-frills, small-bills" Rockville Northern Chinese are so "terrific" that diners
don't "worry about the lack of decor"; satisfied fans advise
neophytes to "navigate carefully" among the "authentic"
choices (which draw an Asian clientele) because the
staff can't always "explain the menu in English"; N.B. the
Virginia branch is unrated.

Aaranthi 🅂　　　　　∇ 19 | 14 | 17 | $19
*Dana Plaza, 409 Maple Ave. E. (Beulah Rd.), Vienna, VA,
703-938-0100*
◪ A "fresh, reasonably" priced lunch buffet helps this "strip
mall" Indian "compete" for local biz in Vienna, even if the
menu garners mixed reactions from surveyors; likewise,
reports on the service range from they "really care"
to merely "perfunctory."

Addie's 🅂　　　　　23 | 14 | 19 | $33
*11120 Rockville Pike (Edson Ln.), Rockville, MD,
301-881-0081*
■ "Whimsical and creative", this "service-minded"
New American "gem" earns applause for "cheerfully"
delivering "unexpected quality on the [Rockville] Pike"
in a "sweet" cottage setting; though a few grouches gripe
that it's "a tad too rustic" (it's "like eating a gourmet meal
in your dining room"), the majority regard it as "one of the
best" in the area.

Aditi 🅂　　　　　22 | 14 | 19 | $21
3299 M St., NW (33rd St.), 202-625-6825
Amma 🅂
3291 M St., NW (33rd St.), 202-625-6625
Amma Vegetarian Kitchen 🅂
*344A Maple Ave. E. (bet. Beulah Rd. & Park St.), Vienna,
VA, 703-938-5328*
◪ Known for "consistently good" food and "reasonable"
prices, Aditi is perhaps "the best Indian" in "hard-to-park"
Georgetown, albeit that's "not saying much" according to
critics of its "Americanized" spicing and "uninspired" decor;
relocated a few doors away is Amma, its Vegetarian cousin,
and there's a new second cousin in Vienna, VA.

Agrodolce S ▽ 22 | 18 | 21 | $25
21030J Frederick Rd. (Father Hurley Blvd.), Germantown, MD,
301-528-6150
■ Find "real" Italian food, "beautiful courtyard" dining and a "pleasant" interior at this "up-and-comer" "north of the Beltway"; Germantown locals appreciate the "fresh and reliable" dishes, as well as the "friendly" servers.

Akasaka S ▽ 21 | 14 | 18 | $23
Van Dorn Station Shopping Ctr., 514C S. Van Dorn St.
(bet. Edsall & S. Pickett Rds.), Alexandria, VA, 703-751-3133
■ Tucked away in a strip mall near Alexandria's Landmark Plaza, this little-known spot provides "good" Japanese food (including some of the "best cold noodles in town") in "orderly" surroundings at "affordable prices"; sushi seekers know to sit at the counter to watch the chef in action.

Al Tiramisu S 23 | 18 | 22 | $40
2014 P St., NW (bet. 20th & 21st Sts.), 202-467-4466
☑ Romantic couples at this "dark", "intimate" Dupont Circle Italian love nest "cuddle up" and then "loosen their belts" in anticipation of the "delectable" dishes served by an "enthusiastic" staff; but while the owners are "personable", some find their "schmooze" a bit "overbearing" and others warn of "sticker shock" when those "marvelous specials" turn out to be much "more expensive than the menu items."

America ◑S 12 | 16 | 13 | $21
Union Station, 50 Massachusetts Ave., NE (N. Capitol St.),
202-682-9555
☑ The all-American menu at this "too loud" Union Station "tourist haunt" is as "huge" as the room is "big", but while it offers lots of "variety", it gets better ratings for the "great" people-watching than for the "mass-produced" quality.

Andalucia S 21 | 18 | 20 | $34
4931 Elm St. (Arlington Rd.), Bethesda, MD, 301-907-0052
12300 Wilkins Ave. (Park Dr.), Rockville, MD, 301-770-1880
☑ "Basic but very good" "garlicky" food and flamenco music (Rockville only) provide a mostly convincing "touch of Spain" at these separately run Iberians; the "more formal" Bethesda branch "lights up" when owner Joaquin Serrano is there supervising, though others prefer Maria Serrano's (his ex-wife) "comforting" Rockville locale.

Andaman S – | – | – | M
4828 Cordell Ave. (Woodmont Ave.), Bethesda, MD, 301-654-4676
Thai tapas are featured at this striking new Bethesda Asian whose two-story bar and dining areas use bay windows, plush fabrics and dark wood accents for a serenely dramatic effect; named for the sea southwest of Thailand, its wide-ranging, seafood-strong menu lists over 30 small plates, plus entrées, 'wild things' (wok-fried frogs legs), a veggie section and sizzling platters to keep the kids enthralled.

Angelo & Maxie's/Generation 2 S | – | – | – | E |
901 F St., NW (9th St.), 202-639-9330
Reston Town Ctr., 11911 Democracy Dr. (Reston Pkwy.),
Reston, VA, 703-904-4313
Deliberate decadence sets the tone at this high-energy
Downtown steakhouse, an over-the-top '30s supper club
recreation with oversized steaks, a raw bar, an extensive
roster of starters, a whimsically-themed cigar bar and every
trendy libation known to twenty- and thirtysomething
professionals – if its New York moxie doesn't make it in
DC, it won't be because it hasn't tried; N.B. Reston's high-
end demographics just generated another 'Gen 2' branch.

Arbor S | – | – | – | M |
2400 18th St., NW (Belmont Rd.), 202-667-1200
Perched on Adams Morgan's prime people-watching corner,
this engaging Contemporary American offers a a primo
destination for affordable, everyday eating, with entrées
ranging from beef filet to compositions with lots of garden
stuff in the center of the plate (think salad in a pizza crust);
lovely greenery and chic white-washed simplicity make it
feel like spring inside, while those outdoor tables should
keep this spot 'action central' at brunch.

Ardeo S | 22 | 21 | 20 | $40 |
3311 Connecticut Ave., NW (Macomb St.), 202-244-6750
■ "Ardent admirers" give this bastion of "Cleveland Park
chic" solid marks all around for its "appealing" New
American food, "avant-garde" decor, "attentive" service
and "almost too animated" atmosphere; it's one of those
places where the "whole is greater than the sum of its
parts", not to mention that it's a "favorite of media celebs";
N.B. look for Bardeo, a smart wine bar with its own tasting
menu, to open next door.

Argia S | ▽ 23 | 23 | 20 | $28 |
124 N. Washington St. (bet. Broad St. & Park Ave.),
Falls Church, VA, 703-534-1033
■ Falls Church supporters salute this "good" young Italian
"in a dining-poor area" near the State Theatre for its
"authentic" cooking, "lively" vibe and "remarkable" value
(with single and table-size serving options); though it's still
"working out the kinks", optimists are ready to "go back."

Arigato | ▽ 23 | 15 | 16 | $21 |
13039 Fair Lakes Shopping Ctr. (Fair Lakes Blvd.), Fairfax,
VA, 703-449-8404
11199 Lee Hwy. (Rust Rd.), Fairfax, VA, 703-352-9338 S
■ At these "comfortable" Fairfax Japanese twins, the "witty
sushi chefs" and "attentive" staff will make you "feel
welcome" as they serve you "great" appetizers (some
quite "unique") and "awesome" raw fish; local boosters
also say *arigato* (thanks) for "highly recommended"
specialties like *tonkatsu*.

Artie's S 21 | 17 | 20 | $25
3260 Old Lee Hwy. (south of Fairfax Circle), Fairfax, VA,
703-273-7600
■ A "consistent crowd-pleaser", this "dark", clubby
American – one of "too few decent eateries in Fairfax" – is a
"working lunch" staple and a "regulars' sort of place" at
night, thanks to its "well-prepared" fare (especially the
"distinctive" ozzie rolls) and "friendly" service; popularity
has its price though, so prepare for a "long wait."

Arucola S 17 | 15 | 16 | $29
5534 Connecticut Ave., NW (Morrison St.), 202-244-1555
☑ "Cosmopolitan yet neighborly", this Italian trattoria in
Chevy Chase is an "indispensable" resource for "something
light outdoors", an early family dinner or a bite "after the
movies"; detractors, however, are "disappointed" with the
"inconsistent food and service" and "chaotic" ambiance;
P.S. it's "cheaper and less crowded at lunch."

ASHBY INN S 25 | 24 | 24 | $47
692 Federal St. (Rte. 759), Paris, VA, 540-592-3900
■ "See the stars at Sky Meadows, then have dinner in Paris
(VA, that is)" at this New American inn that's definitely
"worth the drive"; owners John and Roma Sherman "do it
all" and do it "right", providing a "well-thought-out" menu
matched with "great" wines in "unstuffy" surroundings;
P.S. check out the "great romantic" Sunday brunch and
ask about the winery tours nearby.

Asia Nora 23 | 23 | 21 | $43
2213 M St., NW (bet. 22nd & 23rd Sts.), 202-797-4860
☑ The "phenomenal" tasting menu at this "cool and
sophisticated" "exotic treat" in the West End showcases
"adventurous" Asian fusion cuisine based on "organic"
ingredients and enhanced by "jewel-like" presentations; the
"beautiful" room adds to the experience, though critics cite
the "precious" ambiance and "too-small portions."

Austin Grill S 18 | 17 | 18 | $21
750 E St., NW (bet. 7th & 8th Sts.), 202-393-3776
2404 Wisconsin Ave., NW (bet. Calvert & Hall Sts.), 202-337-8080
7278 Woodmont Ave. (Elm Ave.), Bethesda, MD, 301-656-1366
8430A Old Keene Mill Rd. (Rolling Rd.), Springfield, VA,
703-644-3111
South Austin Grill S
801 King St. (Columbus St.), Alexandria, VA, 703-684-8969
☑ Amigos of this wildly popular Tex-Mex chain "go for the
swirlies [margaritas] and stay for the fun", as well as for
the kitchen's "fresh" takes on Southwestern standards, such
as portobello fajitas; purists, however, pan the "bland" fare,
"frat-scene" atmosphere and "inexperienced" service.

Bacchus
21 | 17 | 19 | $28

1827 Jefferson Pl., NW (bet. 18th & 19th Sts.), 202-785-0734
7945 Norfolk Ave. (Del Rey Ave.), Bethesda, MD,
301-657-1722 S

■ "Make a meal" out of the "marvelous" "meze, meze, meze" at these Lebanese meccas in Dupont Circle and Bethesda, which are ideal for "sharing" small plates; sure, their "authentic" decor is starting to "show wear" (right "down to the crooked pictures"), but surveyors agree they remain "dependable", "urbane" sites for both diplomatic and "corporate outings."

Bailiwick Inn S
_ | _ | _ | VE

4023 Chain Bridge Rd. (Main St.), Fairfax, VA, 703-691-2266
At their civilized, Downtown Fairfax landmark inn, Ann and Christopher Sheldon help grown-ups unwind over French- and American-accented Continental dinners (prix fixe $55–$65, wine not included), formally served in an intimate, 19th-century dining room or on the terrace; afternoon tea (Thursday and Sunday), à la carte lunches (Wednesday and Friday) and monthly Wine Master Dinners (reserve early) provide more ways to decompress; N.B. children under 18 are welcome for private functions only.

Bambulé S
14 | 18 | 15 | $32

5225 Wisconsin Ave., NW (Jennifer St.), 202-966-0300
◪ This trendy Chevy Chase bistro's "heated terrace", "billowy curtains" and "big" "fluffy sofas" help make it a "relaxing", "upscale" place for an "after-work" or late-night rendezvous; critics, however, argue that the Mediterranean food is "pedestrian" and note that while the setting is "good for people-watching, there's no one interesting to watch."

Banana Cafe S
17 | 17 | 16 | $20

500 Eighth St., SE (E St.), 202-543-5906
■ Cubanos call this "cheery" Capitol Hill spot a "charming" "letter from home", a haven with hearty Latino food ("morsels of pork, black beans, rice and plantains equal heaven"), "colorful characters", a humming piano bar upstairs (with "wonderful" atmosphere) and a "different" kind of Sunday brunch; tip: in warm weather try to "sit outside" on the patio.

Bangkok Bistro S
21 | 18 | 19 | $22

3251 Prospect St., NW (bet. 33rd St. & Wisconsin Ave.),
202-337-2424
■ Folks looking for affordable Georgetown dining "Thai a ribbon around" this "very hip" taste of Bangkok, which is "too often forgotten" but pleases plenty of partisans with a menu chock-full of "spicy goodness", "cool" "funkadelic" decor and "friendly" service; "great" sidewalk cafe seating and speedy delivery are bonuses.

Bangkok Garden § 20 | 14 | 19 | $21
4906 St. Elmo Ave. (Old Georgetown Rd.), Bethesda, MD,
301-951-0670

▣ Long known as a "casual", "comfortable" Bethesda
ethnic stalwart where it's "easy to get seated and served
quickly", this Thai veteran's amiable staff will also happily
"advise novices" about the "very good" dishes on the
menu; while the decor used to be a weak point, a "lovely
renovation" (with new carpeting, tables and lighting) has
ameliorated the situation.

Barolo 21 | 18 | 22 | $40
223 Pennsylvania Ave., SE (bet. 2nd & 3rd Sts.),
202-547-5011

▣ Perhaps the "last lobbyist restaurant on the House side",
this pricey Piedmontese "hideaway" is "worth going to
even if you're not" wining and dining a pol swear Hill
insiders; located on the second floor of a townhouse, it
features *"alta cucina"* preparations (notably "innovative
pastas") and "personal service with style"; "romantic"
types recommend a table in the "great" front room, which
boasts a fireplace and view of the Capitol.

BD's Mongolian BBQ § 16 | 13 | ◄15 | $19
7201 Wisconsin Ave. (bet. Bethesda Ave. & Willow Ln.),
Bethesda, MD, 301-657-1080

☒ Since you assemble your own meal from the salad bar–
style setup of ingredients (a choice of meats, poultry,
vegetables, sauces, oils and spices) at this "crowded"
all-you-can-eat Mongolian BBQ in Bethesda, "students,
families and cheapskates" say "you have no one to blame" if
your stir-fry disappoints; while party poopers pontificate
that "if I wanted to cook my own meal I would've stayed
home", more find it a "fun" "interactive" concept.

BeDuCi § 19 | 18 | 19 | $36
2100 P St., NW (21st St.), 202-223-3824

☒ "Warm", "delightful" owners who "work the room" and
"great" Dupont Circle people-watching from an enclosed
"street veranda" lend a "European feel" to this "quiet"
Mediterranean; the prix fixe lunch is a "bargain", but
otherwise it can be a tad "pricey" for a little local place.

Bella Luna § ▽ 19 | 17 | 17 | $22
9401 Lee Hwy. (Blake Ln.), Fairfax, VA, 703-383-6968

☒ "Hidden" in a Fairfax office building, this Italian's location
might discourage some from trying what many locals tout
as "good-to-excellent" eating; for a virtually risk-free way
to find out whether the cooking is truly *bella*, consider the
inexpensive serve-yourself lunch spread ($6.95) or the
champagne buffet brunch ($12.95).

Benjarong S
— — — M
Wintergreen Plaza, 885 Rockville Pike (Edmundson Dr.),
Rockville, MD, 301-424-5533
The reopening of what many consider Rockville's top Thai
at a different, larger locale in the same shopping center
has fans angling for weekend tables, especially now that
its subdued, elegant decor and handsome bar add another
dimension to the meal; early reports are that the hiatus
didn't dampen the kitchen's fire as it still turns out spirited
versions of regional dishes that play off nicely against the
polite and soothing ambiance.

Ben's Chili Bowl ● S ⌿
20 12 17 $9
1213 U St., NW (bet. 12th & 13th Sts.), 202-667-0909
■ Beloved as "a great DC landmark", this "historic" "late-
night oasis" can be found "on a stretch of U Street that's
getting better all the time"; the kitchen satisfies with "sinfully
tasty", "low-cost, high-cholesterol" diner food highlighted
by "the best" chili dogs, cheese fries and milk shakes.

Bertucci's S
17 15 16 $17
1218-20 Connecticut Ave., NW (Jefferson Pl.), 202-463-7733
2000 Pennsylvania Ctr., 2000 Pennsylvania Ave., NW
(bet. 20th & 21st Sts.), 202-296-2600
6525 Frontier Dr. (Franconia Rd.), Springfield, VA, 703-313-6700
8027 Leesburg Pike (off Rte. 495), Tysons Corner, VA,
703-893-5200
725 King St. (Columbus St.), Alexandria, VA, 703-548-8500
◨ Nearly 1,000 surveyors weighed in on this Italian chain,
so there's bound to be disagreement: defenders call them
"dependable" "family places" (youngsters "love to play with
the dough") for "great" rolls and "cheap" salads, pastas and
"tasty" brick-oven pizzas, but naysayers find the romper-
room atmosphere "too noisy" and the food too "unexciting."

Big Bowl S
— — — M
Reston Town Ctr., 11915 Democracy Dr. (bet. Dulles Toll Rd. &
Reston Pkwy.), Reston, VA, 703-787-8852
This big, bold blockbuster in Reston needed its reservation
beepers virtually from Day One; an Asian-themed production
of the Chicago-based Lettuce Entertain You Enterprises,
its Chinese, Vietnamese and Thai dishes rely on pedigreed
foodstuffs and last-minute preparations, and the wood-and-
tropical-greenery interior is cleverly crafted to seat techies,
suits and parents with strollers in an array of settings,
including an eat-in bar and a sidewalk cafe.

Bilbo Baggins S
17 18 17 $26
208 Queen St. (Lee St.), Alexandria, VA, 703-683-0300
◨ "Fantastic" breads, a "nice brunch" and a winning wine
list win kudos for this "quirky" Eclectic set in an Old Town
townhouse; even if the "imaginative" seasonal menu items
"sometimes don't work" and the seating feels "cramped",
that doesn't diminish this "chummy" spot's "rustic" appeal.

Bis 🅂 | 25 | 24 | 22 | $44 |

Hotel George, 15 E St., NW (bet. New Jersey Ave. & N. Capitol St.), 202-661-2700

■ "Political electricity" sparks this "stunning" French bistro, a strong "vote-getter on Capitol Hill" whose "superb" American-influenced Gallic classics (including escargots "bursting with flavor"), "chic bar" and "seductive lighting" have made it a "trendy" "star-watching" destination; the bottom line: "this one's a real comer."

Bistro 🅂 | 20 | 19 | 20 | $33 |

Washington Monarch Hotel, 2401 M St., NW (24th St.), 202-457-5020

■ Some surveyors feel that this pleasant West End hotel dining room doesn't "get the credit it deserves" for its "impressive brunch" buffet (served in a separate banquet room), solid seasonal New American cuisine, "exquisite courtyard" and lovely ambiance.

Bistro Bernoise 🅂 | – | – | – | M |

5120 MacArthur Blvd., NW (Arizona Ave.), 202-686-3939

Daily promotional specials display this young European-themed bistro's range: Sunday is paella night, Tuesday it's fondue, followed by seafood (Wednesday), half-priced wines (Thursday), appetizers (Friday) and desserts (Saturday); set in a cozy Palisades storefront that's brightened by sponged walls and warm lighting, its pluses also include Swiss-born chef-owner Herbert Kerschbaumer, who goes all out to woo a neighborhood with lots of hungry families and active seniors, and few gemütlich feeding zones.

Bistro Bistro 🅂 | 17 | 17 | 16 | $26 |

Villages at Shirlington, 4021 S. 28th St. (Hwy. 395), Arlington, VA, 703-379-0300

Reston Town Ctr., 1811 Library St. (Dulles Toll Rd., Reston Pkwy. exit), Reston, VA, 703-834-6300

▰ While its once-pioneering "formula" – modern American "comfort food" served in a "casually chic" setting – is still popular with many, dissenters feel these "bustling" Northern Virginia bistros have become a bit of a "suburban cliché" ("nothing exciting"); N.B. now under separate ownership.

Bistro Francais ⬤🅂 | 21 | 18 | 19 | $31 |

3128 M St., NW (bet. 31st St. & Wisconsin Ave.), 202-338-3830

■ For a "Parisian fix", it's hard to beat this quintessential French bistro on M Street, which features "dependable" bourgeois "classics", an open-to-the-street entrance and polished wood-and-brass interior and "generally" fast service; while it also draws the "ladies who shop" and "out-of-towners with kids", it's at its best "really late", when it becomes the "meeting place for chefs" and revelers who like to order "snails at 2 AM."

Bistro 123
20 | 17 | 20 | $35

246 Maple Ave. E. (bet. Glyndon & Park Sts.), Vienna, VA,
703-938-4379

☑ Expect "solicitous" service and "good early-bird" deals at
this "quiet" "oasis in the suburbs"; it's a "dark", "intimate"
"neighborhood" spot in Vienna with a long bar, beam
ceilings and a "solid" modernized French bistro menu, along
the lines of duck breast with a brandy–sour cherry sauce.

Bistrot du Coin S
– | – | – | M

1738 Connecticut Ave., NW (bet. R & S Sts.),
202-234-6969

'French, fun and friendly' is the motto of this young Parisian-
feeling enclave above Dupont Circle that aims to live up to
Le Petit Larousse's definition of a bistro as a place to eat
good food and drink good wine at a reasonable price; it
certainly looks the part – with characteristic yellowish-
brown walls, polished woods and a zinc-topped bar, and a
menu of onion soup, pâtés and steak frites – but it needs
time to work out some kinks.

BISTROT LEPIC S
25 | 19 | 21 | $40

1736 Wisconsin Ave., NW (S St.), 202-333-0111

■ "You could be in France and not do better" than this
"charming", "high-energy" Upper Georgetown transplant,
which serves up "delicious calf's liver", pig's feet and other
"succulent", "flavorful" bistro classics to a devoted old-
guard clientele; the *"très petit"* storefront can get "noisy"
and "cramped", but there is the option of renting out the
private room upstairs (seats eight to ten) or stopping by
for afternoon tea.

Blackie's S
– | – | – | E

1217 22nd St., NW (bet. M & N Sts.), 202-333-1100

It's not their father's (or your father's) steakhouse anymore –
not since 'Blackie' Auger's kids spent $5 million updating
this Golden Triangle staple with deluxe decor, a French chef
to oversee its sauces and imported foodstuffs, and some
3,500 bottles of wine; but loyalists will still find its signature
dry-aged beef (and traditional trimmings), seasoned waiters,
stained-glass windows and those nostalgic photos of the
good old days and pols – after all, Dad taught them not to
fix what ain't broke.

Black's Bar & Kitchen ◑ S
22 | 17 | 19 | $35

7750 Woodmont Ave. (bet. Cheltenham Dr. &
Old Georgetown Rd.), Bethesda, MD, 301-652-6278

☑ Jeff and Barbara Black (of Addie's) "do it again" at this
"energetic" Bethesda venue with "innovative" Gulf Coast–
influenced American seafood dishes (especially "ethereal"
fish), an "upbeat" oyster bar, a nicely appointed room and
some of the most desirable patio and deck seating around;
as might be expected of an 'in' place, it's often "crowded."

Bleu Rock Inn [S] 23 | 23 | 23 | $49
Rte. 211 (5 mi. west of Hwy. 522N), Washington, VA, 540-987-3190
◪ "Great views" of a "beautiful pond, vineyards" and the Blue Ridge mountains beyond supplement the solid French-inspired New American fare at this rural Virginia retreat; though a meal here isn't cheap, this lovely B&B is sometimes spoken of as a "runner-up" to the phenomenal Inn at Little Washington nearby, especially at Sunday brunch.

Blue Iguana [S] 17 | 16 | 17 | $23
12727 Shoppes Ln. (Fair Lakes Pkwy.), Fairfax, VA, 703-502-8108
◪ Surrounded by ubiquitous chains, Western Fairfax residents say it's "nice to have" this "bright" Eclectic venue around for "something different"; the "exotic combos" are equally "good" at brunch, lunch or dinner (there's a $17.95 prix fixe Sundays–Thursdays), but dissenters get their licks in over "spotty" service and warn that later at night this chameleon becomes a "very smoky hot spot."

Blue Point Grill [S] 23 | 18 | 20 | $37
600 Franklin St. (Washington St.), Alexandria, VA, 703-739-0404
■ "A gem" located next door to Alexandria's Sutton Place gourmet shop (which shares the same owner), this "hidden" catch-of-the-day specialist lures in fin fanatics with its "fabulous fresh seafood", "knowledgeable" staff and a "delightful" "colonnaded terrace for warm-weather dining"; though the frugal find the "big check" daunting, the kitchen "gives simple and straightforward a good name."

Blue Stone Cafe [S] ▽ 21 | 19 | 18 | $30
327 Seventh St., SE (Pennsylvania Ave.), 202-547-9007
■ Lauded as a "terrific addition" to the Eastern Market neighborhood, this apricot-colored New American cafe has prettied up its share of a former post office into an airy, "easygoing" canteen with an "outstanding" weekend brunch; since the consensus is that Capitol Hill "needs a place" like this, everyone hopes it "lives up to its potential."

Bob & Edith's Diner ◐ [S] 16 | 11 | 17 | $10
2310 Columbia Pike (S. Wayne St.), Arlington, VA, 703-920-6103
■ "Campy" and funky, this "unmarked monument" to "white-trash cooking" "will have you in and out in a dash"; a 24-hour Arlington "truck stop without the truckers" it's the "place to go to at 3 AM" "after a hard night out" when you want nothing more than "cheap", "greasy" diner eats.

Bobby Van's Steakhouse [S] ▽ 18 | 16 | 17 | $37
809 15th St., NW (bet. H & I Sts.), 202-589-0060
◪ One of a rash of recently opened boardroom steakhouses dotting the Downtown business district, this NYC import's "warm and stylish" setting (with dark paneling and replicas of Remington bronzes), "macho" meat menu and extensive wine list may seem "not so different from the competition", but it draws its share of pols and celebs.

Bombay Bistro S
22 14 19 $21

Bell's Corner, 98 W. Montgomery Ave. (Washington St.),
Rockville, MD, 301-762-8798
3570 Chain Bridge Rd. (Lee Hwy.), Fairfax, VA, 703-359-5810
■ "Terrific", "authentic Indian cuisine in unassuming
surroundings" sums up these suburban subcontinentals,
which offer an "excellent" bargain lunch buffet and "great
help" in understanding the multiregional menu; but
popularity has its price, meaning "long waits" for a table.

BOMBAY CLUB S
25 26 25 $38

815 Connecticut Ave., NW (bet. H & I Sts.), 202-659-3727
■ "You don't need a sari to be treated like a rani" by the
truly "impeccable" staff at this "sophisticated Indian" near
the White House, a "quiet", "civilized" "power lunch" haunt
with "well-spaced tables" and a "British colonial" club feel
that make for an "elegant" backdrop for the "wonderful"
cuisine (the tandoori salmon is terrific).

Bombay Curry Co. S
21 12 20 $18

Calvert Shopping Ctr., 3110 Mt. Vernon Ave. (W. Glebe Rd.),
Alexandria, VA, 703-836-6363
■ "Affordable", "spicy" Indian cuisine, a "fab Sunday
buffet" and a "gracious" welcome help overcome an
unassuming strip mall location at this "neighborhood"
dining spot in Alexandria.

Bombay Gaylord S
▽ 20 12 14 $18

8401 Georgia Ave. (Bonifant St.), Silver Spring, MD, 301-565-2528
■ While plain-looking, this "bargain" Indian enriches the
ethnic dining mix in Silver Spring with its "tasty" lunch buffet;
most seem satisfied with the dishes' "nice spices", but those
who want it hotter need only ask.

Bombay Palace S
23 20 21 $30

2020 K St., NW (bet. 20th & 21st Sts.), 202-331-4200
◪ One wag quips that the kitchen fire that temporarily
closed this "businesslike" K Street Indian only "proves
the spiciness of its chiles", as exemplified by its signature
vindaloo; while fans crave the "authentic" dishes (including
the lamb tandoori that may be the "best on earth"), others
find the fare "uneven" and decry "condescending" service.

Bombay Tandoor S
_ _ _ M

8603 Westwood Ctr. Dr. (Tyco St.), Tysons Corner, VA,
703-734-2202
Tysons Corner dot-coms and briefcase-toters fill the nicely
spaced tables at this big, new office-building subcontinental
whose lunchtime buffet (recession-priced at $8.95) and
lengthy menu provide lots of options for veggie-lovers,
carbo-loaders, carnivores and those whose net worth has
taken a nosedive; it's favored by the area's Indian high
techies who go for the fiery lamb vindaloo, while timid
palates let yogurt and rice tame the fire.

Bonsai [S] ▽ 21 | 18 | 20 | $26

4040 S. 28th St. (bet. Quincy & Randolph Sts.), Shirlington, VA, 703-824-8828

■ Petite and "pretty", this family-run Japanese brightens Shirlington's restaurant row with its "top-quality" appetizers (particularly the "live clam to die for" and *edamame*, fresh soybeans) and "very fresh" sushi and cooked traditional dishes; it's all served by an "attentive" staff at fair prices.

Bread Line 21 | 12 | 14 | $12

1751 Pennsylvania Ave., NW (bet. 17th & 18th Sts.), 202-822-8900

■ Mark Furstenberg is a "perfectionist" who brings "four-star talent" to the "$10 lunch" trade, and his "astronomically good" breads and sandwiches have "revolutionized the White House–area lunch scene"; yes, his bakery is "a bit frenzied" and "minimalist", but the "long lines are testimony" to DC's "appreciation of quality."

Broad Street Grill [S] 19 | 15 | 18 | $24

132 W. Broad St. (N. Washington St.), Falls Church, VA, 703-533-1303

◪ One of a number of "improving choices in the 'burbs", this Falls Church New American's "inventive combinations", convivial bar and "relaxing" atmosphere please most of its "local" clientele; but despite "friendly" service, it's "still searching for itself" and thus remains "kind of streaky."

B. Smith's [S] 20 | 23 | 19 | $32

Union Station, 50 Massachusetts Ave., NE (N. Capitol St.), 202-289-6188

◪ "Movers and shakers" dig into "gussied-up Sunday supper Southern fare" at this "stately" Union Station haunt; when the eponymous Barbara Smith is there, "she makes everyone feel special" so even if the "food lags behind" the setting, that surely doesn't stop a diverse "thirtysomething" crowd from gathering at the active bar.

Bua [S] 20 | 14 | 18 | $21

1635 P St., NW (bet. 16th & 17th Sts.), 202-265-0828

■ It's a "no-frills Thai", but it's located in hip Dupont Circle East, so it offers some of the area's best people-watching from its outdoor deck; choose among "reliable" standards or "interesting specials", all brought by a "quick" staff.

Buca di Beppo [S] 15 | 19 | 18 | $23

1825 Connecticut Ave., NW (Florida Ave.), 202-232-8466
122 Kentlands Blvd. (Great Seneca Hwy.), Gaithersburg, MD, 301-947-7346

◪ Bring the gang to this "wonderfully tacky" Italian above Dupont Circle, where the "huge", family-style portions of red-sauce eats will leave you "breathing garlic for days"; the food and service, however, are secondary to the "gimmicky" fun, and if you have a taste for "kitsch", you must "check out the men's room"; N.B. the Kentlands branch is new.

Buon Giorno [S]
20 | 19 | 21 | $37

8003 Norfolk Ave. (Del Rey Ave.), Bethesda, MD, 301-652-1400

■ "Faded glory"? – only if "fresh ingredients", "delicious" (albeit "predictable") cooking, "comfortable" surroundings that permit conversation and "pleasant" service go out of style insist loyalists of this Bethesda Italian; despite its rep, you don't really need "gray hair and a hearing aid" to get in.

Burma [S]
20 | 8 | 16 | $18

740 Sixth St., NW (bet. G & H Sts.), 202-638-1280

◪ "That pungent smell" wafting down the staircase is "authentic green tea leaf salad" and you can sample it along with other "enjoyably offbeat" Burmese dishes at this "funky little" second-floor Chinatown spot; notwithstanding some gripes about "uneven" food and service, it's "one of the few bargains left" in a rapidly gentrifying area.

Burrito Brothers
15 | 8 | 12 | $9

1718 Connecticut Ave., NW (Florida Ave.), 202-332-2308 [S]
Union Station, 50 Massachusetts Ave., NE (N. Capital St.), 202-289-3652 [S]
205 Pennsylvania Ave., SE (2nd St.), 202-543-6835 🚫
1825 I St., NW (bet. 18th & 19th Sts.), 202-887-8266
1815 M St., NW (bet. 18th & 19th Sts.), 202-785-3309
2418 18th St., NW (bet. Belmont St. & Columbia Rd.), 202-265-4048 [S] 🚫
7505 E. Leesburg Pike (Pimmit Dr.), Falls Church, VA, 703-356-8226 [S]
11690 Plaza America Dr. (Sunset Hills Rd.), Reston, VA, 703-478-6394 [S] 🚫

◪ For "quick", "cost-efficient" carbo loading, these Tex-Mex "Gen Y hangouts" with fake pueblo decor "get the job done" with "burritos as big as a hacienda"; amigos say the grub is as "fresh and healthy as fast food" gets, but critics rap the wraps as "bland"; P.S. seating is "limited."

Burro [S]
16 | 8 | 13 | $8

1621 Connecticut Ave., NW (bet. Q & R Sts.), 202-483-6861
2000 Pennsylvania Ave., NW (20th St.), 202-293-9449

◪ "Pit stops" for "junk food that isn't made of junk", this "healthy" "good-deal" Tex-Mex pair goes beyond "huge" burritos to also include "tasty" soups, chili, tacos and salads; dissenters, though, conclude "no fat, no flavor."

Busara [S]
21 | 22 | 20 | $24

2340 Wisconsin Ave., NW (south of Calvert St.), 202-337-2340
8142 Watson St. (International Dr.), Tysons Corner, VA, 703-356-2288

■ Accented with the "lush colors of Thailand", these twins in Upper Georgetown and Tysons Corner "set the decor standard" for upscale ethnic dining and draw a clientele that appreciates the artful "nouvelle" dishes and "professional" service; even if some feel that the DC interior looks "dated", its "soothing" garden remains a perennial "joy."

Butterfield 9 [S] — | — | — | E

600 14th St., NW (bet. F & G Sts.), 202-289-8810
Calling power players, theatergoers and sybarites, this svelte Downtown sophisticate carved out of the defunct Garfinkel's department store and inspired by the classic flick *The Thin Man,* is run by real pros (notably Umbi Singh of New Heights) who showcase what's billed as New American cuisine with a classic twist (think rack of lamb with black olive crust); word is, when it's good, it's very good, but the kitchen can be uneven.

Cactus Cantina [S] 18 | 16 | 16 | $20

3300 Wisconsin Ave., NW (Macomb St.), 202-686-7222
■ Just "try to not have fun" at this "festive" Tex-Mex sidewalk cafe in Cleveland Park where there's "always a crowd" downing "fresh" chips with "great" salsa, "tasty" "south-of-the-border" basics and "powerful" margaritas; it's all delivered with "assembly-line efficiency" and the long lines only "reflect its appeal to everyone."

Cafe Asia [S] — | — | — | M

1134 19th St. NW (bet. L & M Sts.), 202-659-2696
1550 Wilson Blvd. (N. Pierce St.), Arlington, VA, 703-741-0870
Ever "bustling", this "funky" Dupont Circle Pan-Asian proved to be such a winning formula – offering a "something- for-all" menu of "high-quality" dishes, $1 apiece sushi from 5 to 7 PM and "efficient" service – that it cloned itself into a big, "modern" site in Rosslyn; note, however, that the new offshoot hasn't at all eased the crush at the "always-packed" DC flagship.

CAFE ATLANTICO [S] 23 | 23 | 20 | $35

405 Eighth St., NW (bet. D & E Sts.), 202-393-0812
■ Though James Beard nominee Jose Ramos Andres, the founding chef, has moved on from this "voguish" "Rio de Janeiro on Eighth Street" to Jaleo, word is that his successor continues to turn out "cutting-edge" Latin American creations that are "tops"; the Penn Quarter setting is just as "dramatic" as ever and the bar continues to mix "wonderful" Latin cocktails; P.S. try the "amazing dim sum brunch."

Cafe Bethesda [S] 24 | 20 | 21 | $40

5027 Wilson Ln. (Cordell Ave.), Bethesda, MD, 301-657-3383
■ "All coziness and romance", this "sweet place" in Bethesda showcases "imaginative", "delicately prepared" New American cuisine, served by an "unpretentious and professional" staff; a few gripe about "cramped conditions" at peak times, resulting in too "little comfort for the price", but the "charming" sidewalk seating is an option and lunchtime is always pleasant.

Cafe Dalat S
21 | 9 | 18 | $18

3143 Wilson Blvd. (Highland St.), Arlington, VA, 703-276-0935

■ Rapidly developing Clarendon may no longer be an ethnic enclave, but this "personable", "family-run" Vietnamese "dive" still cooks up "reliable", cheap "classics" (including "fabulous" spring rolls and "great vegetable options") for a cast of "regulars of all descriptions"; "don't let the atmosphere fool you", because "year after year" this is a "solid" choice.

Cafe Deluxe S
19 | 19 | 18 | $25

4910 Elm St. (bet. Arlington Rd. & Woodmont Ave.), Bethesda, MD, 301-656-3131
3228 Wisconsin Ave., NW (Macomb St.), 202-686-2233

■ Albeit "more cafey than deluxey", this Cleveland Park American "clubhouse" is as "competitive" as ever when it comes to its major "pickup scene"; Bethesda's "stand-and-model set" now has its own version (and plans are to open a Tysons Corner clone in late summer '01); despite complaints about the "noisy meet-market" vibe, those who "get there early" find them to be quite "kid-friendly."

Cafe Marianna S
21 | 18 | 21 | $28

1201 N. Royal St. (Bashford Ln.), Alexandria, VA, 703-519-3776

■ Displaying "real attention to details", this "charming" Alexandria bakery/cafe treats everyone like "old friends"; the kitchen delivers "flavorful", "lovingly made" Eclectic dishes "with a touch of New Orleans" spunk in a "quirky" antique-filled room and out on the "lovely" patio; the few grumbles about "spotty food" are drowned out by a chorus of fans proclaiming "you've got to love this place."

Cafe Midi S
∇ 20 | 17 | 19 | $15

1635 Connecticut Ave., NW (R St.), 202-234-3090

■ North of Dupont Circle, this "upscale" Mediterranean "carryout with seating" adds a "French flair" to its "fresh" breads, "great veggie sandwiches" and soups prepared in an open kitchen; many choose to dine in the "sun-drenched" upstairs room with a "calm and inviting" atmosphere, but those who feel that the "cafeteria" setup is "a minus" get it to go.

Cafe Milano ●S
21 | 19 | 17 | $41

3251 Prospect St., NW (Wisconsin Ave.), 202-333-6183

◪ La Dolce Vita "scene" – think celebrities, Euro-trendies, "50ish politicians and their trophy girlfriends" – at this "hellaciously noisy", recently gussied up Georgetown hot spot is as Italian as the "sophisticated" pastas; of course, where one's seated for dinner ("older diners upstairs", "eye candy at the bar") and how one's treated "depend on the chicness of the guests", which is why locals opt to go here for lunch (or breakfast, served weekends).

Cafe Mileto ▣   ▽ 19 | 15 | 18 | $22
Cloppers Mill Village, 18056 Mateny Rd. (Great Seneca Hwy.),
Germantown, MD, 301-515-9370
■ A shopping center "haven" for families (expect "lots of
kids after soccer practice"), this Germantown Italian does
a "good" job with its wood-fired pizzas and solid pastas,
served by an "eager" staff; even if it stands out primarily
because of the lack of competition, so be it because most
think "the 'burbs need more places like this."

Cafe New Delhi ▣   ▽ 20 | 13 | 20 | $17
1041 N. Highland St. (Clarendon Blvd.), Arlington, VA,
703-528-2511
◪ Bargain hunters advise "lunch is the best time to go"
to this largely "undiscovered" Arlington Indian, when
the three-dish *thali* combination platters are offered at
the "super-cheap" price of $6.95; but don't expect any
glamour or glitz, because this is one of those unimpressive-
looking places that focuses instead on "quality" edibles
and "friendly" service.

Cafe Oggi ▣   18 | 16 | 18 | $34
6671 Old Dominion Dr. (bet. Lowell & Whittier Sts.),
McLean, VA, 703-442-7360
◪ "Lawrence Welk would've been at home" with the
mature crowd that frequents this "nice" McLean Italian, a
"convenient" "neighborhood" spot that gets some polite
notices for its "fine fish" and pasta dishes; naysayers,
however, pan the "dull" menu of "ordinary" standards
and the "aging" '70s setting.

Cafe Ole ▣   19 | 13 | 16 | $19
4000 Wisconsin Ave., NW (Upton St.), 202-244-1330
■ "Very convenient" as the double bill after a movie at the
theater around the corner, this Tenleytown Mediterranean
with "zip" features a "nice outdoor dining" area where
diners like to "assemble a meal from the bite-size options"
(40 meze choices are offered); during the daytime, it's a
sunny cafeteria-style spot for a sandwich or a "light" entrée,
or for weekend brunch.

Cafe Parisien Express ▣⊄   20 | 12 | 15 | $16
4520 Lee Hwy. (bet. Woodrow & Woodstock Sts.), Arlington,
VA, 703-525-3332
■ "An odd hybrid of fast food and bourgeois cuisine" is
the bill of fare at this French-accented "self-serve cafe"
in Arlington, where many feel the edibles "can't be beat
for the price"; even more impressive, however, is the fact
that the "attentive owner" has turned the simple strip-mall
space into a "friendly" "neighborhood meeting place."

Cafe Promenade [S] 21 | 23 | 19 | $34

Mayflower Hotel, 1127 Connecticut Ave., NW (bet. L & M Sts.), 202-347-2233

■ "Forever *the* power breakfast and lunch" haunt, where every newsmaker from Franklin Roosevelt to J. Edgar Hoover to Monica Lewinsky has been sighted, this "great", dignified room set in a conveniently located Downtown hotel is an "elegant" lobby cafe serving "consistent" Mediterranean cuisine; equally "a treat" is the afternoon tea and the lavish Friday night seafood buffet.

Cafe Royal [S] 17 | 15 | 16 | $32

Potomac Village, 9812 Falls Rd. (River Rd.), Potomac, MD, 301-299-3000

◪ Advocates feel that this Potomac French bistro is a "pleasant" enough lunch spot for "some terrific dishes" (such as the salmon paillard and New York strip steak); the unconvinced, though, counter that the food is too "pricey" and "uneven", especially since owner Fritz Siegfried opened Matisse.

Cafe Taj [S] 21 | 18 | 21 | $24

1379 Beverly Rd. (Old Dominion Dr.), McLean, VA, 703-827-0444

■ "In Northern VA and want Indian? – Cafe Taj you go"; it's as simple as that for McLean *masala* fans who rely on this "modern" "sleeper" for the "best variety" of dishes on the "spur of the moment"; its "excellent buffet lunch" (Monday–Saturday), "inviting atmosphere" and "friendly service" seal the deal.

Cajun Bangkok [S] 20 | 13 | 18 | $21

907 King St. (Alfred St.), Alexandria, VA, 703-836-0038

■ A "great little Old Town find", this storefront features a menu that gets its "kick" from a "surprisingly compatible" "Cajun-meets-Thai" marriage; "it works" because the "snazzy", "spicy" combination respects each cuisine and invites the adventurous to "experiment", and the "menu suggestions and jokes" from the staff further enliven the "interesting" mix.

California Pizza Kitchen [S] 15 | 12 | 14 | $17

1260 Connecticut Ave., NW (N St.), 202-331-4020
Montgomery Mall, 7101 Democracy Blvd. (Westlake Dr.), Bethesda, MD, 301-469-5090
1201 S. Hayes St. (12th St.), Arlington, VA, 703-412-4900
Tysons Corner Ctr., 7939L Tysons Corner Ctr. (Rte. 7), McLean, VA, 703-761-1473

◪ "Take the kids and still eat like an adult" at this "souped-up" Cal-Italian "fast-food" chain, home to "fresh", "creative pizzas", pastas and salads that attract plenty of mouths; but the jaded say the once-"novel" concept has "gone ordinary", with a "sterile" look and "sketchy" service.

California Tortilla S   21 | 13 | 18 | $10

Rockville Town Ctr., 199E E. Montgomery Ave. (Maryland Ave.),
Rockville, MD, 301-610-6500
4862 Cordell Ave. (bet. Norfolk & Woodmont Aves.), Bethesda,
MD, 301-654-8226

■ Every "quick and easy", "freshly" rolled burrito at this
family-run counter stop is seasoned with "a sense of fun"
and a "huge choice of hot sauces"; though "not fancy", it's
part of a "weekly meal plan" for "many loyal customers"
in Bethesda who appreciate "healthy food on a budget";
N.B. there's a new and unrated branch in Rockville.

Calvert Grille S   16 | 11 | 17 | $17

Calvert Apts., 3106 Mt. Vernon Ave. (bet. Commonwealth Ave. &
Glebe Rd.), Alexandria, VA, 703-836-8425

▨ New owners have made some changes at the "friendly"
"neighborhood" *Cheers* of Alexandria by standardizing
the schedule of "good" American specials (e.g. prime rib
on Fridays) and converting the former kids' play area into
a banquet room; nonetheless, it's still a "homey" spot for
a "Saturday brunch" with the family.

CAPITAL GRILLE S   23 | 23 | 23 | $45

601 Pennsylvania Ave., NW (6th St.), 202-737-6200
1861 International Dr. (Leesburg Pike), Tysons Corner, VA,
703-448-3900

■ "When Congress is in session", this "posh" "power
haunt" near the Capitol is *the* place to "experience DC" in
action; known for its "first-rate" steaks, seafood and cigars,
as well as senator-spotting and service that dramatically
improves "if your picture is in the *Post*", its "rich", "dark"
surroundings will "make you feel like a Republican,
regardless of your party affiliation"; N.B. the Tysons
Corner branch is unrated.

Capitol City Brewing Co. S   14 | 16 | 16 | $19

Postal Sq., 2 Massachusetts Ave., NE (1st St.), 202-842-2337
1100 New York Ave., NW (11th St.), 202-628-2222
2700 S. Quincy St. (28th St.), Shirlington, VA, 703-578-3888

▨ Carved out of cavernous, high-traffic spaces, these "loud"
brewpubs draw tourists and post-preppies alike for after-
work "fun and good beers"; foodwise, hop-heads advise
stick with the "great" soft pretzels, burgers and other
simple bar nibbles.

Caravan Grill S   ▽ 16 | 11 | 16 | $18

1825 18th St., NW (bet. S & T Sts.), 202-518-0444

■ "When you're in the mood for a different" kind of buffet at
lunch or dinner, consider the Persian spread – everything
from yogurt soup to "excellent" lamb shanks – offered at this
Adams Morgan ethnic; despite its unimpressive decor score,
it's a "clean, well-lit place" with a "nice courtyard" out back.

CARLYLE GRAND CAFE S   24 | 21 | 21 | $29

4000 S. 28th St. (Quincy St.), Shirlington, VA,
703-931-0777

■ This "classy" New American surely "put Shirlington on
the culinary map" thanks to its "consistently" "excellent"
seasonal menu, "beautiful" surroundings and "affordable"
pricing; the service is "fast-paced", but regulars warn it
draws such big crowds that there are often "long waits",
so call ahead to reserve; N.B. check out their bakery, Best
Buns, located next door.

CASHION'S EAT PLACE S   24 | 21 | 21 | $38

1819 Columbia Rd., NW (bet. Biltmore & Mintwood Sts.),
202-797-1819

■ Surveyors say that dinner at chef-owner Ann Cashion's
"always-buzzing" New American in Adams Morgan is a
"delightful adventure" because of her "delectable" dishes
that make "inventive" use of regional, seasonal ingredients;
moreover, the warm setting with earth-tone colors, an
elevated bar and an open kitchen helps make it a "hip"
"home away from home" for "grown-ups."

Caucus Room   – | – | – | E

401 Ninth St., NW (D St.), 202-393-1300

It would be hard to find a more stately setting for doing the
nation's business than this polished mahogany Downtowner,
with its see-and-be-seen glass-walled dining rooms, clubby
booths and barroom; it's run by pros Michaeil Sternberg and
Larry Work (Sam & Harry's), whose specialties are VIP
cosseting and prime-aged beef, and sponsored by political
heavies (Tom Boggs and Haley Barbour) and big biz (the
Carlyle group); the well-rounded American menu attracts the
likes of the King of Jordan and Chicago's William Daley.

Centro S   – | – | – | M

4838 Bethesda Ave. (bet. Arlington Rd. & Woodmont Ave.),
Bethesda, MD, 301-951-1988

Bethesda goes upscale Italian with this handsome young
grill where the airy atrium provides a pleasant, modern
backdrop for a well-tuned Northern Italian menu; dining
on fashionable pastas and up-to-date fish specials brought
by personable servers, patrons have been proclaiming
tutto bene from Day One.

Cesco S   22 | 19 | 18 | $41

4871 Cordell Ave. (Norfolk Ave.), Bethesda, MD,
301-654-8333

◪ Regarded by some as Bethesda's most "sophisticated"
and "best" Italian, this polenta-colored favorite cooks up
"classic" Tuscan "dishes not readily found" in the suburbs,
along with such crowd-pleasers as "superb osso buco and
risotto", but it garners a few brickbats for "erratic" service;
N.B. now that it's established, executive chef Francesco
Ricchi splits his time with his other venture, Etrusco.

C.F. Folks 🚫 | 22 | 10 | 18 | $13 |
1225 19th St., NW (bet. M & N Sts.), 202-293-0162
■ "Good specials and witty repartee" are dished out at this "gourmet" but inexpensively priced lunch counter below Dupont Circle where "real characters" sit cheek by jowl over the best crab cakes, meat loaf and grilled fish; N.B. open weekdays for lunch only.

Chardonnay [S] ▽ | 21 | 22 | 21 | $39 |
Doubletree Park Terrace Hotel, 1515 Rhode Island Ave., NW (Scott Circle), 202-232-7000
■ "Untrendy" but oh "so soothing", this "cosmopolitan little dining room" tucked away in a Downtown hotel off Scott Circle matches its "good" New American menu with an "interesting wine list" and a "romantic" ambiance that includes a "charming" garden.

CHEESECAKE FACTORY ◐ [S] | 21 | 18 | 17 | $23 |
Chevy Chase Pavilion, 5345 Wisconsin Ave., NW (bet. Jennifer St. & Western Ave.), 202-364-0500
White Flint Mall, 11301 Rockville Pike (Nicholson Ln.), Rockville, MD, 301-770-0999
◪ Yes, "the wait is a permanent fixture" at these "mobbed" American "monuments to gluttony" that offer "too much" of everything – an encyclopedic menu, "gigantic portions" and a "loud" volume; skeptics may sniff "'factory' says it all", but the addicted willingly wrestle with the eternal dilemma: "the meals are so huge that it's tough to make it to the best part – cheesecake!"

China Garden [S] | – | – | – | M |
Gannett Bldg., 1100 Wilson Blvd. (N. Lynn St.), Arlington, VA, 703-525-5317
Everything about this glitzy Hong Kong–style banquet hall in Rosslyn shouts authenticity – from the Cantonese seafood and weekend dim sum frenzy to the stage designed for wedding receptions; go early for "terrific" dishes and "people-watching" (but not for pampering service).

Ching Ching Cha [S] ▽ | 19 | 25 | 24 | $18 |
1063 Wisconsin Ave., NW (bet. K & M Sts.), 202-333-8288
■ "Shangri-la in DC" is the word on this "serene", "unique" tearoom in Georgetown; surrounded by "interesting" Asian collectibles (all for sale), patrons can go "light" with a brewed pot and "wonderful, tiny Chinese pastries" or opt for a "simple" meal, attended to by a "gracious" staff.

Christopher Marks | 17 | 18 | 19 | $30 |
1301 Pennsylvania Ave., NW (13th St.), 202-628-5939
◪ Converted from a sports bar, this Downtown hangout near the Warner Theatre is now a "clubby scene" serving Contemporary American food; the "attractive" setting is fine for "standard business" dining, though holdouts call it a work in progress that's "still finding its way."

Chutzpah 🅂   – | – | – | I

Fairfax Town Ctr., 12214 W. Ox Rd. (bet. Monument Dr. & Rte. 50), Fairfax, VA, 703-385-8883
This Fairfax fledgling's tongue-in-cheek name acknowledges skepticism of a place that calls itself a deli, yet looks newly-minted and acts nice – but try an overstuffed pastrami sandwich before you scoff; its display case filled with heartburn classics like homemade chopped chicken liver, house-cured corned beef and herring in cream or wine sauce makes ex-pat NYers drool.

Cities 🅂   19 | 23 | 17 | $36

2424 18th St., NW (Columbia Rd.), 202-328-7194
🔳 "Striking" decor that "keeps changing" to capture the spirit of a different "hip" destination draws a "good-looking" "Euro crowd" to this "slick" Adams Morgan Eclectic; the "urban" vibes are as appealing as the "revolving" cuisines (currently 'World'), which, though "unpredictable", are "great when they hit"; N.B. dinner only.

CITRONELLE   27 | 25 | 25 | $61

(aka Michel Richard's Citronelle)
Latham Hotel, 3000 M St., NW (30th St.), 202-625-2150
⬛ "Michel stays – we win"; chef-owner Michel Richard's full-time dedication to his Georgetown "splurge" destination ensures that this is "everything a restaurant should be" with "exceptional", "cutting-edge" New French cuisine (ranked tops in DC) accompanied by a "superb wine list"; the "elegant yet understated" approach comes off as "cool" to some, though not for those dining stoveside at the chef's table in the spectacular glass-walled kitchen.

City Lights of China 🅂   22 | 12 | 17 | $20

1731 Connecticut Ave., NW (bet. R & S Sts.), 202-265-6688
🔳 Long a beacon for "a-cut-above" Chinese food at "bargain" prices, this Dupont Circle "hole-in-the-wall" is beloved in spite of its "Formica and vinyl interior", "crowded tables" and tendency to "rush" its clientele (thus, takeout is a popular option); but now that its former owners are running nearby Meiweh, doubters say its light has "dimmed."

Clyde's 🅂   17 | 20 | 18 | $25

Georgetown Park Mall, 3236 M St., NW (Wisconsin Ave.), 202-333-9180
70 Wisconsin Circle (bet. Western & Wisconsin Aves.), Chevy Chase, MD, 301-951-9600
1700 N. Beauregard St. (Seminary Rd.), Alexandria, VA, 703-820-8300 ◐
Reston Town Ctr., 11905 Market St. (Reston Pkwy.), Reston, VA, 703-787-6601 ◐
⬛ "Upbeat" and "steady", these modern, crowd-pleasing American bistros with "slightly upscale" design themes are "good in a no-nonsense way", dishing up "classic" saloon eats; legions of regulars reckon them "handy" "standbys."

Coco Loco [S] 18 | 19 | 16 | $31

817 Seventh St., NW (bet. H & I Sts.), 202-289-2626

◪ There's "always a party going on" at this "club-type" Chinatown Brazilian "extravaganza" where the "fun" is fueled by potent drinks and the *churrasco* (a "parade" of "meats on a sword" "served tableside") is augmented by "tasty" tapas; but despite the "nifty concept", foes aren't *loco* about the "uneven" food or "slam-bang" service.

Coeur De Lion [S] 23 | 25 | 25 | $50

Henley Park Hotel, 926 Massachusetts Ave., NW (10th St.), 202-414-0500

■ Soft jazz sets the tone at this "intimate" Downtown hotel dining room, which is favored for "any occasion", thanks to its "romantic", medieval ambiance and "delicious" Chesapeake-accented, New American cuisine; regulars miss its longtime maitre d' Ralph Fredericks (now in New Orleans), but his "gracious staff" still "makes you feel special", and it's hard to feel anything but mellow when you're dancing cheek-to-cheek (Friday and Saturday nights).

Connaught Place [S] 22 | 18 | 22 | $24

10425 North St. (bet. Rte. 236W & University Dr.), Fairfax, VA, 703-352-5959

■ Curry connoisseurs confirm that this Fairfax Indian's "authentic" cooking is on a par with "London or Delhi" – "wonderfully spiced" and served with a "touch of elegance" in "peaceful" surroundings by a "friendly" staff; it's a "pleasant surprise" awaiting "off the beaten track" and suitable for a business lunch or a pre-theater dinner.

Coppi's [S] 19 | 18 | 17 | $26

1414 U St., NW (bet. 14th & 15th Sts.), 202-319-7773

◪ "Cozy" (read "cramped") and "casual", this U Street spot is "a great find" for "yummy" "wood oven–fired" pizza with a "crisp" crust and "unusual" toppings; its famed Nutella calzone sweetens the deal for the many surveyors who regard it as the "best dessert in town", though critics chide the "lackadaisical" service.

Così Sandwich Bar [S] – | – | – | I

1700 Pennsylvania Ave., NW (17th St.), 202-638-6366

Xando Così ◐ [S]

301 Pennsylvania Ave., SE (3rd St.), 202-546-3345

1647 20th St., NW (R St.), 202-332-6364

1350 Connecticut Ave. (Dupont Circle), 202-296-9341

2050 Wilson Blvd. (bet. N. Courthouse Rd. & Vietch St.), Arlington, VA, 703-522-0300

Fans of this "NYC export" and its Eclectic sandwiches built on "fresh-baked flatbread" hail the "cool concept" and "tasty eats", although critics claim the "novelty wears off" fast, and it's "a little pricey"; the Xando Così branches morph into bar/lounges with designer pizzas (aka "Gen X headquarters") later at night.

Cottonwood Cafe [S] 19 18 18 $29
4844 Cordell Ave. (bet. Old Georgetown Rd. & Wisconsin Ave.), Bethesda, MD, 301-656-4844
◪ Supplying "consistently fine" Southwestern fare (note that they're definitely "not afraid" to make it "*mucho* spicy") and satisfying thirsty souls "in need of a great margarita", this lively and popular pueblo in Bethesda attracts plenty of compadres with its menu of "unusual twists"; skeptics, however, claim it's "no big deal."

Crisfield [S] 21 11 17 $29
8012 Georgia Ave. (East-West Hwy. & Railroad St.), Silver Spring, MD, 301-589-1306
◪ For nostalgia buffs, this "original" Chesapeake fish house in Silver Spring epitomizes "grungy greatness" with its "fresh" basic seafood (much of it fried) served up amid "dive decor"; even if this edible piece of history doesn't come cheaply, loyalists say it's "still worth it" to sit at the bar and order oysters on the half-shell or a classic oyster stew.

Crisfield at Lee Plaza [S] 16 13 14 $27
Lee Plaza, 8606 Colesville Rd. (Georgia Ave.), Silver Spring, MD, 301-588-1572
◪ At this independent Silver Spring spin-off of Crisfield, the "traditional" seafood clearly "loses something in the translation", albeit its signature crab cakes and a few other "bright spots" on the menu can make it a "good value for lunch"; not helping matters is the "inattentive" service.

Crisp & Juicy [S] 22 6 15 $11
Sunshine Sq., 1331G Rockville Pike (Congressional Plaza), Rockville, MD, 301-251-8833
Leisure World Plaza, 3800 International Dr. (Georgia Ave.), Silver Spring, MD, 301-598-3333
Lee Hts., 4540 Lee Hwy. (Lorcom Ln.), Arlington, VA, 703-243-4222 ⊄
913 Broad St. (bet. N. Oak & Spring Sts.), Falls Church, VA, 703-241-9091
■ Bare-bones accurately describes the "fast-food" settings of these Latin rotisseries, as well as the carcasses left on your plate after digging into a "fabulous" BBQ bird; dip the clucker in your choice of sauces and pair it with "unusual" ethnic sides; they're a "perfect", "cheap" meal to "take out", making this "great poultry in motion."

Crystal Thai [S] 22 16 21 $20
Arlington Forest Shopping Ctr., 4819 Arlington Blvd. (Park Dr.), Arlington, VA, 703-522-1311
■ "The best soft-shell crabs anywhere" (prepared in eight succulent ways) would surely be reason enough to "go back" often to this "bright" Thai near Rosslyn, but regulars are also drawn by the "classy" service and "comfortable" atmosphere; consequently, it's very "well attended on weekends", so expect "tightly spaced tables" and lots of din.

Da Domenico 21 | 18 | 21 | $36

1992 Chain Bridge Rd. (Rte. 123), Tysons Corner, VA, 703-790-9000

◪ One of the few remaining "freestanding" restaurants left in Tysons Corner, this "clubby" and conveniently located Italian attracts "local businessmen" and the "over-50" set with its "excellent", hefty veal chops, old-fashioned "private booths" and an operatic proprietor who breaks into impromptu song; it may look "a bit dated", but it's a "comfortable" place where "you'll feel welcome."

Daily Grill [S] 16 | 18 | 17 | $25

Georgetown Inn, 1310 Wisconsin Ave. NW (M St.), 202-337-4900
1200 18th St., NW (M St.), 202-822-5282
Tysons Galleria, 2001 International Dr. (Rte. 123), Tysons Corner, VA, 703-288-5100

◪ While there may be "no daily thrills" behind the "polished doors" of these "upper-middle-class" grills, their "broad menu" of modernized American "comfort food" is good enough to generate constant lunchtime "waits"; come evening, their "large" boardroom-cum-bar spaces are "buzzy" with "cigar-and-martini" meetings.

Dante [S] 23 | 24 | 23 | $41

1148 Walker Rd. (Colvin Run Rd.), Great Falls, VA, 703-759-3131

◪ A moneyed clique is simply "charmed" by this "lovely" Great Falls Northern Italian set in a Victorian-style house with a "countryside" feel, "intimate" and "romantic" rooms and a staff that extends a "warming welcome"; as ratings attest, the rich cuisine is "very respectable" too, featuring such signature items as rabbit legs and veal scaloppini.

DC COAST 25 | 24 | 23 | $44

1401 K St., NW (14th St.), 202-216-5988

■ *The* "hip Downtown place" for "A-list" "young pros", this "stylish" New American makes "sophisticated dining" fun with its "wonderful", "original" seafood dishes, "great energy", "stargazing potential" and a "soaring" space with striking sight lines; it's also one of DC's toughest reservations, but be forewarned that if you don't nab a table on the "quieter" balcony, the "only way to have a conversation will be over your cell phone."

Dean & DeLuca Cafe [S] 18 | 13 | 13 | $16

3276 M St., NW (33rd St.), 202-342-2500
1299 Pennsylvania Ave., NW (bet. E & 13th Sts.), 202-628-8155

◪ Those looking for "gastronomy-a-go-go" in Georgetown should consider this "European"-style sidewalk cafe and takeout shop that offers terrific people-watching along with its "fancy" sandwiches, "creative" salads and sweet finales; even though many find it "way overpriced", with an "unhelpful" staff and few amenities, it's still "a treat" for "a snack" on a sunny summer day; N.B. there's also a small Downtown commissary for suits.

Delhi Dhaba [S] 18 | 10 | 15 | $15

7236 Woodmont Ave. (bet. Bethesda Ave. & Elm St.), Bethesda, MD, 301-718-0008
2424 Wilson Blvd. (bet. Barton St. & Clarendon Blvd.), Arlington, VA, 703-524-0008
K-Mart Shopping Ctr., 454 Elden St. (Grant St.), Herndon, VA, 703-467-8484

■ "Paper plates, plastic forks" and Indian music videos add up to a "strictly cafeteria-style" setup at the Arlington outlet of these "Taj Mahals of cheap eats" where the "spicy" and plentiful dishes come "quickly"; the Bethesda branch features a wee bit more ambiance, as well as full service and real silverware.

Del Ray Garden & Grill [S] 20 | 14 | 19 | $20

4918 Del Ray Ave. (bet. Cordell Ave. & Old Georgetown Rd.), Bethesda, MD, 301-986-0606

■ Solid food and service "shine through" the "simple" decor at this "quiet", "reasonably priced" Vietnamese "hidden" in Bethesda; it's the kind of place where management will gladly "spice to a diner's specification" and it's sweet "proof that family-owned restaurants can thrive."

Diner, The 🌙 [S] – | – | – | I

2453 18th St., NW (bet. Belmont & Columbia Rds.), 202-232-8800

Adams Morgan clubgoers rejoiced when nearby Tryst, the oh-so-happening Adams Morgan cafe/bar/living room, opened this 24/7 feeding station that sports lines at 4 AM; its cool diner look (chrome-and-red stools at the shiny counter, deep booths, worn tile floor and pressed-metal ceiling), hip vibe and realistically-priced (mostly under $10) meat loaf, mac 'n' cheese and old fashioned breakfasts make it welcome at any hour.

District ChopHouse & Brewery [S] 19 | 20 | 18 | $29

509 Seventh St., NW (bet. E & F Sts.), 202-347-3434

◪ Before or after "a game at the MCI" Center, beef eaters crowd this "dark", "noisy" Downtown chain chophouse for "big" "slabs of meat", "tasty burgers" and "don't-miss" onion rings, washed down with a specialty brew; dark booths, pool tables and plenty of TVs for endless sports viewing further enhance this "guy's paradise", even if critics counter that its "convenient" location is its "best feature."

Dolce Vita [S] 23 | 15 | 20 | $25

10824 Lee Hwy. (bet. Main St. & Rte. 123), Fairfax, VA, 703-385-1530

■ A whimsically decorated brick oven dominates "Fairfax's Italian treasure", which turns out "great" crusty pizzas, salads and pastas to complement its "good" wine list and "wandering minstrel", who "adds to the evening" pleasure; but "get there early" because prices are such "a bargain" that everyone wants to go at least "once a week" and they don't take reservations for less than four people.

Dominique's ⓢ   – | – | – | E

Watergate South, 600 New Hampshire Ave. (Virginia Ave.), 202-337-5890

Rattlesnake, Senate bean soup, Liz Taylor's chocolate truffles and Diana Damewood's warm greetings are back at this polished French-Continental bistro that reincarnates retired restaurateur Dominique D'Ermo's legendary fun spot; with a prime location across the street from the Kennedy Center and a $29 pre- or post-theater prix fixe dinner, its tables are bound to be jammed.

Donatello ●Ⓢ   21 | 18 | 20 | $35

2514 L St., NW (bet. Pennsylvania Ave. & 25th St.), 202-333-1485

◪ Frequented both by tourists drawn to its inviting patio and Kennedy Center patrons who stop in for early- or late-night prix fixe deals, this West End Italian garners polite applause for its "consistently good" traditional menu, "personal warmth" and "romantic" upstairs room, even if detractors shrug "mediocre."

Donna's Coffee Bar ⓢ   – | – | – | I

St. Gregory Hotel, 2033 M St. NW (20th St.), 202-223-2981

Baltimore's sleek coffeehouse empire goes to Washington, setting up shop in a casual indoor/outdoor Dupont Circle South site; catering to a biz and media clientele, it offers trendy Med- and Californian-inspired eats centered around upscale sandwiches, salads, pastas and light plates.

Duangrat's ⓢ   25 | 21 | 22 | $27

5878 Leesburg Pike (Glen Forest Rd.), Falls Church, VA, 703-820-5775

■ This dressed-up Thai featuring "elegant" costumed waitresses and "pastel"-painted rooms offers "terrific, authentic" regional dishes, drawing crowds to its Northern Virginia locale; fans advise "forget the pad Thai and explore" the rest of the menu (try the three-flavored fried flounder); P.S. on most weekends, there's classical dancing upstairs.

Dusit ⓢ   21 | 14 | 19 | $19

2404 University Blvd. W. (Georgia Ave.), Wheaton, MD, 301-949-4140

■ Regulars at this "very Wheaton-y" Thai don't mind that it's "not much on decor" because they're "never rushed" through their meal; "enjoy" a variety of "solid" renditions and specials that "are always good."

Ecco Cafe ⓢ   20 | 17 | 18 | $25

220 N. Lee St. (Cameron St.), Alexandria, VA, 703-684-0321

◪ Diana Damewood (of Dominique's) is now gone from this cafe with "endless rooms", which she transformed into Old Town's "definitive" gathering place, but the generally positive comments and "long weekend waits" suggest that the Italian menu remains "fulfilling", and the service still reflective of her "warmth", if not her sparkle.

eCiti Cafe & Bar   - | - | - | E

1524 Spring Hill Rd. (Leesburg Pike/Rte. 7), Tysons Corner, VA, 703-760-9000

Abuzz from Day One, this high-tech playroom in Tysons Corner fills a former warehouse with big *citi* club vibes and high-glam pleasure platforms – a huge bar, a separate sushi bar and various eating environments (including a glass-enclosed upstairs room for the ultimate see-and-be-seen scene) to suit most any mood; plus, the imaginative food, billed as American baroque, is very user-friendly.

Eiffel Tower Cafe S   ▽ 19 | 21 | 20 | $36

107 Loudoun St., SW (King St.), Leesburg, VA, 703-777-5142

■ Escargots, *navarin d'agneau* (lamb stew) and the "best crème brûlée anywhere" are among the Gallic classics served at this "nice French addition" to Leesburg's historic district; at lunchtime, it's considered "a lady's place", while in the evening worker bees gather for a quick bite.

El Gavilan S   ▽ 20 | 11 | 15 | $17

8805 Flower Ave. (Pine Branch Rd.), Silver Spring, MD, 301-587-4197

■ Gringos feel like they're in "another country" at this "lively" Silver Spring Central American, which welcomes with "bargain" dining, a "lively" "down-to-earth" vibe and a staff that's willing to bridge borders.

El Pollo Rico S⊅   23 | 7 | 15 | $10

2541 Ennalls Ave. (Viers Mill Rd.), Wheaton, MD, 301-942-4419
2917 N. Washington Blvd. (10th St.), Arlington, VA, 703-522-3220

■ Crispy-skinned and "deliciously tender", the rotisserie chicken cooked at these "rough-and-ready" Peruvian BBQ pits are "simply awesome"; the decor ain't much, but the prices are "rock bottom" and the takeout option is fast.

El Tamarindo S   18 | 10 | 16 | $16

7331 Georgia Ave., NW (Fessenden Rd.), 202-291-0525
1785 Florida Ave., NW (bet. 18th & U Sts.), 202-328-3660 ☾
4910 Wisconsin Ave., NW (42nd St.), 202-244-8888 ☾

◪ Hard to beat for a "late-night meal" or "margs anytime", these low-rent Salvadorans epitomize "no-hassle", low-budget eating; the "totally authentic" Latin "home cooking" may be "too spicy for mom and dad, but it's just right" for the "starving students" who populate these joints.

Elysium S   ▽ 23 | 26 | 24 | $48

Morrison House Hotel, 116 S. Alfred St. (bet. King & Prince Sts.), Alexandria, VA, 703-838-8000

■ "Special occasions" become even more so when commemorated amid the "elegant" appointments (including tapestries and chandeliers) at this "formal", dimly lit Federal-style destination in Old Town, which serves a "great" prix fixe New American dinner by a staff that's "attentive beyond the call of duty"; lunch at the bar is also recommended.

Equinox 🅂   24 | 19 | 22 | $45

818 Connecticut Ave., NW (I St.), 202-331-8118

◪ "Rising star" chef-owner Todd Gray is in the kitchen at this Farragut Square New American – a most "welcome addition" to the neighborhood – creating "exciting" but "refreshingly unpretentious" seasonal dishes, while his wife, Ellen, works the front of the house and attends to "Washington's power" elite.

ESPN Zone 🅂   15 | 20 | 16 | $21

555 12th St., NW (E St.), 202-783-3776

See review in Baltimore Directory.

Espresso Bar, The 🅂   ▽ 13 | 16 | 11 | $16

(fka Cascade Cafe)

National Gallery of Art, Constitution Ave. & Fourth St., NW, 202-737-4215

◼ Aptly located near the cascading waterfall in the National Gallery of Art, this "hidden treasure" is essentially an oak-and-steel Italian espresso bar and gelateria, though it also sells some sandwiches, salads and desserts; it's "crowded and not personal", but at least it's "quick."

Etrusco 🅂   – | – | – | E

1606 20th St., NW (bet. Connecticut Ave. & Q St.), 202-667-0047

Chef Francesco Ricchi (of Cesco) "is back in DC where he belongs" at this soothing Dupont Circle Italian yearling whose "great room" (a barrel-vaulted atrium) beautifully complements his personalized take on the cuisine of the red, white and green; predictions that "this could be a favorite" are borne out by the well-known faces and bec fins.

Evening Star Cafe 🅂   20 | 19 | 18 | $28

2000 Mt. Vernon Ave. (Howell St.), Alexandria, VA, 703-549-5051

◪ "Funky" and "lively", this New American cafe fits in very nicely in the "interesting", changing neighborhood of Del Rey; look for a seasonal menu that's smartly backed up by a 1,000-bottle selection of modestly priced wines, as well as a "retro" lounge-cum-fun room and an active bar, which strains to accommodate all the "yuppies"; N.B. there's a wine bar upstairs.

Faccia Luna Pizzeria 🅂   20 | 15 | 17 | $17

2400 Wisconsin Ave., NW (Calvert St.), 202-337-3132
823 S. Washington St. (Green St.), Alexandria, VA, 703-838-5998
2909 Wilson Blvd. (Fillmore St.), Arlington, VA, 703-276-3099

◼ "Creative" brick-oven pizzas that evoke "shades of the Bronx", as well as crowd-pleasing pastas and salads, earn plaudits from the kids and postgraduates who frequent these Italian joints; they're very "reasonably priced" and their interesting photo display and outdoor tables liven up their otherwise "uninspired" spaces.

Fadó Irish Pub S   15 | 21 | 16 | $19
808 Seventh St., NW (bet. H & I Sts.), 202-789-0066
☑ Though it may be a "Disney version of an Irish pub, the lads here know how to pull a pint of Guinness" say guzzlers at this "crowded", "realistic"-looking chain watering hole near Downtown's MCI Center; even if the food is only "decent", it's still a "fun", "friendly" place.

Fairmont Bar & Dining S   21 | 21 | 24 | $26
4936 Fairmont Ave. (Old Georgetown Rd.), Bethesda, MD, 301-654-7989
■ Surveyors say that this "real neighborhood restaurant" in Bethesda is "off to a "promising" start, thanks to its "nicely executed" American comfort food; it also features a bargain early-bird, "adorable and delicious" bite-size desserts and 30 selections of wine by the glass, a "wine lover's dream."

Faryab Afghan Cuisine S   22 | 16 | 20 | $24
4917 Cordell Ave. (bet. Norfolk Ave. & Old Georgetown Rd.), Bethesda, MD, 301-951-3484
■ "Stimulating appetites" in Bethesda is this Afghan, known for its "excellent kebabs", signature pumpkin stew and other savory but "not too exotic" dishes; "nice" digs and a "gracious" staff further explain why this is "among the best ethnics" in town, especially "when you want to be coddled."

Felix S   20 | 19 | 18 | $32
2406 18th St., NW (Belmont Rd.), 202-483-3549
■ "Amazing matzo ball soup on Friday nights" is one of the many reasons why crowds head to this "funky" Eclectic, which "tries hard to be" "hip", Adams Morgan–style, and succeeds; along with a choice of 26 designer martinis, there's also "innovative" cooking and live nightly music; N.B. they've opened Spy Lounge, a chic new cocktail destination, next door.

Filomena Ristorante S   21 | 20 | 19 | $33
1063 Wisconsin Ave., NW (bet. K & M Sts.), 202-338-8800
☑ "Campy" "holiday decorations, "generous" servings of "basic", "rich" Italian fare and buffet deals at lunch and brunch draw tourists, "festive" groups and "the occasional celebrity" to this Georgetown venue; dissenters, however, note that there's "not much finesse" to the preparations and warn of the "noisy", "crowded" conditions.

Firehook Bakery & Coffeehouse   22 | 14 | 16 | $11
3411 Connecticut Ave., NW (bet. Macomb & Newark Sts.), 202-362-2253 S
1909 Q St., NW (19th St.), 202-588-9296 S
912 17th St. (bet. I & K Sts.), 202-429-2253
214 N. Fayette St. (bet. Cameron & Queen Sts.), Alexandria, VA, 703-519-8020 S

(continued)

Firehook Bakery & Coffeehouse
105 S. Union St. (King St.), Alexandria, VA, 703-519-8021 🅂
3241 M St., NW (bet. Potomac St. & Wisconsin Ave.),
202-625-6247 🅂
◼ "Otherwise viceless" mavens are hooked on the "great" breads, cakes and cookies made at these ever-proliferating "carbo paradises" that are also lunch"hangouts"; P.S. the Cleveland Park sib, with a "secret" garden, is a "treasure"; ditto the spacious new Georgetown branch serving brunch.

Five Guys 🅂⊘   25 | 9 | 17 | $8
107 N. Fayette St. (King St.), Alexandria, VA, 703-549-7991
4626 King St. (Beauregard St.), Alexandria, VA, 703-671-1606
6541 Backlick Rd. (Old Kingmill Rd.), Springfield, VA,
703-913-1337
14001 Jefferson Davis Hwy. (Longview Dr.), Woodbridge, VA,
703-492-8882
◼ "Incredible", "big bad burgers" "stacked high with fixin's" and teamed with "fantastic" fresh-cut Cajun fries are why these Northern Virginia "kids-and-guys" patty places win accreditation as the *Survey's* top Bang for the Buck; sure, the grease may "drip off your elbows", there's "no decor" and it's counter service only, but these eats are actually "worth a drive around the Beltway in rush hour."

Flat Top Grill 🅂   – | – | – | M
4245 N. Fairfax Dr. (Taylor St.), Ballston, VA, 703-528-0078
This flashy corporate eatery's 'unlimited' stir-fry features a salad bar of fresh ingredients and some 40 sauces for a create-your-own meal that is cooked for you on a special grill; its healthy eating concept is buttressed by some less virtuous but ambitious appetizers (shrimp and cream cheese–filled wontons with raspberry jalapeño sauce), sinful sweets, Asian beers and trendy tipples, creating quite a buzz with Ballston cliff dwellers and office workers.

Florida Ave. Grill   21 | 14 | 19 | $15
1100 Florida Ave., NW (11th St.), 202-265-1586
◼ "Wonderful Soul Food" and good-natured "banter" "give comfort" to the famous and the famished who visit this Northwest '40s-era diner; its "fascinating" photos, reminders of DC's Southern heritage, will entertain you as you dig into the "best breakfast for the money", but there's fatback aplenty on the menu so have your "cardiologist on call."

Food Factory 🅂   19 | 7 | 12 | $11
8145G Baltimore Ave. (University Blvd.), College Park, MD,
301-345-8888
4221 N. Fairfax Dr. (Glebe Rd.), Arlington, VA, 703-527-2279
◼ "Huge chunks of well-marinated kebabs" for virtually pennies and "weekend specials that are even better" garner praise for these cafeteria-style Pakistanis; but given their "uninviting" digs and hectic pace, some prefer to take out.

Foong Lin
18 | 14 | 18 | $21

7710 Norfolk Ave. (Fairmont Ave.), Bethesda, MD,
301-656-3427

■ "One of the most popular Chinese restaurants in
Bethesda's hot dining scene", this "solid", if unexciting,
staple has a few "very good" dishes, some "healthy"
choices and a "nice" staff that handles "kids in high chairs"
and a "40th birthday party" with equal aplomb.

Fortune S
21 | 13 | 16 | $20

N. Point Village Ctr., 1428 Reston Pkwy. (bet. Baron Cameron Rd. &
Rte. 7), Reston, VA, 703-318-8898
6249 Arlington Blvd. (Patrick Henry Rd.), Seven Corners, VA,
703-538-3333

◪ Be patient and "don't fill up too early" on whatever small
plate is "flying by" your table at these Hong Kong–style
banquet halls, which roll out a huge variety of some of "the
best" dim sum around (they feature a "large" seafood
menu as well); while the relocation of the Falls Church
branch may have shortened the wait, the atmosphere at
both is still more "warehouse" than glitz.

Four & Twenty Blackbirds S
25 | 21 | 23 | $41

650 Zachary Taylor Hwy./Rte. 522 (Rte. 647), Flint Hill, VA,
540-675-1111

■ It's "great to get out of town" for a "romantic" dinner or
"super" brunch at this "charming", "unpretentious" New
American snugly set in the "bucolic" Virginia foothills; the
"cozy" interior and "caring" staff make it a "popular"
spot for power players to decompress over a "creative",
"delicious" meal made entirely from scratch, from breads
and starters to dessert.

Frogs & Friends S
▽ 22 | 16 | 23 | $28

7391 John Marshall Hwy. (Rectortown Rd.), Marshall, VA,
540-253-5399

■ An "excellent place to stop on the way to the mountains",
even "worth" a special trip on its own, this "quaint" roadside
French bistro in the Virginia horse country makes friends
easily, with its "intimate" woody surroundings and solid
menu, including such seasonal menu items as duck with
oranges and tangerines.

Full Kee ◐S
21 | 6 | 14 | $15

509 H St., NW (bet. 5th & 6th Sts.), 202-371-2233 ⊉
5830 Columbia Pike (Rte. 7), Falls Church, VA, 703-575-8232

■ "Chinatown's best dive" (and one of the few left), this
veteran Asian appeals with "terrific" Cantonese specialties
like "fabulous shrimp-dumpling soup", budget prices and
late hours (till 1 AM on weekdays, 3 AM weekends), which
make it a magnet for local chefs and night owls; but a non-
English-speaking staff means it's "better to go with Chinese
people"; N.B. the Virginia branch is unrated.

Full Key ◐ [S] ▽ 22 7 13 $15
Wheaton Manor Shopping Ctr., 2227 University Blvd. W. (Georgia Ave.), Wheaton, MD, 301-933-8388
■ One of the best of Wheaton's "authentic", no-atmosphere Asians, this Chinese joint features "don't-miss" Hong Kong–style soups and roast pork, along with Cantonese specialties like *congee* (rice gruel with savory toppings); it can be "difficult to communicate" with the staff, but just watch what the other tables are having and "order the same."

Gabriel [S] 23 20 21 $33
Radisson Barcelo Hotel Washington, 2121 P St., NW (bet. 21st & 22nd Sts.), 202-956-6690
■ "Complex and earthy" Spanish and Southwestern flavors can be found at this "very European" hotel dining room off Dupont Circle; the "outstanding" champagne Sunday brunch (starring its famed centerpiece roast suckling pig) is a definite treat, but the "wonderful tapas", paired with a "nice sherry list", make it worth considering at other times too.

Gaffney's Restaurant, Oyster & Ale House [S] – – – M
4301 N. Fairfax Dr. (Utah St.), Ballston, VA, 703-465-8800
Restaurant pros Mike Soper (ex Soper's on M), Ralph Capobianco (Stella's, King Street Blues) and Pat Gaffney's (Union Street Public House) latest venture brings an old-timey saloon feel to Ballston, with a classic raw bar paired with a seafood and all-American grill menu featuring some interesting regional twists (shrimp-and-sausage gumbo); no alehouse would be complete without its house brew (oyster stout), plus there's a roomy eat-in bar and courtyard.

GALILEO [S] 26 24 24 $57
1110 21st St., NW (bet. L & M Sts.), 202-293-7191
IL LABORATORIO
1110 21st St., NW (bet. L & M Sts.), 202-293-7191
■ "Elegant", if "a little stuffy", Roberto Donna's "power" destination has long been considered the "best of the best for that important lunch or dinner" Downtown, thanks to "outstanding" Italian cuisine and "top-notch" service; he's earning even more applause at hot, hot Laboratorio (his "spectacular" showcase restaurant within Galileo) where several nights a week he crafts a tasting menu "extravaganza", an "out-of-this-world" experience.

Garden Cafe [S] ▽ 19 18 19 $28
State Plaza Hotel, 2117 E St., NW (bet. 21st & 23rd Sts.), 202-861-0331
■ "Tucked away" in a "discreet location" in Foggy Bottom, this courtyard cafe has introduced some interesting Asian touches to its "appealing" New American menu (along the lines of lemongrass mahi mahi with orange miso); at lunch it's full of "State Department wonks", while its "good-value" pre-theater menu draws Kennedy Center ticket-holders.

Generous George's [S] 17 | 15 | 16 | $15

3006 Duke St. (Cambridge Rd.), Alexandria, VA, 703-370-4303

◪ Kids and "kitsch" are George's passion, which explains why this "garish" Italian "amusement park" is always wall-to-wall with birthday parties; and he "really is generous", piling pasta on top of pizza and pouring "beverages by the gallon"; foes, though, sniff merely "mediocre."

Georgetown Seafood Grill [S] 20 | 18 | 19 | $29

1200 19th St., NW (bet. M & N Sts.), 202-530-4430

■ Young Connecticut Avenue types descend upon this Golden Triangle raw bar and seafood house "after work" for "perfect happy hour specials" like oysters (50 cents apiece), steamed mussels and popcorn shrimp (both $3 a plate); a few dissenters find it "unremarkable", but most feel it's "pleasant", especially if you "eat outside" in nice weather.

Georgia Brown's [S] 23 | 23 | 21 | $35

950 15th St., NW (bet. I & K Sts.), 202-393-4499

■ "Stunning" and "sophisticated", this Downtown Southerner entices "Washington insiders", "celebrities" and visiting firemen with its "y'all-come"-by hospitality; even if its "delectable" Soul Food "clogs some arteries", the staff's "energy" and professionalism "warm" all hearts; P.S. check out the "great jazz brunch."

Geranio [S] 20 | 19 | 22 | $35

722 King St. (bet. Columbus & Washington Sts.), Alexandria, VA, 703-548-0088

◪ The changing of the guard a few years back at this "classy" Old Town Italian still evokes mixed reactions: most agree the "new chef has breathed life back" into the menu by adding lighter, more modern dishes, though others regret that it's "not what it used to be"; nevertheless, most still regard it as a "favorite", made even more "romantic" by fireside tables appointed with candles and flowers.

GERARD'S PLACE 27 | 23 | 25 | $59

915 15th St., NW (bet. I & K Sts.), 202-737-4445

■ "Simple elegance" distinguishes this Downtown knockout where eponymous chef Gerard Pangaud masterminds a "brilliant" New French menu; his "gourmet" innovations are proffered by a highly "knowledgeable" staff in a "quiet", "intimate" environment that's ideal for power meals and romantic rendezvous alike; of course it's "pricey", but it's "outstanding in every regard" and "well worth the splurge."

Giovanni's Trattu – | – | – | M

1823 Jefferson Pl., NW (bet. M & N Sts.), 202-452-4960

"Noisy basement eating on tasty Italian dishes" has been the story of this "wonderful little local" brick-walled trattoria in Dupont Circle South for more than two decades; recently revived by accomplished owner Giovanni (former manager of Cafe Milano), it retains a refreshingly untrendy appeal.

Good Fortune ●🄢   21 | 13 | 16 | $19
2646 University Blvd. (bet. Georgia Ave. & Veirs Mill Rd.),
Wheaton, MD, 301-929-8818
◪ "Dim sum magna cum laude" is the widespread appeal
of this modest Wheaton Cantonese, so "come early" (before
noon) on weekends or you'll have to battle long lines of
"Asian diners" who appreciate the "authentic" chow; first-
timers should note that the extensive menu and hectic
atmosphere can be daunting.

Gordon Biersch Brewery   – | – | – | M
Restaurant 🄢
900 F St., NW (9th St.), 202-783-5454
Downtown professionals and MCI ticket-holders find a
sophisticated yet casual setting for midday to midnight
dining (but 11 PM weeknights) at this New American
brewery offering an internationally accented menu along
with German-style lagers and fashionable strong drinks;
set in a wonderful turn-of-the-century bank building, its
ornate ceiling is offset by cream walls, olive leather and
marbleized columns, which divide the place into bar, lounge,
dining room and private spaces.

Grapeseed   – | – | – | M
4865 Cordell Ave. (Norfolk Ave.), Bethesda, MD,
301-986-9592
At this attractive, modish New American bistro and wine bar
in Bethesda, most of the dishes on the user-friendly menu
are available in tapas-size portions, each with a grape
recommendation (such as cornmeal-dusted fried oysters
with Muscadet); the intriguing pairings of food and wine,
offered in an airy open-to-the-street setting, make it a great
place to hook up with friends and sample lots of matches.

Greenfield Churrascaria 🄢   16 | 14 | 17 | $28
1801 Rockville Pike (Randolph Rd.), Rockville, MD,
301-881-3397
◪ "Even inveterate carnivores will get their fill" at this set-
price Brazilian meat-for-all on Rockville Pike, where the
"gargantuan" salad-and-sides buffet is a mere preview to
the real show; sit down, strap on the feed bag and let the
"roving waiters" endlessly slice off cuts from the skewered
slabs of BBQ onto your plate; it's "a lot of food", but critics
warn of "mediocre flavors" and "sporadic" service.

Green Papaya 🄢   – | – | – | M
4922 Elm St. (Arlington Rd.), Bethesda, MD, 301-654-8986
Warm tones, a soothing waterfall, clever lighting effects –
even a mock banana tree – create a stylish backdrop at this
young Bethesda Vietnamese, whose artistic presentations
play up the characteristic freshness of this cuisine; novices
might try squid salad incorporating its namesake fruit or
lemongrass pork with vermicelli, while curries and pepper-
sauced selections provide old-hands with plenty of heat.

Greenwood S
       –   –   –   E

5031 Connecticut Ave., NW (Nebraska Ave.), 202-364-4444
Art abounds at chef Carol Greenwood's new venue in Upper
Northwest – starting with the idiosyncratic, market-driven
New American cuisine that has earned her a loyal following
and extending to designer digs and a daily-changing food
centerpiece on the 22-person communal table; deep rose
walls, arresting photos, custom-blown glass and even the
filmy curtains accenting the booths add to the effect.

Grillfish S
       –   –   –   M

1200 New Hampshire Ave., NW (M St.), 202-331-7310
*4866 Cordell Ave. (bet. Norfolk & Woodmont Ave.), Bethesda,
MD, 301-941-9058*
Just like in Downtown DC, it sure didn't take long for
Bethesda to catch onto this "casual" seafood house
concept – choose your fish and your sauce, then let the
kitchen "simply" grill or sauté your entrée; both branches
are "lively" (read "very noisy") spaces with "candles
everywhere" and "fake distressed walls" and add up to
"tasty and fun" "healthy alternatives."

Grill from Ipanema S
       20   18   18 $28

1858 Columbia Rd., NW (Belmont Rd.), 202-986-0757
■ Full of "high energy" and "good humor", this "dark", hip
spot in Adams Morgan is a "home away from home" for
Brazilian expatriates, who gather for "spicy and appealing"
"authentic" cooking washed down by "deadly caipirinhas";
though it's a bit "inconsistent", fans swear it's often
a "wonderful" "adventure."

Haad Thai S
       22   17   19 $17

1472 Beauregard St. (Reading St.), Alexandria, VA, 703-575-1999
1100 New York Ave., NW (bet. 11th & H Sts.), 202-682-1111
■ "No one does lunch Thai better" than these "top-quality"
Asians opposite the Convention Center in DC and the Mark
Center in VA, where the "unusually" "delicious and fragrant"
preparations are served by a "fast and competent" staff
in "pleasant" surroundings; consequently, they're always
packed, but the tropical decor provides a mini getaway at
a "cheap" price.

Haandi S
       23   16   20 $24

*4904 Fairmont Ave. (Old Georgetown Rd.), Bethesda, MD,
301-718-0121*
*Falls Plaza Shopping Ctr., 1222 N. Broad St. (Rte. 7), Falls Church,
VA, 703-533-3501*
■ The pungent "aromas as you enter" these pink-colored
suburban Northern Indians are "an indication of wonderful
food to come"; tandoori specialists, they're also "kind to
vegetarians" and they "can be trusted to offer good value"
for relatively upscale dining; the "solicitous" staff is helpful
in explaining dishes to novices, though more experienced
palates quibble that the menu holds "no surprises."

Hakuba S　　　　─│─│─│M│
Kentland Mkt. Sq., 706 Center Point Way (Great Seneca Hwy.), Gaithersburg, MD, 301-947-1283
In Kentlands, Montgomery County's new, high-end enclave, this serene Japanese has found its niche, with a setting mixing earth tones and cushy seats with decorative servings of sushi, tempura, noodles, *ochazuke* (fish or seaweed on rice with hot tea) and grills; its uncommon-for-the-'burbs raw fish selections (gizzard shad, sea eel) and authentic touches like serving sake in a cedar box draw cognescenti.

Hama Sushi S　　　　▽ 24│21│21│$25│
2415 Centreville Rd. (Fox Mill Rd.), Herndon, VA, 703-713-0088
■ Blond woods and paper lanterns set the stage at this Herndon Japanese that prides itself on its "fresh, fresh, fresh fish" and turns expert cuts from familiar and unusual species into "superb sushi"; the list of specials deserves particular attention, plus the chef makes creative rolls based on cooked ingredients.

Harambe African Cafe ◐S　　　　─│─│─│ I │
1771 U St., NW (Florida Ave.), 202-332-6435
It's a "rare treat in Adams Morgan" (or anywhere) to find a "good, cheap and friendly" place that's "not crowded"; not only does this "small, family-run" storefront cafe offer visitors an authentic taste of Eritrean cooking, with its spicy dishes, scooped up with the traditional spongy bread (*injera*), but it also features some Italian dishes.

Hard Rock Cafe S　　　　13│19│15│$20│
999 E St., NW (10th St.), 202-737-7625
◪ "Been there, done that, bought the T-shirt" sums up most grown-ups' reactions to this "noisy" rock 'n' roll shrine in prime tourist territory in DC; but when "teenage birthday parties" provoke visits, some concede that the burgers are "ok" and the "memorabilia" worth seeing at least once.

Hard Times Cafe S　　　　19│14│17│$14│
Woodley Gardens, 1117 Nelson St. (Rte. 28), Rockville, MD, 301-294-9720
1404 King St. (West St.), Alexandria, VA, 703-837-0050
3028 Wilson Blvd. (Highland St.), Arlington, VA, 703-528-2233
K-Mart Shopping Ctr., 428 Elden St. (bet. Herndon Pkwy. & Van Buren St.), Herndon, VA, 703-318-8941 ◐
1021 Washington Blvd. (Montrose Ave.), Laurel, MD, 301-604-7400
6362 Springfield Plaza (Commerce St.), Springfield, VA, 703-913-5600 ◐
4920 Del Ray Ave. (Rte. 187), Bethesda, MD, 301-951-3300
■ "Patsy Cline on the jukebox", a bowl of heartwarming (some say heartburning) chili and a cold beer or two add up to a "good and filling" time at these "grubby" American joints; while they're not for every taste, regulars like it that they're "down-to-earth", "cheap and cheerful."

Hautam Kebobs 🅂 ▽ 18 | 15 | 18 | $18

Ritchie Ctr., 785D Rockville Pike (Wooton Pkwy.), Rockville, MD, 301-838-9222

☑ An "unpretentious" and "nice family place", this Rockville Middle Eastern is a "good" spot to visit to learn about Persian cuisine, because the kitchen pays careful attention to seemingly simple dishes like grilled meat kebabs, accompanied by "great" rice and bread; it's "value"-priced and frequented by local Iranians, yet it remains relatively undiscovered by others.

Havana Breeze 18 | 10 | 12 | $12

1401 K St., NW (14th St.), 202-789-1470

■ Favorable winds brought this colorful Cuban to town, where it's providing a "good, fast and affordable" shirtsleeve lunch for Downtown suits; order the "perfect Cuban sandwiches", "great empanadas" and other eats at the counter downstairs, then find a table; P.S. be warned that the "lines may make you think you're in Castro's Cuba", but the DJ featured on Friday and Saturday nights in the appealing upstairs bar is "great fun."

Heart In Hand 🅂 19 | 21 | 21 | $27

7145 Main St. (Church St.), Clifton, VA, 703-830-4111

☑ Blessed with a "lovely setting and a romantic country atmosphere" that make it an ideal "getaway", this "quaint" Southerner in Clifton features a rich menu of classics such as Tennessee ham, chicken Suzanne and catfish that's fine for a "ladies' lunch"; the disappointed, however, sigh it "could be a great out-of-the-way restaurant but it needs some life."

Hee Been 🅂 ▽ 22 | 15 | 19 | $22

6231 Little River Tpke. (Beauregard St.), Annandale, VA, 703-941-3737

■ Popular with many Asians who regard it as the "best traditional Korean restaurant around", this Annandale spot offers "authentic" favorites such as tableside BBQ, as well as "lots of new things to try"; though the staff tries to be "helpful", Westerners may find it "hard to understand" the "unusual" choices without an experienced guide, but the "great lunch buffet" is an easy option.

Heritage India 🅂 23 | 23 | 19 | $34

2400 Wisconsin Ave., NW (Calvert St.), 202-333-3120

■ Lined with fascinating historical photos on the walls of its "serene", "elegant" rooms, this "aristocratic" Indian exposes Washingtonians to a wider "range" of its culinary and cultural heritage; the kitchen turns out "top-notch" dishes, both familiar and exotic, and by most accounts the staff is now as "wonderfully seasoned" (albeit a few complaints arise about "pushy" treatment) as the food; N.B. they've recently added a downstairs bar.

Hermitage Inn [S] ▽ 22 | 22 | 22 | $37

7134 Main St. (next to RR tracks), Clifton, VA, 703-266-1623

■ Located on Clifton's Main Street, this "lovely" historic hotel (circa 1869) that once welcomed presidents Ulysses Grant and Teddy Roosevelt is now a "special-occasion" destination for prix fixe Provençal meals that incorporate local ingredients; whether seated upstairs in the restored dining room or out on the "pleasant" patio, most laud the "excellently prepared" menu, country ambiance and "flowing" service; one or two, however, say "overrated."

Hinode [S] 20 | 17 | 19 | $23

4914 Hampden Ln. (Arlington Blvd.), Bethesda, MD, 301-654-0908
134 Congressional Ln. (bet. Jefferson St. & Rockville Pike), Rockville, MD, 301-816-2190

◪ These "simple", traditional Japanese eateries in suburban Montgomery County function as "extensions of our kitchen" admit locals bent on its "consistently good" sushi, bento box bargains and "healthy" grilled Asian dishes; detractors, however, yawn "boring" and suggest the smiling staffers "need to communicate better."

Hogate's [S] 12 | 12 | 13 | $28

800 Water St., SW (bet. Maine Ave. & 9th St.), 202-484-6300

◪ At this "tourist trap on the waterfront", "busloads of blue-hairs" find it comforting that everything here seems the "same as it was" when it opened in 1938 – from the "wonderful" "view of the river" and its famed (and "still good") rum buns to, alas, its "Soviet-style" seafood meals and "threadbare" surroundings.

Hollywood East Cafe ◐ [S] 22 | 9 | 17 | $17

2312 Price Ave. (Elkin St.), Wheaton, MD, 301-942-8282

■ "Hidden" on a side street is Wheaton's "best bet" for "genuine" "Hong Kong–style cuisine"; the interior may be "seedy" (some regulars warn "don't look below your knees"), but the dishes are "distinctive" (particularly the "outstanding specials"), "delicious" and available till late at night; N.B. the above decor rating may not take into full account a recent updating.

Hope Key ◐ [S] 20 | 8 | 17 | $16

3131 Wilson Blvd. (Highland Ave.), Arlington, VA, 703-243-8388

■ "As close to going to a Hong Kong dive as one gets" in Clarendon, this "authentic" "bargain" "favorite" boasts "a plethora of interesting dishes", including "terrific noodle soups", and draws a "high proportion of Asian diners"; get recommendations from the "waiters, who know what's best" among the Cantonese choices, though it's hard to go wrong.

Horace & Dickie's ◐S⊄   ▽ 27 9 18 $9
809 12th St., NE (H St.), 202-397-6040
■ Possibly the "best fried fish ever", paired with a few
Southern sides, can be devoured at this down-home
"carryout" "institution" in Northeast DC; it's "always
crowded" with "repeat customers" who willingly "wait on
long lines" for a "cheap" fix, but be warned that it's located
in a sketchy neighborhood, so exercise caution.

Houston's S   19 17 18 $23
7715 Woodmont Ave. (bet. Cheltenham Dr. &
Old Georgetown Rd.), Bethesda, MD, 301-656-9755
12256 Rockville Pike (Montrose Rd.), Rockville, MD, 301-468-3535
■ "Rock steady", this immensely popular chain of "brass-
and-fern" eateries is a "solid" "standby" for "outrageous"
spinach dip, "satisfying" burgers and other "bar food"
basics; the service team is mostly "efficient", but be advised
of the "punishing wait at all times of the day" for a table.

Hunan Chinatown S   19 14 17 $21
624 H St., NW (bet. 6th & 7th Sts.), 202-783-5858
☑ Veterans of this Chinatown Chinese lament that it has
"lost its sense of adventure" and "needs to freshen up" its
act, but the staff's "speedy pre-game" execution of "tasty"
standard plays like General Tso's chicken still scores with
many MCI Center ticket-holders.

Hunan Lion S   20 20 20 $22
2070 Chain Bridge Rd. (Old Courthouse Rd.), Tysons Corner, VA,
703-734-9828
■ Tysons Corner's "haute" Chinese is an "attractive" choice
for a "consistently high-quality" menu, "pleasant" setting
and "VIP" treatment for all; though a handful of doubters
think it's "decent" but "getting old", the majority keeps
returning and thus ensures that it remains a "popular place."

Hunan Number One ◐S   21 15 18 $20
3033 Wilson Blvd. (Garfield St.), Arlington, VA, 703-528-1177
■ "Singapore noodles are a big hit" at this red-and-gold
Arlington Chinese, as are its "excellent" daily dim sum
and "delicious, spicy" seafood dishes; the "standard"
menu selection is "huge", but still, the "obliging" staff
"will make you anything you want."

Hunan Palace S   ▽ 19 14 18 $18
Shady Grove Shopping Ctr., 9011 Gaither Rd. (Shady Grove Rd.),
Gaithersburg, MD, 301-977-8600
☑ Despite the kitchen's "uneven" execution at this
Gaithersburg Chinese, the "enormous" multiregional
selection does hold some "surprising" treats, notably "good"
Taiwanese and Shanghai-style "standards" (the best dishes,
however, are the "exotic off-the-menu specialties"); even
if some find it "nothing memorable", it's "cheap and fast."

Hunter's Inn [S] 13 | 15 | 15 | $26
917 Quince Orchard Rd. (Great Seneca Hwy.), Gaithersburg, MD, 301-527-1400
10123 River Rd. (Falls Rd.), Potomac, MD, 301-299-9300
◪ Dark woods, etched glass and cozy booths make these American steak and seafood houses "clubby" spots, and since they're in "suburban" neighborhoods without many such options, they're very popular; but some advise "hunt elsewhere" because these eats are "very ordinary."

Huong Que [S] ▽ 23 | 13 | 21 | $19
Eden Ctr., 6769 Wilson Blvd. (Clarendon Rd.), Falls Church, VA, 703-538-6717
■ Reputedly a haunt of local celebrity chefs, this Falls Church Vietnamese set in the bustling Eden Center is an "interesting" Asian social center and marketplace that delivers "generous servings" of "great" food; the room is bare-bones, but it's made inviting by the "charming owners."

Ice House Cafe [S] 18 | 15 | 17 | $26
760 Elden St. (Spring St.), Herndon, VA, 703-471-4256
◪ This Herndon "hangout" boasts an Eclectic menu, a rustic interior adorned with old photographs and "good" live jazz on weekends; it can get "noisy" when crowded, but that doesn't deter the throngs that gather at the old-style bars.

Il Borgo [S] 21 | 19 | 21 | $36
1381A Beverly Rd. (bet. Elm St. & Old Dominion Dr.), McLean, VA, 703-893-1400
◪ "Warm-hearted" chef-owner Vittorio Testa's personal welcome, "rich" and "hearty" Italian fare and willingness to "make anything you want" transform this "standard-issue commercial building space" in McLean into a "festive", "comfortable" dining room; but while most locals appreciate this close-to-home option, some feel that this "throwback" is a bit "overdone for the 'burbs."

Il Cigno [S] ▽ 19 | 19 | 19 | $31
Lake Anne Plaza, 1617 Washington Plaza (N. Shore Dr.), Reston, VA, 703-471-0121
◪ On a lovely summer afternoon, diners love to sit on the patio and take in the "great view" of Lake Anne (and the splashing fountain) at this "romantic" Reston Italian where the "good" pasta, seafood and veal dishes are enhanced by "friendly" service and a Tuscan-accented interior; critics, however, are "not impressed" with the "ordinary" fare.

Il Lupo [S] – | – | – | M
4009 Chain Bridge Rd. (Main St.), Fairfax City, VA, 703-934-1655
This cute trattoria in Old Town Fairfax (formerly Il Radicchio) turns out agreeable, affordable pastas, pizzas and other Italian fare, as well as daily specials; at lunchtime, lots of local biz gets done at its tables, while later, families and twosomes make themselves at home.

Ilmee S　　– | – | – | M
14015 Lee Jackson Hwy. (Centreville Rd.), Chantilly, VA,
703-631-3400
Upon entering this spacious Chantilly Korean, expect to find
families and techies mixing and matching condiments to
spice up the already fiery BBQ cooked on tabletop grills,
digging into hearty casseroles and nibbling on a variety of
raw fish specialties at the sushi counter.

Il Pizzico　　23 | 16 | 20 | $27
Suburban Park, 15209 Frederick Rd. (Guide Dr.), Rockville, MD,
301-309-0610
■ "Everyone has a good time" at this "superior" Rockville
Italian where diners dig into "marvelously authentic pastas
and good seafood" delivered by a "knowledgeable" staff in
a "sunny", "warm" atmosphere; but as you'd expect from
a "great", "reasonably priced" "neighborhood place", it
often gets "crowded" and the "no-reservations" policy
can lead to "frustrating" waits.

Il Radicchio S　　17 | 14 | 15 | $21
223 Pennsylvania Ave., SE (C St.), 202-547-5114
1801 Clarendon Blvd. (Rhodes St.), Arlington, VA,
703-276-2627
■ When you "don't feel like cooking" but want something
"affordable and filling" to share while "relaxing" with
friends, consider the pizzas, sandwiches and all-you-can-
eat bowls of spaghetti "dressed up" with a choice of
"tantalizing" sauces at these "easygoing" Italians; but be
forewarned that while these venues definitely fill a niche
with their "urban flair", the food and service can "vary
greatly" by location.

I Matti S　　21 | 18 | 19 | $34
2436 18th St., NW (bet. Belmont & Columbia Rds.),
202-462-8844
☑ Feel like you're in a trattoria in Italy at this "lively" Adams
Morgan spot with popular open-to-the-street tables that
are ideal for people-watching; it's a smart choice for a
"long, romantic" Saturday lunch or a casual dinner over
"earthy", "inventive" pastas.

Inn at Glen Echo S　　18 | 19 | 19 | $34
6119 Tulane Ave. (MacArthur Blvd.), Glen Echo, MD,
301-229-2280
☑ Because this former roadhouse "in the woods" near Glen
Echo Park is blessed with such a picturesque setting, it's
no surprise that brunchers all vie for an outdoor deck
table; nighttime has its special appeal too, as couples
snuggle in the "cozy", "romantic" rooms, while music
lovers listen to live jazz in the bar on Sundays; the less
impressed, however, find the American home cooking and
service too "variable."

INN AT LITTLE WASHINGTON [S] 29 | 29 | 29 | $90

Main & Middle Sts., Washington, VA, 540-675-3800

■ "In a class of its own" and once again the *Washington Survey's* No. 1 restaurant for Food, Decor and Service, this "national treasure" in the Virginia countryside epitomizes a "sybaritic dining experience" with "exquisite" New American cuisine that's the "gastronomic equivalent of sex"; an "extravagant" "gold mine of an interior" and a "phenomenal" staff; given its high visibility, it's a tribute to owners Patrick O'Connell and Reinhardt Lynch that so many "salute" this inn as "absolutely" "unforgettable."

Iota [S] ▽ 15 | 16 | 15 | $17

2832 Wilson Blvd. (Edgewood & Fillmore Sts.), Arlington, VA, 703-522-8340

◪ While this Clarendon club is best known for its live nightly bands (and monthly poetry readings), hot tunes aren't all that's cooking here; some Gen Xers sup on "interesting" American dishes with International accents in the spiffed-up side cafe, but the more critical "go for the music", period.

I RICCHI 25 | 23 | 23 | $48

1220 19th St., NW (bet. M & N Sts.), 202-835-0459

◪ At Christianne Ricchi's Tuscan villa below Dupont Circle, pampered clients and their expense-account patrons "loosen their belts" for "first-class", "artfully done" Florentine specialties (like handmade tortellini with ricotta and spinach) served in a convincingly "rustic setting"; moreover, the staff is "knowledgeable" and when this place is "on top of its game" (as it often is), it's "one of the best Northern Italians around."

It's About Thyme ▽ 20 | 16 | 19 | $31

128 E. Davis St. (Main St.), Culpeper, VA, 540-825-4264

■ Located in the "quaint Civil War town" of Culpeper, this "neat" storefront bistro with hospitality aplenty serves up rustic Continental dishes on old wooden tables in a countrified milieu; it's a "pleasant lunch stop" for tourists and a local resource too, which means that with "no other good restaurants" nearby, there can be "a wait."

JALEO [S] 23 | 20 | 19 | $28

480 Seventh St., NW (E St.), 202-628-7949
72-71 Woodmont Ave. (Elm St.), Bethesda, MD, 301-913-0003

■ The "food and atmosphere pulse with excitement" at this Penn Quarter Spanish "scene" where the "sangria's a must", as are the "scrumptious" tapas; though the limited-reservation policy and "waits" at prime times are drawbacks, the majority thinks that this is a seriously "fun" "place to gather with friends"; N.B. José Andres' new Bethesda location is a runaway hit.

Japoné ◐ [S] – | – | – | E
2032 P St., NW (21st St.), 202-223-2573

Cafe Japoné ◐ [S] – | – | – | M
2032 P St., NW (21st St.), 202-223-1573
Stark contrasts distinguish the formal all-white boîte downstairs, with its flowing draperies, high-backed booths, long onyx table for 20, and Japanese and French fusion fare, from the mod black-and-neon, sake-sushi-and-karaoke cafe upstairs where trendy young 'uns mix 'n' match; meanwhile, at the dress-up-and-go-all-out fine dining venue, a hybrid menu runs from rockfish sashimi to luxury-priced kobe beef; N.B. dinner only, and they both stay up late.

Jasmine Cafe [S] ▽ 23 | 18 | 20 | $27
1633A Washington Plaza (N. Shore Dr.), Reston, VA, 703-471-9114
■ Overlooking Reston's Lake Anne, this "creative" New American isn't really a "secret", but its "off-the-beaten-path" location in the Washington Plaza and "intimate" size certainly make it feel that way; while it's rather "cramped" inside, the terrace is a "charming" place to dine on beef tenderloin with a Gorgonzola cream sauce.

Jean-Michel [S] 23 | 19 | 22 | $42
Wildwood Shopping Ctr., 10223 Old Georgetown Rd. (Democracy Blvd.), Bethesda, MD, 301-564-4910
■ "Tucked away" in a Bethesda strip mall, this "great neighborhood" restaurant "warms" up its older clientele on "a cold winter day" with "extremely reliable" Classic French cooking; it's run by a real "pro" who treats "you like an old friend" and it offers additional inducements like "easy parking", "quiet" tables at lunch and a chocolate soufflé that alone is "worth the trip."

JEFFERSON RESTAURANT [S] 25 | 26 | 25 | $48
Jefferson Hotel, 1200 16th St., NW (M St.), 202-833-6206
■ Countless famous faces have sought refuge at this "quiet", "private" hotel dining room near the White House, which draws a following with "superb" New American cuisine (especially "inspired" on holidays) turned out by an "excellent", "discreet" staff in "romantic alcoves"; also appealing is the "elegant" afternoon tea and the "great bar" (order the "best screwdriver around").

Jeffrey's at the Watergate [S] – | – | – | E
Watergate Hotel, 2560 Virginia Ave., NW (New Hampshire Ave.), 202-298-4455
Transplanted Texans find ground zero at this posh Watergate hotel dining room (formerly Aquarelle), a sib of Jeffrey's Restaurant in Austin (reputedly a First Eater's fave); here, Contemporary Texas cuisine (think: crispy oysters on yucca root chips with habanero-honey aioli), warmed-up decor and 'ya'll come' hospitality add a southwestern twang to a cosmo spot that's popular with Kennedy Center patrons.

Jerry Seafood   25   12   20 $40
9364 Lanham Severn Rd. (¾ mi. west of Rte. 495, exit 20A), Seabrook, MD, 301-577-0333

■ Despite the fact that it's a shirtsleeve "suburban" seafood "joint", this Seabrook spot earns a Top 40 food ranking for its rightfully famous 'Bomb', an "excellent" no-filler crab cake made with the "lumpiest, best meat" (its "huge" slabs of "fabulous" fish get kudos too); but while most find the family environment "fun", a few carp that the menu is "too expensive" relative to the ambiance.

Joe's Place Pizza & Pasta S   16   11   16 $12
430 N. Frederick Ave. (Odenhall Rd.), Gaithersburg, MD, 301-417-6602
5555 Lee Hwy. (bet. N. Harrison & Jefferson Sts.), Arlington, VA, 703-532-0990
3922 Old Lee Hwy. (Main St.), Fairfax, VA, 703-691-0222
5870 Leesburg Pike (Columbia Pike), Falls Church, VA, 703-820-5181
435 Maple Ave. W. (Nutley St.), Vienna, VA, 703-281-1111

◪ Parents and "kids love" these bright pizza-and-pasta parlors for their "romper-room atmosphere" and family-friendly eats, while the "office bunch" goes for the "bargain buffets"; even critics who call them "uninspired" "red-sauce factories" concede that they're "cheap" and handy.

John Harvard's Brew House S   16   16   17 $21
1299 Pennsylvania Ave., NW (bet. E & 13th Sts.), 202-783-2739

◪ "Mobbed" at lunch for working meals, at happy hour and at dinner (it's close to the theater and the mall), this "noisy", "subterranean" Downtown brewpub often feels "like a big fraternity house" for adults; the "decent" pub grub, including "good burgers", offered at "reasonable prices" will do if you keep your expectations in check.

Johnny's Half Shell   24   18   21 $32
2002 P St., NW (bet. 20th & 21st Sts.), 202-296-2021

■ A "rising star" in Dupont Circle, this "hip" but "completely unpretentious" bistro is creating quite a buzz with its "sparkling" fresh, "creatively" prepared seafood, matched by a "first-rate" international wine list; but be warned that it doesn't take reservations and it's "too small" to squeeze in all comers, so "get there early" or try to snag a seat at the white marble bar.

J. Paul's S   18   18   17 $23
3218 M St., NW (bet. Potomac St. & Wisconsin Ave.), 202-333-3450

◪ The young and single descend upon this "fun" perch in Georgetown for its prime people- and sports-watching and "raw bar scene"; the menu features a "wide selection" of American eats – hot pretzels, crab cakes, burgers, ribs – and even if some think it "could be better", most are content with the "festive" atmosphere.

Kabul Caravan 🖸 ▽ | 21 | 19 | 20 | $24 |

Colonial Shopping Ctr., 1725 Wilson Blvd. (bet. Quinn & Rhodes Sts.), Arlington, VA, 703-522-8394

■ Located on the "silk route" through Rosslyn, this "top-notch" Afghan evokes its "mysterious" homeland with "delicious", "interesting" fare (particularly the "wonderful pumpkin dishes"), "exotic" artifacts and plenty of hospitality; overall, it's a jet lag–free getaway that's worth taking.

Kawasaki ▽ | 20 | 12 | 16 | $35 |

1140 19th St., NW (bet. L & M Sts.), 202-466-3798

■ Well known to Asian businessmen and sophisticated travelers for its uncompromisingly "authentic" Japanese cuisine, notably its "great, traditional" sushi offerings, this Golden Triangle venue is less frequented by nearby residents, perhaps because they're discouraged by the "expense-account" prices.

Kazan | 22 | 19 | 22 | $33 |

Cambridge Corner Shopping Ctr., 6813 Redmond Dr. (Bridge Rd.), McLean, VA, 703-734-1960

■ "Bright decor" and new sidewalk seating make the atmosphere at this McLean standby even more "cheerful"; enjoy "great Turkish cooking", such as marvelous meze and a "must-try" doner kebab (spit-roasted pressed lamb and veal with yogurt sauce and bread), served by a "friendly", "accommodating" staff.

KAZ SUSHI BISTRO | 25 | 20 | 21 | $32 |

1915 I St., NW (bet. 18th & 20th Sts.), 202-530-5500

■ Chef-owner Kaz Okochi delights the "eye and the palate" with "fresh, creative appetizers", "terrific, imaginative" raw fish creations ("waiter, there's a mango in my sushi") and delightful desserts (the green tea tiramisu is "to die for") at this "minimalist", "postmodern" Japanese near the World Bank; it pulls in a "hip, young crowd" and major "foodies" and chefs who overlook the occasionally "slow" service as they anticipate the "truly exciting choices."

King Street Blues 🖸 | 18 | 19 | 18 | $19 |

112 N. St. Asaph St. (bet. Cameron & King Sts.), Alexandria, VA, 703-836-8800
5810 Kingstowne Center Dr. (bet. Kingstowne Blvd. & S. Van Doren St.), Kingstowne, VA, 703-313-0400

☑ "Frat boys" watch sports on TV, listen to tunes (live on Sunday nights) and chow down on ribs, "great garlic mashed potatoes" and other "filling, messy" Southern barbecue eats at this "youthful" Old Town "hangout" with "interesting", "wacky" decor (think lots of papier-mâché); P.S. the Kingstowne annex is even more of a "neighborhood place" and also lures in crowds with live music on Thursday nights.

KINKEAD'S [S] 27 | 24 | 25 | $49

2000 Pennsylvania Ctr., 2000 Pennsylvania Ave., NW (I St., bet. 20th & 21st Sts.), 202-296-7700

■ Bob Kinkead's "original" seafood-slanted New American cooking has made this power-central spot the *Washington Survey*'s Most Popular restaurant and one of the toughest reservations in town; its "no-kinks" perfectionism "instantly impresses" with "stylish" surroundings, a "knowledgeable" (if "arrogant") staff and "superb fish dishes" (ranked "the best" in DC); N.B. his soon-to-open Colvin Run Tavern has Tysons Corner abuzz.

Kobalt [S] – | – | – | VE

Ritz-Carlton, The, 1150 22nd St., NW (bet. L & M Sts.), 202-835-0500

Deep-blue stemware, fresh flowers and ultra-luxurious appointments accent this ritzy hotel dining room near the West End, providing a posh backdrop with lots of privacy for VIP guests; its state-of-the-art, see-in kitchen turns out beautifully plated Contemporary American cuisine, while the obliging servers are what you would expect from this brand-name host – however, it's still young and working out a few kinks.

Konami [S] ▽ 21 | 23 | 21 | $25

8221 Leesburg Pike (Rte. 123), Tysons Corner, VA, 703-821-3400

■ Tysons Corner techies find "great sushi hiding" out in a commercial strip mall (it's in its own building) at this high-gloss Japanese whose owners did a "fantastic job redecorating" (nice *feng shui* makes "everything feel right" here) what was a fast-food joint; the sophisticated layout includes smart lighting and a soothing garden patio.

Kramerbooks & Afterwords Cafe ☾ [S] 16 | 14 | 14 | $19

1517 Connecticut Ave., NW (bet. Dupont Circle & Q St.), 202-387-1462

◪ "Browsing" for reading, feeding and dating material is the story behind this Dupont Circle bookstore/cafe where the colorful characters and late hours are further attractions; most treat its American fare as "convenient" fillers and focus instead on the 'dysfunctional' family sundae, which could also describe the "preoccupied" servers.

Krupin's [S] 18 | 10 | 14 | $17

4620 Wisconsin Ave., NW (Chesapeake St.), 202-686-1989

◪ The 202 area code's "sole service provider for sour pickles, belly lox", corned beef sandwiches and other Jewish-style items according to mavens is this Upper NW deli (which "looks the part too"); it's also "the place to be on Sundays" for big breakfasts and "personal abuse", but though it may be "as close" as DC gets to the gold standard, Gotham expats insist that it "pales in comparison."

LA BERGERIE [S] 25 | 23 | 24 | $49
218 N. Lee St. (bet. Cameron & Queen Sts.), Alexandria, VA, 703-683-1007
■ "Old-world charm" and "old-fashioned French-Basque" cooking explain the appeal of this Old Town treasured link to a time when one dined out "with family" in a "quiet and elegant atmosphere"; nowadays, it's the youngsters (relatively speaking) who are trying their "parents' fancy restaurant" and they're raving about the "awesome" cuisine (the "duck confit and soufflé are fit for a dream") and "formal", professional service that's as "serious", but as "caring", as dad.

La Brasserie [S] 21 | 18 | 19 | $38
239 Massachusetts Ave., NE (bet. 2nd & 3rd Sts.), 202-546-9154
◪ A "longtime Capitol Hill standby" for lobbyists, with a "lovely", sunny terrace that makes persuading a pol that much easier, this Gallic veteran continues to do the trick with "reliable" bistro fare (especially the "delicious soups"), "personalized" manners and a "completely French feel"; nonetheless, a few dissenters think it's "holding on to yesteryear."

La Chaumiere 23 | 23 | 22 | $41
2813 M St., NW (bet. 28th & 29th Sts.), 202-338-1784
■ Francophiles and what's left of Georgetown's old guard find this "cozy" country French restaurant a "winter favorite" "by the fireplace" for "authentic" quenelles and cassoulet; Geraldine Pain, the founding owner's daughter, has continued the tradition of "caring", "inviting" service while adding "new twists" like updated specials.

La Colline 22 | 19 | 22 | $43
400 N. Capitol St., NW (bet. D & E Sts.), 202-737-0400
◪ Synonymous with "networking", "fundraisers" and "fine dining on Capitol Hill", this spacious Classic French venue is being "rediscovered" by young power brokers for its "honest" value and "understated" ways; it may "deserve a better setting" (it's a bit "staid"), but "TV reporters sitting up front" and senators lining the room help boost the ambiance.

La Cote d'Or Cafe [S] 23 | 21 | 22 | $42
6876 Lee Hwy. (bet. Washington Blvd. & Westmoreland St.), Falls Church, VA, 703-538-3033
◪ This "cozy" Falls Church bistro may be "hard to find but it's easy to come back to", thanks to its "charming", "romantic" atmosphere ("fresh roses on every table") and impressive citified French fare; since some find it a "bit pricey for the locale", consider the early-bird special.

LAFAYETTE [S] 23 | 27 | 24 | $49 |

Hay Adams Hotel, 800 16th St., NW (H St.), 202-638-2570

■ Located across the square from the White House, this "delightfully dignified" hotel dining room features "elegant" "old-world decor" (fresh flowers, candlelit tables, nightly piano music) and a power clientele that alone makes it "worth the price of admission"; chef Frederic Lange turns out New American food with a French flair, as well as an "almost absurdly civilized" afternoon tea, but the real house specialty is the pampering that makes "you feel like a VIP."

La Ferme [S] 21 | 23 | 22 | $43 |

7107 Brookville Rd. (East-West Hwy. & Western Ave.), Chevy Chase, MD, 301-986-5255

◪ "Perfect for older folks and family gatherings", this "calm" Chevy Chase Country French set in an old farmhouse is graced with a very "pretty" dining room and an arbor-replete deck; moreover, don't be surprised if the staff turns your lunch with friends over sweetbreads, Dover sole and "outstanding" soufflés into an occasion.

La Fourchette [S] 21 | 18 | 19 | $34 |

2429 18th St., NW (bet. Columbia Rd. & Kalorama St.), 202-332-3077

■ In nice weather, the sidewalk dining at this "homey", "reasonably" priced family-run staple provides an experience as Left Bank as it gets in Adams Morgan, while during the cold months the French bistro fare (along the lines of "great" rabbit and "delicious" sweetbreads) makes for "good winter eating"; after many "years of experience", the house can "assure consistency", despite "a little attitude."

La Madeleine French Bakery [S] 18 | 17 | 14 | $16 |

3000 M St., NW (30th St.), 202-337-6975
7607 Old Georgetown Rd. (Commerce St.), Bethesda, MD, 301-215-9142
Mid-Pike Plaza, 11858 Rockville Pike (Montrose Rd.), Rockville, MD, 301-984-2270
500 King St. (Pitt St.), Alexandria, VA, 703-739-2854
Bailey's Crossroads, 5861 Crossroads Ctr. (Columbia & Leesburg Pikes), Falls Church, VA, 703-379-5551
1833 Fountain Dr. (bet. Baron Cameron Rd. & Reston Pkwy.), Reston, VA, 703-707-0704
1915C Chain Bridge Rd. (Rte. 7), Tysons Corner, VA, 703-827-8833

◪ Say what you will about "French fast food", but these "pseudo-quaint" bakery/cafes fill a "niche" with their "comforting", semi-"authentic" offerings (don't miss the "wonderful tomato-basil soup"), "moderate" prices and "convenient" locations; though many dislike the "confusing cafeteria format" and "disorganized" service, nobody complains about the "free" "crusty" bread.

La Miche 22 | 20 | 22 | $43

7905 Norfolk Ave. (bet. Old Georgetown Rd. & Wisconsin Ave.), Bethesda, MD, 301-986-0707

■ A "steady" performer whose virtues are "never out of style", this "traditional" Bethesda French "standard" can be counted on for "solid", "well-prepared" "classic" dishes (the "heavenly soufflés are a treat") served in a "charming" candlelit setting; detractors, however, find it "a little stuffy" and "old-fashioned."

Landini Brothers [S] 20 | 18 | 19 | $35

115 King St. (Union St.), Alexandria, VA, 703-836-8404

◪ "Everyone in town" seems to frequent the bar at this "too-dark" hangout in Old Town with a "*Godfather*" feel before "squeezing" into the back room for the "best linguine with white clam sauce" and other "straightforward" dishes delivered by an "accommodating and humorous" staff; dissenters, though, warn that this is "tourist central."

La Provence 22 | 19 | 20 | $42

Vienna Shopping Ctr., 144 W. Maple Ave. (bet. Center St. & Courthouse Rd.), Vienna, VA, 703-242-3777

◪ Subdued lighting and "pretty" touches create a sweet "little surprise" for visitors to this "surprisingly good" French "gem" set in the Vienna Shopping Center; locals know to take advantage of the "bargain prix fixe lunch" since it "becomes crowded and hectic as the evening progresses", which means that "quality and service vary" at dinner.

L'AUBERGE CHEZ FRANÇOIS [S] 27 | 27 | 27 | $55

332 Springvale Rd. (2 mi. north of Georgetown Pike), Great Falls, VA, 703-759-3800

■ "Who doesn't love this woodsy outpost of Alsatian cooking" in Great Falls with its "adorable Provençal decor, warm " ambiance and "romantic" garden?; the Haeringer family is to be commended for its "leaving well enough alone" by continuing to offer a "glorious" five-course prix fixe Classic French menu (top-ranked in the *Washington Survey*) that may be the "best fine dining value" around; in sum, it's an "unparalleled experience" that's appreciated even more since it reopened after last year's fire.

L'AUBERGE PROVENCALE [S] 27 | 26 | 26 | $63

13630 Lord Fairfax Hwy. (Rte. 50), Boyce, VA, 540-837-1375

■ Chef-owner Alain Borel and his wife, Celeste, are "delightful" hosts and their antique-filled pre–Revolutionary War manor house set in the Virginia Hunt Country is a "hopelessly romantic" destination for Classic French dining; whether you linger over an "absolutely fabulous" five-course prix fixe dinner in the "beautiful" garden room or out on the patio, it promises to be "lovely all the way."

Lauriol Plaza S
21 | 22 | 18 | $24

1835 18th St., NW (S St.), 202-387-0035

☑ Relocated to a spacious Dupont Circle East venue with an eye-catching industrial-chic interior, this "happening" Latin has been a "mob scene" from day one; still relatively "cheap", with the "same great" menu of Mexican, Cuban and Spanish dishes, it also offers "lively" rooftop and sidewalk dining; but the "too-long waits" and "rushed" service make some miss the "funky" "charm" of the old site.

Lavandou S
21 | 18 | 19 | $36

3321 Connecticut Ave., NW (bet. Macomb & Newark Sts.), 202-966-3002

☑ Renovated a couple of years ago, this "trusted" Cleveland Park French bistro sports a "brighter" look, but the food's "as rich as ever"; though it's "still too crowded", fans say it's "worth" dealing with the "noise" to dine on the "gutsy" country fare, including "sunny" Provençal specialties.

LEBANESE TAVERNA S
23 | 18 | 20 | $25

2641 Connecticut Ave., NW (bet. Calvert St. & Woodley Rd.), 202-265-8681

5900 Washington Blvd. (McKinley Rd.), Arlington, VA, 703-241-8681

Congressional Plaza, 1605 Rockville Pike (Congressional Ln.), Rockville, MD, 301-468-9086

■ "Success hasn't spoiled" this "family-friendly" Lebanese trio, which appeals with "consistently excellent" "comfort" food, "great" locations and "affordable" prices; sample an assortment of the "garlicky" and "delicious" meze, or let the "dedicated" waiters "help you decide."

Legal Sea Foods
20 | 17 | 18 | $31

2020 K St., NW (bet. 20th & 21st Sts.), 202-496-1111

Tyson Galleria, 2001 International Dr. (Rte. 123), Tysons Corner, VA, 703-827-8900 S

Montgomery Mall, 7101 Democracy Blvd. (270 Frwy.), Bethesda, MD, 301-469-5900 S

Washington-Reagan National Airport (New North Terminal/ Terminal C), Arlington, VA, 703-413-9810 S

☑ Massachusetts-based "chowdah champions", these "corporate" seafood houses "know how to treat a fish" according to fin fans who are hooked on their "dependably" "fresh" fare and kid-friendly ways; critics of the "generic" setup carp "what they do to a crab cake should be illegal."

Le Gaulois
22 | 20 | 19 | $35

1106 King St. (bet. Fayette & Henry Sts.), Alexandria, VA, 703-739-9494

☑ "Well-priced Classic French fare that doesn't bankrupt you" earns strong support for this "rustic" Old Town bistro with a "treat" of a garden patio and old-school standards; the unenchanted, however, "mark it down for service" and suggest the "gruff" staff "could use some warmth."

Le Jardin
     – | – | – | E

1207 19th St., NW (bet. M & N Sts.), 202-833-4800

The intimate townhouse setting below Dupont Circle invites collegial conversation and whispered endearments at this Contemporary French (Yannick Cam, ex Provence and El Catalan, has a hand in this venture), where guests are seated at banquettes or a window table framed by floral-patterned glass; well-chosen wines, a fireplace and terrace tables maintain a year-round romantic ambiance.

Le Mannequin Pis S
     ▽ 25 | 16 | 20 | $37

18064 Georgia Ave. (Rte. 108), Olney, MD, 301-570-4800

■ "Belgians eat really well" conclude first-timers at this "tiny" Olney bistro after they've devoured "fantastic mussels and frites" washed down with "beer that's treated like wine" by a staff that's "eager to please"; though a few quibble that the "prices are high" for the 'burbs and its performance sometimes falters, most think it's "worth the pilgrimage."

Le Petit Mistral S
     22 | 17 | 21 | $40

6710 Old Dominion Dr. (Chain Bridge Rd.), McLean, VA, 703-748-4888

■ A "cute little place" offering "surprising quality and elegance in the middle of McLean", this French bistro's "excellent" prix fixe meals are "a treat" for those looking for a "bargain", as well as a "lovely" atmosphere and "attentive" service; in sum, it's a "welcome" local "treasure."

Le Refuge
     23 | 20 | 21 | $38

127 N. Washington St. (bet. Cameron & King Sts.), Alexandria, VA, 703-548-4661

■ "Refugees from the Left Bank of the Potomac" gather at this "charming" Old Town French "hideaway" for "good" old-fashioned "comfort" food, but be prepared to get "up close and personal" because these quarters are "cramped."

Le Relais S
     ▽ 25 | 24 | 24 | $49

Seneca Sq. Shopping Ctr., 10251 Seneca Rd. (bet. Georgetown Pike & Rte. 7), Great Falls, VA, 703-444-4060

■ "Stylish" and "modern" in a Frank Lloyd Wright kind of way, this "great addition to Northern Virginia" provides the Great Falls gentry with a "pretty" setting for "wonderful" French-American cuisine accompanied by a "fabulous wine list"; its "strong team" (ex the defunct Maison Blanche) ensures an "exceptional" experience "in all respects."

Le Rivage S
     18 | 19 | 20 | $36

1000 Water St., SW (bet. Maine Ave. & 9th St.), 202-488-8111

◪ Especially "beautiful at sunset", this Contemporary French on the SW waterfront features an "early" prix fixe dinner emphasizing "worthwhile" seafood, which, combined with timely service, makes it an Arena Stage ticket-holder's "salvation"; but though it's widely considered to be one of the area's "best choices", there's "still room to improve."

Les Halles ◐ [S] 19 | 17 | 17 | $35
1201 Pennsylvania Ave., NW (12th St.), 202-347-6848
◪ Take a trip to the 6th arrondissement by dining at this "fast and boisterous" Downtown French brasserie where the waiters are "cavalier", cigar smoke fills the air and the action keeps up till late; snag a table on the sidewalk terrace for prime people-watching while you dig into a "competently" done steak and the "best frites in DC."

Le Tarbouche 22 | 24 | 22 | $38
1801 K St., NW (18th St.), 202-331-5551
■ "Dramatic" and "exotic", this "fashionable" K Street Middle Eastern draws a global crowd with its "gorgeous" decor, "curiously successful blend" of French and Lebanese cuisines and "good humor"; the "graceful" ambiance at lunchtime seamlessly segues into a secluded feel at night, making it a "great place to try something different."

L'Etoile [S] ▽ 21 | 21 | 20 | $35
Clarion Hampshire Hotel, 1310 New Hampshire Ave., NW (N & 20th Sts.), 202-835-3030
■ The menu at this modish French-Moroccan hotel dining room off Dupont Circle lists steak béarnaise, cassoulet and lamb tagine, so it can be a "real surprise" to learn that it's strictly non-dairy kosher; since it's the "only such one in DC", it's less surprising that the staff, albeit "accommodating", sometimes "can't cope with the Saturday night crowds."

Levante's [S] 17 | 18 | 16 | $25
1320 19th St., NW (Dupont Circle), 202-293-3244
7262 Woodmont Ave. (Elm St.), Bethesda, MD, 301-657-2441
◪ "Appetizing" *pides* (boat-shaped pizzas) and "people-watching" are equal highlights at these Mediterranean-flavored Euro imports off Dupont Circle and in Bethesda, where the "sleek", casual settings, outdoor seating and "wide choices" of "different" Levantine items keep them full; a vocal minority, however, find them "faux" and only "fair."

Le Vieux Logis 22 | 20 | 20 | $44
7925 Old Georgetown Rd. (Auburn Ave.), Bethesda, MD, 301-652-6816
■ Behind "delightful exterior" murals, this "adorable" Country French cottage in Bethesda "charms" "urbane", "older" regulars by serving them "very good" "classics" in cozily "romantic" surroundings and being "responsive" to their needs; a few yawn "decent" but "unexceptional."

Lightfoot Cafe [S] ▽ 23 | 25 | 21 | $35
11 N. King St. (Market St.), Leesburg, VA, 703-771-2233
■ Relocated to "stunning" new quarters in a vintage "high-ceilinged bank", this "stylish" Leesburg Eclectic is making its mark with its "fabulous" atmosphere and "inventive" dishes (don't miss the desserts); despite a few gripes about "erratic" service, most laud it as a "great addition."

Little Saigon 🅂   – | – | – | I
6218B Wilson Blvd. (Patrick Henry Dr.), Falls Church, VA, 703-536-2633
This plain strip mall dining spot near Falls Church's Eden Center fills with local Vietnamese sampling its large repertoire of their homeland's dishes; inexpensive and authentic, it's worth checking out, especially with a crowd – its menu lists several good-value party dinners.

Little Viet Garden 🅂   20 | 14 | 17 | $20
3012 Wilson Blvd. (Garfield Rd.), Arlington, VA, 703-522-9686
☑ The "pleasant" "alfresco option" "makes everything taste better" at this "popular" Vietnamese "yuppie" hangout in Clarendon; still, expect dishes that are as "hit-or-miss" as the "uneven" service.

Los Chorros 🅂   ▽ 18 | 12 | 18 | $18
2420 Blue Ridge Ave. (Georgia Ave.), Wheaton, MD, 301-933-1066
◼ "Deservedly popular" with Salvadorans who create their own lively atmosphere, these suburban Central Americans offer authentic regional cooking, along with a broad menu of familiar Mexican dishes.

Lotte Plaza Market 🅂   ▽ 18 | 8 | 11 | $12
325 Old Lee Hwy. (Rte. 50), Fairfax, VA, 703-352-1600
◼ Housed in a sprawling Asian market in Fairfax, this "food court" provides a "variety" of "cheap", "tasty" adventures, from "fresh sushi" to "authentic" Korean soups; the tables in the mock interior courtyard offer great people-watching too.

Louisiana Express Co. 🅂   20 | 9 | 15 | $17
4921 Bethesda Ave. (Arlington Rd.), Bethesda, MD, 301-652-6945
◼ "Exercise more and eat here" at Bethesda's answer to Big Easy cravings – the "terrific" po' boys, "Cajun" chicken, jambalaya and bread pudding are worth any extra miles on the bike; service can be "slower than molasses on a praline", but the eats are "not to be missed."

Luigino 🅂   19 | 18 | 18 | $34
1100 New York Ave., NW (H & 12th Sts.), 202-371-0595
☑ At lunch, this "enjoyable" "Downtown business hangout" hums along as "hearty" pastas, pizzas and "sophisticated" Northern Italian specialties fuel "unhurried" meetings, while solos grab a "quick" bite at the dining bar; at night, however, the postmodern premises become (too?) quiet.

Luna Grill & Diner 🅂   18 | 15 | 16 | $18
1301 Connecticut Ave., NW (N St.), 202-835-2280
4024 28th St. S. (Quincy St.), Arlington, VA, 703-379-7173
☑ Favored by the "granola-and-Birkenstock crowd" for their "green plates" filled with fresh veggies, these "hip" American diners in Dupont Circle and Arlington are "good and cheap" and so popular that getting seated at lunch can seem like "an exercise in frustration"; foes say that "inconsistent quality and mediocre service are big turn-offs."

Madras Palace [S] — | — | — | I

Diamond Sq., 74 Bureau Dr. (Quince Orchard Rd.), Gaithersburg, MD, 301-977-1600

A royal treat for Montgomery County herbivores, not to mention locals looking for good cheap eats, this Vegetarian Indian's repertoire boasts enough variety to keep the curious busy for many visits, sampling *uthapams* (sourdough pancakes), *dosas* (large crêpes) and non-alcoholic drinks; its lunch buffet is one of the best meal deals around.

Maestro [S] — | — | — | VE

(fka Ritz Carlton, The Restaurant)

Ritz-Carlton, 1700 Tysons Blvd. (International Dr.), Tysons Corner, VA, 703-917-5498

Masters of the art of pampering at this posh Tysons Corner power preserve just spent $1.5 million on a svelte makeover of the dining room, an impressive demonstration kitchen and a wall of wine; its new contemporary Italian cuisine can be sampled through choose-your-own tasting menus, or by letting ambitious chef Fabio Trabocchi (ex London's Floriana) demonstrate his creativity; megadeal lunches or the wildly popular Sunday brunch are other ways to go.

Maggiano's Little Italy [S] 19 | 18 | 18 | $25

5333 Wisconsin Ave., NW (Western Ave.), 202-966-5500
Tyson Galleria, 1790M International Dr. (Rte. 123), Tysons Corner, VA, 703-356-9000

◪ Go "for the happy gluttony of it" all say fans of these Italian-American eateries, which are filled with "noise, garlic" and groups chowing down on "monstrous"-sized (and "heavy") family-style meals; opponents, however, call them the triumph of "quantity over quality."

Majestic Cafe [S] — | — | — | M

911 King St. (Patrick St.), Alexandria, VA, 703-837-9117

Chef-partner Susan Lindeborg's (ex Morrison-Clark Inn) warm-hearted tribute to Old Town Alexandria's 'good eats' restaurant legacy sports a personal-size dining room, blending art deco elements (from its former New Majestic Cafe days) and modern comforts, that suits anything from a casual burger to a celebration; its a perfect match for Lindeborg's highly regarded, regionally-inspired Contemporary American dishes; plus, there's a spiffy bar for sipping, supping and scoping the street.

MAKOTO [S] 28 | 23 | 26 | $49

4822 MacArthur Blvd., NW (Reservoir Rd.), 202-298-6866

■ "Wear respectable socks" when taking "visiting dignitaries" and guests to this top-rated, "authentic" Japanese in the Palisades, where patrons sit shoeless in a "tiny", "exquisitely simple" "traditional" dining room as a "charming" staff serves "outstanding" tidbits that amount to "food as art"; P.S. if "little cubes at little tables" aren't your thing, there's also a "gem" of a little sushi bar.

Malaysia Kopitiam S   – | – | – | I
1827 M St., NW (bet. 18th & 19th Sts.), 202-833-6232
An exciting source of exotic dishes at (literally) bargain-basement prices, this former Wheaton Malaysian relocated a while back to a basic step-down space below Dupont Circle, where the picture menu and proud proprietor help novices explore the extensive Malay, Chinese and Indian offerings; experienced diners give noodles and appetizers the nod, but prices are low enough to encourage sampling.

Malibu Grill Brazilian Steakhouse S   18 | 15 | 17 | $22
4516 Fair Knoll Dr. (Fair Lakes Pkwy.), Fairfax, VA, 703-222-5555
5715 Columbia Pike (Rte. 7), Falls Church, VA, 703-379-0587
◪ These ranch-sized Northern Virginia feeding stations have a "great gimmick" – an all-you-can-eat salad bar that precedes a Brazilian meat-fest where spear-wielding gauchos slice a variety of meats onto your plate; while beloved by always- hungry teenage boys and a "fun place to go with a group" "to pig out on a protein power diet", it definitely helps to "pace yourself."

Mama Lucia S   – | – | – | I
Olney Village Mart, 18224 Village Mart Dr. (bet. Rte. 108 & Georgia Ave.), Olney, MD, 301-570-9500
Federal Plaza, 12274 Rockville Pike (Twinbrook Pkwy.), Rockville, MD, 301-770-4894
NY-style pizza (the real deal), pastas, subs, salads and other familiar Italian-American entrées are the draw at these suburban shopping center eateries, which are notable for their cheap prices, huge portions and simple, pleasant surroundings; in Rockville, the lunchtime counter service moves with Big Apple speed, while the Olney location has table service (optional at lunch), and lots more space; N.B. a new Bethesda branch was set to open at press time.

M & S Grill S   19 | 20 | 19 | $30
600 13th St., NW (F St.), 202-347-1500
◪ Decorated with lots of mahogany, brass and leather, this "classy", "masculine" replica of a Traditional American saloon feeds the Downtown "suited set" a "very business"-oriented lunch, then loosens up a bit for happy-hour martinis and meal-sized munchies; despite some barbs about how "service could be better", its well-thought-out design and "varied" menu of mostly "good" food make it "difficult to get a reservation."

Mango Mike's S   – | – | – | M
4580 Duke St. (Jordan St.), Alexandria, VA, 703-370-3800
"Festive" and funky, this Caribbean-themed "end-of-the-day place" moved its sunset beach party to another locale on Duke Street over a year ago, but the hot island kitchen still keeps things cooking with its popular jerk chicken and Tuesday lobster special, and the "live steel drum" brunch keeps the beat going on Sundays.

MARCEL'S 27 | 24 | 24 | $58

2401 Pennsylvania Ave., NW (24th St.), 202-296-1166

■ "Talented" chef Robert Wiedmaier's "wonderful" West End French-Belgian quickly rocketed "into an elite class" (it's in the Top 10 for food) shortly after it opened not long ago in the space that formerly housed Provence; anticipate a "gracious maitre d'", "hearty" and "adventurous" cuisine ("the duck is a treat") paired with "outstanding" wine service, "mouthwatering desserts", a "romantic" (albeit sometimes "loud"), "provincial" ambiance and a beckoning sidewalk cafe; in sum: "a winner."

Mare e Monti [S] ▽ 21 | 15 | 17 | $25

Free State Mall, 15554B Annapolis Rd. (Hwy. 197), Bowie, MD, 301-262-9179

■ Buried in a suburban mall in Bowie but well worth unearthing is this white-walled, arch-filled Italian "treasure" with interesting appetizers such as mozzarella *en carozza* (a deep-fried sandwich with an anchovy-garlic sauce), solid seafood dishes and unusual "homemade" pastas like *timballo*, a lasagna from the Abruzzi region; not only is it "unexpectedly delightful", it's a decent "value" too.

Mark, The 20 | 20 | 20 | $36

401 Seventh St., NW (bet. D & E Sts.), 202-783-3133

◪ "Always interesting" combinations that "know no boundaries" is how surveyors describe Allison Swope's New American creations at this Penn Quarter bistro with a "lively Downtown look" and a location that's "perfect" before attending the Shakespeare Theater; naturally, with so many "inventive" dishes, a few are bound to "miss the mark", but even critics go on Monday nights (and Saturdays in summer), when bottled wine is half off.

Market St. Bar & Grill [S] 21 | 19 | 20 | $36

Hyatt Hotel, 1800 President St. (Market St.), Reston, VA, 703-709-6262

◪ Versatile is an apt word to describe this "surprisingly sophisticated" New American hotel dining room in Reston, which works for "telecom business deals" at lunchtime, weekend jazz suppers in the lounge and an "excellent Sunday brunch"; a few note "too many chef changes", but most think it's still the "best choice" in the area.

Mark's Duck House ◐ [S] 22 | 10 | 17 | $21

6184A Arlington Blvd. (Patrick Henry Dr.), Annandale, VA, 703-532-2125

■ "Serious" Hong Kong–style cooking draws local toques and Chinese foodies to this "stripped-down" Falls Church ethnic, which may "lack style and pizazz" but more than makes up for it with its "phenomenal specialties" (ask for a translation of the Chinese-language listings); seafood is its strong suit along with "the best" BBQ meats and "unbelievable" daily dim sum.

Martin's Tavern S
| 16 | 19 | 17 | $27 |

1264 Wisconsin Ave., NW (N St.), 202-333-7370

◪ Since FDR's presidency, this "dark" "Georgetown classic" has been a "neighborly" watering hole, offering a "cool place to duck into on a hot day" for basic American pub grub and a frosty brew, as well as a cozy spot for an old-fashioned oyster stew "when snow shuts down the city"; the less nostalgic say it's "no big New Deal" and find it "dated."

Matisse S
| 19 | 23 | 18 | $43 |

4934 Wisconsin Ave., NW (42nd St.), 202-244-5222

◪ "Beautifully decorated" with intricate Matisse-inspired ironwork, this "romantic" Upper NW French-Mediterranean otherwise plays to mixed reviews: boosters say it's a "classy" stop that's "just what the neighborhood needs", but dissenters counter that the food and "disorganized" service are "not up to the prices."

Matuba S
| 22 | 13 | 18 | $24 |

4918 Cordell Ave. (Old Georgetown Rd.), Bethesda, MD, 301-652-7449
2915 Columbia Pike (Walter Reed St.), Arlington, VA, 703-521-2811

■ These "safe", straightforward suburban Japanese outfits feature "lots of variations" of "affordable", "fresh" sushi, as well as "other strong options" such as tempura and *katsu*; they also pack "nice budget" bento boxes and deal "efficiently" with kids and crowds; therefore, with so much going for them, most can overlook the unimpressive settings.

Maxim Palace S
| _ | _ | _ | I |

Glen Forest Shopping Ctr., 5900 Leesburg Pike (Glen Forest Dr.), Falls Church, VA, 703-998-8888

On weekends, the dim sum carts at this Falls Church Hong Kong–style banquet hall roll at full speed with a "wonderful assortment" (80 choices) of tempting tidbits to Chinese and Vietnamese families; the morsels, along with an extensive Cantonese menu and buffet lunch, are also available on calmer weekdays, but then you'd miss the frenzied fun.

MCCORMICK & SCHMICK'S S
| 22 | 21 | 21 | $35 |

1652 K St., NW (bet. 16th & 17th Sts.), 202-861-2233
7401 Woodmont Ave. (bet. Montgomery Ln. & Old Georgetown Rd.), Bethesda, MD, 301-961-2626
11920 Democracy Dr. (bet. Discovery & Library Sts.), Reston, VA, 703-481-6600
Ernst & Young Bldg., 8484 Westpark Dr. (Rte. 7), Tysons Corner, VA, 703-848-8000

■ "Any fish, any way you like it", is the deal at these handsome seafood houses, "rendezvous" spots whose "clubby booths" and "old saloon" embellishments lend an air of "privacy" to high-powered meals; despite their "slick", "formulaic" menu and service, they're wildly popular, with most applauding their "beautifully fresh fish."

Medaterra S   18 | 17 | 18 | $25
2614 Connecticut Ave., NW (Calvert St.), 202-797-0400
◪ "Saturated colors" suffuse the interior of this Woodley Park Mediterranean, which specializes in Egyptian-influenced appetizers and French-accented fish dishes; even if the less enthused find the edibles "hit-or-miss", they appreciate the room's "quiet", "homey" appeal.

Mediterranee   22 | 17 | 21 | $31
3520 Lee Hwy. (Monroe St.), Arlington, VA, 703-527-7276
■ "Just right for a low-key romantic dinner" in Arlington, this "tiny", rustic French-Mediterranean's flowery decor, "undiscovered" feel and "attentive" staff complement its "special dishes" (notably couscous and grilled sardines); the seating is "tight" at busy times, but if you go early or late you can pair bargain dining ($18.95 prix fixe) with intimacy.

Mehak S   ▽ 20 | 11 | 18 | $18
817 Seventh St., NW (bet. H & I Sts.), 202-408-9292
7716 Lee Hwy. (Rte. 7), Falls Church, VA, 703-573-8076
■ While this "hole-in-the-wall" Falls Church Moghul and its newer MCI Center sib (the one with the "nice decor") are not well known, those who are familiar with them speak highly of their "deeply flavored classics" cooked with "just enough spice"; it's a "bargain", to boot.

Meiweh S   – | – | – | M
1200 New Hampshire Ave. (M St.), 202-833-2888
Larry La (ex City Lights of China) and his team "have done it again" (but this time with "style") at this "beautiful" new Chinese-American near the West End, which boasts stunning appointments, floor-to-ceiling windows, "less-rushed service" and what early reports call the "same great" multiregional standards that packed his former place.

MELROSE S   27 | 25 | 26 | $51
Park Hyatt Hotel, M & 24th Sts., NW, 202-955-3899
■ Overcome your "anti–hotel" dining room bias at this "spacious", "classy" West End "refuge" that showcases "refined" New American cuisine, museum-worthy art, an "elegant" outdoor courtyard and "gracious" service; it's "a good business restaurant", a "classy spot" for celebratory weekend dining and dancing, a "standard"-setting Sunday brunch pick and a smart choice for "super" holiday dinners; truth be told, it's awfully "hard to fault."

Mendocino Grille & Wine Bar S   22 | 21 | 22 | $42
2917 M St., NW (bet. 29th & 30th Sts.), 202-333-2912
■ Described as a "beautiful blonde" with "California chic", this "innovative" New American's "high-quality" food paired with a "thoughtful" West Coast wine list, "minimalist" setting and "knowledgeable" servers "caught on" fast with date-minded couples; it also works when you just want to "sit by an open window and watch Georgetown go by."

Meskerem ◐Ⓢ   20 | 17 | 17 | $21
2434 18th St., NW (bet. Belmont St. & Columbia Rd.),
202-462-4100
◪ "You either like Ethiopian food or you don't", so if a
"no-silverware experience" of scooping up pungent
stews with spongy bread appeals, then this Adams
Morgan example might be for you; though regarded as a
bit more "Americanized" than its brethren, regulars urge
bring your "family or friends", "sit upstairs" on the beanbags
and "get the sampler" plate.

Metro Center Grille Ⓢ   17 | 16 | 17 | $27
Marriott at Metro Ctr., 775 12th St., NW (bet. H & J Sts.),
202-737-2200
◪ Worth considering for a "moderately priced" business
lunch near the Convention Center, this New American
hotel dining room with an "open feel" and "nicely spaced
tables" presents a menu that runs from simple grilled
items to more "creative" dishes; the clubby downstairs
Regatta Raw Bar offers a more casual (and quicker)
buffet that's a "good value."

Metro 29 ◐Ⓢ   16 | 14 | 16 | $16
4711 Lee Hwy. (Glebe Rd.), Arlington, VA, 703-528-2464
■ "Huge portions" plus late hours are among the reasons
why this big, shiny retro diner in Arlington is a good place
to go "when everyone wants something different" and no
one wants to fuss; it can get "jammed" on weekends and
a so-so food score suggests it's "nothing fancy", but it's a
"basic", "reliable" place to bring the family and you can
get "breakfast at any time."

Mexicali Blues Ⓢ   17 | 17 | 16 | $16
2933 Wilson Blvd. (bet. N. Fillmore & N. Garfield Sts.),
Arlington, VA, 703-812-9352
◪ Though "colorful" and "cute", this Clarendon Central
American "nook" sparks some vocal border disputes:
amigos praise the "cheap", "authentic El Salvadoran and
Mexican" food (it's "not your average tamale"), but foes
fire back that the food doesn't live up to its hype.

Mezza 9 Ⓢ   23 | 22 | 20 | $33
Hyatt Arlington, 1325 Wilson Blvd. (Nash St.), Arlington, VA,
703-276-8999
■ "Wonderfully atypical", this hotel dining room with
"pretty", "appealing decor" features an "ingenious",
"tasty" Mediterranean grazing menu (entrées are offered
as well) and nice touches such as French-press coffee
and complimentary chocolates and dried fruit; thus, this
"unexpected treat" makes a savvy business meal choice,
especially when compared to the rest of the sterile
Rosslyn restaurant scene.

Michael's
— | — | — | E

*Giant Shopping Ctr., 6825 Redmond Dr., Ste. K
(Old Dominion Dr.), McLean, VA, 703-288-4601*
At their glossy, new 'Milan in McLean' Italian, the De Chiari
family draw North Virginia suburbanites with upscale pastas,
seafood and veal, fancy digs and an ability to accommodate
regulars that's already earned them a loyal following at
Renato in Potomac, Md., another high-roller's 'hood; though
early word is in favor of the family recipes, it's likely that
meeting and greeting the neighbors will be as much of a
magnet as eating.

Mike's American Grill S
21 | 20 | 20 | $24

*6210 Backlick Rd. (Old Keene Mill Rd.), Springfield, VA,
703-644-7100*
■ Springfield residents consider themselves "lucky" to
have this "loud", "cavernous" gathering place where an
"attentive", "efficient" young crew serves up addictive
ozzie rolls, crab cakes to crow about, "great burgers",
"excellent" blackened prime rib and other "hearty"
American fare; P.S. the "call-ahead" reservations policy
for groups eases the "long waits."

Mimi's American Bistro ●S
— | — | — | M

2120 P St., NW (bet. 21st & 22nd Sts.), 202-464-6464
Look, that's your waiter at the mike at this DuPont Circle
'theatre restaurant', where enthusiastic singing, dancing,
emoting servers, zingy Med–Middle Eastern fare (from
meze to pastas to grilled duck) and dark, hip decor come
together with late hours (for DC) and a pianist to attract a
mostly young, nightlife crowd; it's also a good bet for an
offbeat business lunch or a bite while scoping the nearby
art gallery scene.

Mi Rancho S
18 | 16 | 18 | $19

*19725 Germantown Rd. (Middlebrook Rd.), Germantown, MD,
301-515-7480*
8701 Ramsey Ave. (Cameron St.), Silver Spring, MD, 301-588-4872
◪ These kid-friendly haciendas provide Germantown and
Silver Spring with lots of "festive" atmosphere plus "real
Mexican" dishes, notably a "wonderful seafood soup (a
frequent special) and "great fresh fish" (on weekends);
while some feel they've grown a tad "complacent", their
village patios and low prices are still "much appreciated."

Miss Saigon S
19 | 15 | 17 | $24

3057 M St. (bet. 30th & 31st Sts.), 202-333-5545
◪ Filled with "twice-a-week" Georgetown wallet-watchers
and tourists recruited by its blackboard specials and
"beautiful" front, this M Street Vietnamese is one of the
neighborhood's "better inexpensive choices" with any claim
to "nice decor"; though not without its critics (it "could
use a bit more zip"), it's nevertheless enjoying a long run.

Miu Kee ◐[S] — | – | – | I

6653 Arlington Blvd. (Annandale Rd.), Falls Church, VA, 703-237-8884

Situated in an unadorned Falls Church strip mall, this Hong Kong–style Chinese is "always crowded" with Asians drawn from miles around by its "excellent BBQ meats", noodle soups and seafood; neophytes should begin with the unthreatening soy-sauce chicken or lobster with ginger and gradually become more adventurous with each visit.

Moby Dick [S]⊄ 21 | 7 | 13 | $12

1070 31st St., NW (bet. K & M Sts.), 202-333-4400
7027 Wisconsin Ave. (Leland St.), Bethesda, MD, 301-654-1838
105 Market St. (Kentlands Blvd.), Gaithersburg, MD, 301-987-7770
Fairfax Town Ctr., 12154 W. Ox Rd. (Main St.), Fairfax, VA, 703-352-6226
6864 Old Dominion Dr. (Rte. 123), Tysons Corner, VA, 703-448-8448

■ What these bare-bones, self-serve Persians lack in amenities they make up for in "unbelievably cheap", "wonderful" fresh-baked bread, "super" hummus, "juicy, fragrant" kebabs and "great" lunch plates; whether you sit down or carry out, expect a "whale of a good meal."

Monocle 17 | 17 | 19 | $31

107 D St., NE (1st St.), 202-546-4488

◪ "A senator at every table" may be a stretch of a claim, but this "clubby" Capitol Hill (Senate-side) mainstay pulls in a regular roster of politicos, lobbyists and Supreme Court justices; while most find the "stargazing" more exciting than the "old-school" American grub, if you're from out of town consider a visit part of your political education.

Montgomery's Grille [S] 13 | 15 | 15 | $23

7200 Wisconsin Ave. (Bethesda Ave.), Bethesda, MD, 301-654-3595

◪ Bethesda twenty- and thirtysomethings say the happy-hour scene on the outdoor deck of this American staple is its main appeal, though it's also conveniently located near movie theaters; as its ratings indicate, it's "nothing special", but it has a "diverse" menu and plenty of tables.

MORRISON-CLARK INN [S] 25 | 25 | 24 | $47

1015 L St., NW (bet. 11th St. & Massachusetts Ave.), 202-898-1200

■ "Soaring windows and floral drapes" add to the "charm" of this "intimate" Victorian New American, "excellent for business gatherings and special events" or a "romantic" "in-town escape"; here, one can go "first-class for a tad less" than at comparable places, though with renowned chef Susan Lindeborg long gone (she's just opened the Majestic Cafe), its stellar food rating may be in question.

MORTON'S OF CHICAGO [S] | 25 | 22 | 23 | $51 |

Washington Sq., 1050 Connecticut Ave., NW (L St.), 202-955-5997
3251 Prospect St., NW (Wisconsin Ave.), 202-342-6258
Fairfax Sq., 8075 Leesburg Pike (Aline Rd.), Tysons Corner, VA, 703-883-0800

■ "Unreconstructed beef eaters" laud the "fantastic" porterhouse and other "decadent", "gut-busting" portions of prime meats served at these "dark", clubby steakhouses; patrons also enjoy being treated like a "power broker and insider" by the "knowledgeable" staff and don't mind signing the expense-account voucher, but they can skip "being introduced to their entrée" as part of the pre-ordering ritual; N.B. a new location is set to open in the Reston Town Center.

Mr. K's [S] | 24 | 23 | 24 | $44 |

2121 K St., NW (bet. 21st & 22nd Sts.), 202-331-8868

◪ "If the French annexed China", the result might be something like this "luxurious" K Street corporate-accounter where some of the "best Chinese food in town" is proffered by a "very formal" staff in an "elegant" setting perfect for "confidential" meetings; critics, though, complain about "overpriced splendor" and one disenchanted wit swears that "the lions out front are ready to run away."

Mrs. Simpson's [S] | – | – | – | E |

2915 Connecticut Ave. NW (Cathedral Ave.), 202-332-8700

The "reincarnation" of this Windsor-Simpson themed restaurant in Woodley Park retains the memorabilia and intimate feel that has always made it a favorite for "sentimental" occasions; reports about "great rack of lamb" from its New American menu sound promising, as do accounts of the "generous brunch."

Nam's of Bethesda [S] | 20 | 15 | 20 | $22 |

4928 Cordell Ave. (Georgetown Rd.), Bethesda, MD, 301-652-2635

◪ "Rarely crowded", this intimate, "quiet" white-tablecloth Bethesda Vietnamese serves "consistently" solid fare (consider the *pho* and the whole fish) by a "gracious" staff; bargain-hunters add that the "great lunch specials" are a "taste bud's delight."

Nam Viet [S] | 22 | 12 | 18 | $20 |

3419 Connecticut Ave., NW (bet. Macomb & Porter Sts.), 202-237-1015
1127 N. Hudson St. (Wilson Blvd.), Arlington, VA, 703-522-7110

■ "Awesome won ton soup", "scrumptious shrimp rolls" and "caramel pork that never disappoints" are the highlights of the "extensive menu of delights" at these Clarendon and Cleveland Park Vietnamese stops; they're best appreciated by folks who "don't require atmosphere" but do want "big portions" of "cheap", "fresh", "excellently balanced" dishes served by "nice" people.

Nathan's S　　　　17　18　18　$34
3150 M St., NW (Wisconsin Ave.), 202-338-2000
◪ The bar at this "popular G-town hangout" attracts a "classy" clientele of second-time-around singles drawn to its drinks and celebrity sightings; the back room is a "hideaway" that remains social "ground zero" for the local old guard, which appreciates the updated American classics; some quibble, however, about "shopworn" decor.

Negril　　　　▽　17　9　12　$18
2301G Georgia Ave. NW (Bryant St.), 202-332-3737
18509 N. Frederick Ave. (Rte. 355), Gaithersburg, MD, 301-926-7220
Mitchellville Plaza, 12116 Central Ave. (Rt. 193), Mitchellville, MD, 301-249-9101
965 Thayer Ave. (Georgia Ave.), Silver Spring, MD, 301-585-3000
◪ Though these Jamaicans aren't big on decor, they work "for people who are there to eat"; look for "reasonably" priced, spicy, tasty island cooking that isn't easily found hereabouts (such as coco bread and curried goat), but also remember that "authentic isn't [always] what you expect."

Neisha Thai S　　　　▽　23　18　22　$22
Zulmore Plaza, 6037 Leesburg Pike (Glen Carlyn Rd.), Bailey's Crossroads, VA, 703-933-3788
7924 LB Tysons Corner Ctr. (Chain Bridge Rd.), Tysons Corner, VA, 703-883-3588
◪ Situated in Bailey's Crossroads, this "psychedelic Thai cave" hopes to give nearby Duangrat's and Rabieng a "run for their money"; enjoy "delicious" food (including passion beef and salmon grilled in banana leaves) served in a "fun" and "glitzy" atmosphere by an "attentive" staff at "reasonable" tabs; N.B. its Tysons Corner sib is new.

New Fortune ◑S　　　　▽　21　13　16　$20
16515 S. Frederick Ave. (bet. N. & S. Westland Drs.), Gaithersburg, MD, 301-548-8886
■ Some of the area's "best "Hong Kong–style dim sum (offered daily), along with a "very broad" compendium of Cantonese, Szechuan and Hunan dishes (listed in a menu with chapter tabs), is served at this Gaithersburg Chinese banquet hall, which is so large you may find yourself accidentally "attending a wedding" reception.

New Heights S　　　　24　23　22　$47
2317 Calvert St., NW (Connecticut Ave.), 202-234-4110
■ Set in a "beautiful", "airy" treetop venue in Woodley Park that's filled with Arts and Crafts furniture, this "quietly hip" New American manages to set a "standard for creativity" "year after year", despite the turnover of talented chefs who have passed through its kitchen; its "loyal patrons" are more than willing to "take the risk of originality" and though occasionally a dish is "too complex" few want it to step back from the edge.

Neyla S
3206 N St., NW (Wisconsin Ave.), 202-333-6353

Expect Mediterranean glam, Las Vegas–style, at this seductive year-old grill in Georgetown, a mysterious stage set (think brilliant hangings, dramatic lighting and clever mirrors) replete with a fashionable communal table to encourage single diners to socialize; its mix of inventive meze, charcoal-grilled items and stylish specialties with Near Eastern flavors is attracting a crowd to a site that has yet to house a winner.

Nibbler, The S
18556 Woodfield Rd. (Muncaster Mill Rd.), Gaithersburg, MD, 301-417-0233

■ If the wonderful rotisserie chicken and intriguing sides at those Incan chicken places have piqued your curiosity about Peruvian food, you should give this "cheap", simple Gaithersburg spot a try; though oddly named and out of the way, regulars recommend it for its "hearty, authentic" cooking and awfully "nice" staff.

Nick & Stef's Steakhouse
MCI Ctr., 601 F. St., NW (6th St.), 202-661-5040

Competing for high stakes at the MCI Center, Joachim and Christine Splichal (Patina, LA) bring their California sensibility to the luxury steakhouse game in a svelte, softly lit enclave, accented with blond wood, leather and silk; and while prime, dry-aged Angus beef is the lead-off player, it's backed by tempting starters and sides, plus designer bar bites; N.B. armchair coaches can dine close to the action in a private room overlooking the Wizards' practice court.

Niwano Hana S
Wintergreen Plaza, 887 Rockville Pike (Edmonston Dr.), Rockville, MD, 301-294-0553

■ "Hidden" on Rockville Pike, this "authentic gem" has Montgomery County sushi freaks swooning over the "large portions of excellent fish" prepared by "experienced masters"; moreover, its "friendly" servers "remember your face" and a smart-looking post-*Survey* redo should improve the above decor score, ameliorating what was its sole drawback.

Nizam's S
Village Green Shopping Ctr., 523 Maple Ave. W. (Rte. 123), Vienna, VA, 703-938-8948

■ The "time-honored tradition" of doner kebab nights (Tuesdays, Fridays and weekends), along with the owner's "warm welcome", distinguishes this "intimate", exotic Turkish bazaar in Vienna; of course, that's not to say that its other specialties aren't equally "delicious", but if forced to make a suggestion loyalists begrudgingly concede that maybe it "could use some new dishes."

NORA
26 24 24 $51

2132 Florida Ave., NW (bet. Connecticut &
Massachusetts Aves.), 202-462-5143
■ Nora Pouillon sure knows how to make "all-organic"
dining taste "so much better than it sounds" at this
"exceptional" New American set in a "romantic" carriage
house above Dupont Circle; it's "very big with official
Washington" and many discerning diners, even if a few
quibblers call it "too politically correct" and "costly."

OBELISK
27 22 26 $57

2029 P St., NW (bet. 20th & 21st Sts.), 202-872-1180
■ For a "superb" experience that's like "eating fine food
at someone's home", indulge in this "gem" off Dupont
Circle that captures the Italian sensibility with its "simple,
pure and satisfying" seasonal cuisine (top-rated in its
category); admirers urge "be open-minded" and let the
chef's "creative prix fixe menus stimulate your palate";
just as "wonderful" as the fare are the wines and a staff
that's intent on making each meal "special."

Occidental, The S
21 23 21 $41

Willard Complex, 1475 Pennsylvania Ave., NW (14th St.),
202-783-1475
◪ A "DC institution" where one goes to "lunch with big
shots", this Downtown New American embodies what
this town "is all about – power"; "clubby" (or "stuffy")
and "professional", it's a place to see and "be seen" in
a room lined with photos of famous politicians; though
dissenters have found it to be "disappointing" in recent
years, we hear it "could be coming back" thanks to the
updated classics of a "fine new chef."

Oceanaire Seafood Room S
– – – E

1201 F St., NW (bet. 12th & 13th Sts.), 202-347-2277
Evocative of a swank ocean liner's dining room, this
seafood-focused American (dry-docked Downtown) is
destined to appeal to a steakhouse crowd with its polished
wood, deft lighting and curved booths suitable for business
and social meetings, backed up by massively-portioned
fresh fin fare, chicken and steak; its retro atmosphere makes
it hard to resist ordering a sidecar or a sea breeze from the
classic cocktail list.

Old Angler's Inn S
22 24 21 $50

10801 MacArthur Blvd. (1 mi. east of Clara Barton Pkwy.),
Potomac, MD, 301-365-2425
◪ "Magical" nights by the patio fountain in the summertime
is the enchanting attraction of this "picturesque" Great Falls
New American that also features a rustic "little garret
upstairs" and a "romantic" fireplace in season; the "pricey"
dishes can be "great", but many detractors think that overall
the food's been taking "a dip."

OLD EBBITT GRILL ◑ [S] 20 | 22 | 20 | $31

675 15th St., NW (bet. F & G Sts.), 202-347-4801

■ DC's big, handsome, neo-Edwardian "public club" (think dark paneling, "period" gas lamps and leather-lined booths) set in a prime Downtown locale provides a highly Washingtonian backdrop for everything from "power breakfasts" to "late-night oysters"; its "huge bar scene" draws plenty of "politicos", as does the "classic" American food and professionally "helpful" staff, but even if they falter, "it's the atmosphere, stupid."

Old Europe [S] 17 | 17 | 19 | $30

2434 Wisconsin Ave., NW (Calvert St.), 202-333-7600

◪ "Bavarian on a budget, all hail sauerkraut" cheer boosters of this "old standby" (circa 1948) in Glover Park where it's "always Oktoberfest"; though the "provincial" German food may be "heavy" and the "dark" decor a bit "worn", it's "reliable" and possibly the "last of its kind" around.

Old Glory BBQ [S] 20 | 18 | 18 | $20

3139 M St., NW (bet. 31st St. & Wisconsin Ave.), 202-337-3406

◪ Amid mock-Southern decor (beer-keg seats, Elvis motifs everywhere), this collegiate BBQ "carnival" housed in an open-to-the-street Georgetown venue offers "messy", "finger-lickin'" fun with "decent" 'cue dished out by a high-energy crew; be warned, however, that it's really "loud" so if you're over 25 you'd better learn to "lip-read" first.

Old Hickory Grill [S] 19 | 11 | 17 | $21

7263 Arlington Blvd. (Allen St.), Falls Church, VA, 703-207-8650

15420 Old Columbia Pike (¼ mi. east of Rte. 29), Burtonsville, MD, 301-421-0204

■ Fans would rather we didn't "tell anyone" about the "good-for-the-money", "down-home" "American dining with a Southern flair" offered at these "friendly" suburban grills, which cook up some of the "best" ribs, grits, meat loaf and "killer shrimp" around; P.S. the Burtonsville flagship still retains a bit of an "old-boy" atmosphere.

Olives 22 | 21 | 18 | $46

1600 K St., NW (16th St.), 202-452-1866

◪ Downtown just "couldn't wait" for Todd English to bring his "trendy" grand cafe to the "K Street dead zone", where an open kitchen and dining bar dominate the "handsome" see-and-be-seen space, making for a "swank" backdrop for his "rich" modern Mediterranean cuisine; but though "everything on the menu sounds great" (and some dishes "will give you chills"), many report that it got "off to a rocky start."

Oodles Noodles   20   14   18 $18
1120 19th St., NW (bet. L & M Sts.), 202-293-3138
4907 Cordell Ave. (bet. Norfolk & Old Georgetown Rds.),
Bethesda, MD, 301-986-8833 S

■ These popular Pan-Asians brighten a "gloomy day" with "hearty", "inexpensive" noodle soups and "quick, healthy" dishes that "get the [bold] flavors right" often enough to keep satisfied slurpers "rubbing elbows" in somewhat "impersonal" settings; still, one or two would've thought that "noodles were foolproof."

Oriental East S   ▽ 21   10   18 $16
1290 E. West Hwy. (Colesville Rd.), Silver Spring, MD,
301-608-0030

■ "Outstanding dim sum" plates are the daily draw at this unprepossessing, "family-friendly" Cantonese in Silver Spring, where serious Sinophiles go "early" on weekends for unusual, authentic treats; dinner, in contrast, can seem less "interesting" – unless you take advantage of the "excellent seafood" and other specialties listed on the (translated) Chinese menu.

Original Pancake House S   19   13   15 $13
370 W. Broad St. (Annandale Rd.), Annandale, VA, 703-891-0148
Discovery Bldg., 7700 Wisconsin Ave. (Old Georgetown Rd.),
Bethesda, MD, 301-986-0285
12224 Rockville Pike (bet. Randolph Rd. & Rolling Ave.),
Rockville, MD, 301-468-0886

◪ "If you're into pancakes", you'll flip for these "breakfast-anytime" suburban diners and their stacks of old-fashioned, "fluffy buttermilk" flapjacks (the "great apple dutch" baby is a best-seller); kids "love" the "homey" American eats, but parents debate whether they're worth the "long weekend waits", not to mention that they'll have to "hit the gym the next day."

Osteria Goldoni S   24   22   21 $53
1120 20th St., NW (bet. L & M Sts.), 202-293-1511

◪ Fabrizio Aielli is the mastermind behind this high-end Dupont Circle Northern Italian that features "fine" "formal" dining (and a chance for "serious talk") just a few blocks from his dramatic Teatro Goldoni; here, you'll find the "great fish" and "inventive" pasta dishes that have earned him plaudits, delivered in a "convivial" setting; though dissenters find the food "slightly uneven" and the service "iffy", admirers insist it's a "wonderful experience."

Outback Steakhouse S   19   15   18 $24
7720 Woodmont Ave. (bet. Old Georgetown Rd. &
Wisconsin Ave.), Bethesda, MD, 301-913-0176
Germantown Sq., 12609 Wisteria Dr. (Great Seneca Hwy.),
Germantown, MD, 301-353-9499
Aspen Manor Shopping Ctr., 13703 Georgia Ave.
(Connecticut Ave.), Silver Spring, MD, 301-933-4385

(continued)
Outback Steakhouse
Beacon Mall, 6804 Richmond Hwy. (Rte. 1), Alexandria, VA, 703-768-1063
Arlington Forest Shopping Ctr., 4821 N. First St. (Park Dr.), Arlington, VA, 703-527-0063
Twinbrook Shopping Ctr., 9579B Braddock Rd. (Twinbrook Dr.), Fairfax, VA, 703-978-6283
10060 Lee Hwy. (Rte. 123), Fairfax, VA, 703-352-5000
Backlick Ctr., 6651 Backlick Rd. (Old Keene Mill Rd.), Springfield, VA, 703-912-7531
☑ Say what you will about chains, but at these Aussie-themed "Morton's for the masses" carnivores can get a "pretty good steak" dinner "for the money", including "great" bloomin' onions and "highly seasoned" sides; sure, many would "pass" on the "Down Under hoopla" and "'G'day mate' business" from the over-friendly staff, yet some find their "predictability" "comforting."

Oval Room   22 | 22 | 22 | $44
800 Connecticut Ave., NW (bet. H & I Sts.), 202-463-8700
■ "Better than the White House mess" nearby, where a number of its customers eat regularly, this classy yet "nonintimidating" New American filled with "lobbyists" at lunchtime will make "you feel powerful just by eating there"; according to admirers, the "lovely food and service" combine with a "beautiful space designed for private conversations" to add up to "really special dining"; N.B. a planned redo will keep it au courant.

Palena   – | – | – | E
3529 Connecticut Ave., NW (Porter St.), 202-537-9250
Frank Ruta and Ann Amernick, two of DC's top toque talents, are delighting foodies with his French- and Italian-influenced Contemporary American menu (inventive but never strange) and her picture-perfect, melt-in-the-mouth desserts at their own Cleveland Park place; veterans of notable kitchens (The White House, Jean Louis), their respect for fine ingredients is legendary, and with a velvet-glove setting, backed by a committed crew, be sure to call early – word is out and prime-time slots are prized.

PALM, THE 🖪   24 | 20 | 24 | $49
1225 19th St., NW (bet. M & N Sts.), 202-293-9091
1750 Tysons Blvd. (International Blvd.), Tysons Corner, VA, 703-917-0200
■ At this legendary Dupont Circle "power meatery", the brash mix of "enormous", "top-notch" steaks, lobster and "fabulous" sides, "fast-paced, irreverent waiters" and bold-name faces is a "hoot" (if you "go with a 'player'", it's better still); in contrast, the "clubby" new Tysons Corner branch draws high-tech "movers and shakers", even "mothers with babies", who say that the "friendlier" staff makes it "easy to enjoy" a meal.

Palm Court
‒ ‒ ‒ E

*Westfield Marriott Hotel, 14750 Conference Ctr. Dr.
(Rte. 7), Chantilly, VA, 703-818-3522*

A lavish Sunday buffet brunch amid the plush splendor of this "bright and airy" formal hotel dining room is a special-event "must"; set in a spacious resort in booming Fairfax County, it's well-rehearsed in handling upscale business lunches and fancy dinners too, with a diverse menu of traditional and modern American and Continental dishes.

Palomino Euro Bistro S
20 25 20 $37

*Reagan Bldg., 1300 Pennsylvania Ave., NW (13th St.),
202-842-9800*

◪ Trading on its showy "multimillion dollar" setting in the Reagan Building Downtown, this Seattle import is fast becoming an after-work and pre-theater "rendezvous" for "dressy or casual" entertaining among the "beautiful people"; fans laud the "different kind" of New American–Med dishes, but foes gripe about the "odd combinations."

Panera Bread S
22 17 17 $12

*Hechinger Commons, 2301 Duke St. (bet. Quaker Ln. &
Yale Dr.), Alexandria, VA, 703-751-1800*
4110 W. Ox Rd. (Rte. 50), Fairfax, VA, 703-246-0056
*Reston Hyatt, 1825 Discovery St. (Market St.), Reston, VA,
703-437-6022*
*Tysons Corner at Pike 7 Plaza, 8365 Leesburg Pike
(Chain Bridge Rd.), Tysons Corner, VA, 703-556-3700*

■ Credit (or blame) this "cheerful" St. Louis–based bakery chain's "great" "formula" of giving "personality" to its American roster of sandwiches (made with "wonderful breads"), soups, salads and sweets for the lunchtime lines out the door; it also provides a "casual" cafe option for a light meal or "after-movie" bite.

Panjshir
21 13 18 $21

924 W. Broad St. (West St.), Falls Church, VA, 703-536-4566
224 W. Maple Ave. (Rte. 123), Vienna, VA, 703-281-4183 S

■ These low-key Northern Virginia Afghans prepare "succulent" ethnic "comfort foods" that are made with "unique flavorings and spices"; an array of "tasty" grilled meats and noodles plus vegetarian options is available, but beware of "dreary" digs that are "low on charm."

Paolo's S
19 19 18 $26

1303 Wisconsin Ave., NW (N St.), 202-333-7353 ◗
*Reston Town Ctr., 11898 Market St. (Fountain Dr.), Reston, VA,
703-318-8920*

◪ Set up in high-traffic locations, these "trendy" Cal-Ital "stop-bys" give away their most popular items – the "amazing" breadsticks and olive dip; as for their pizzas, pastas and salads, they're "reliable" and made even more enjoyable by the walking scenery and outdoor seating; of course, expect crowds, noise and at times "harried" service.

Paradise [S] ▽ 18 | 15 | 17 | $25
7141 Wisconsin Ave. (Montgomery Ave.), Bethesda, MD, 301-907-7500
■ The "fairly extensive" "bargain buffet" at this Bethesda Middle Eastern provides a quick introduction to Persian and Afghan foods, but insiders advise that the "menu is a better" way to explore these complex ancient cuisines; since this storefront "serves the Iranian community" as a gathering place, it's no surprise the fare is very "reliable."

Parkway Deli [S] 20 | 10 | 17 | $15
Rock Creek Shopping Ctr., 8317 Grubb Rd. (bet. Connecticut Ave. & 16th St.), Silver Spring, MD, 301-587-1427
◪ Though "it's a long way from [NYC's] Second Avenue to Silver Spring", this geographically challenged deli still manages to get matzo ball soup, chopped liver, corned beef, lox and eggs and other "Jewish life" supports "to the table quickly"; mavens are happy to feed at this "homey" place, but warn "don't compare it" to the real thing.

Pasha Cafe [S] 21 | 15 | 20 | $21
Cherrydale Shopping Ctr., 2109 N. Pollard St. (Military Rd.), Arlington, VA, 703-528-2126
■ "Share several appetizers" at this Cherrydale "treasure" to discover the "novel" differences in the Egyptian way with familiar Middle Eastern standards and follow with "some of the juiciest chicken this side of Cairo"; it's a "real mom-and-pop" operation, with simple decor accented with ethnic touches and a "pleasant" staff; fans only hope it won't "sacrifice authenticity for Western tastes."

PASTA MIA 25 | 14 | 15 | $18
1790 Columbia Rd., NW (18th St.), 202-328-9114
■ Bring a "big appetite and a clear schedule" to this "wonderful" little pasteria where "mounds" of pasta are "appropriately matched" with "great, flavorful sauces" (don't dare ask for substitutions) at prices so "cheap" it hardly pays to eat at home: nearly every side street in Italy has such a "no-nonsense", "slow"-food "family" operation, but here in Adams Morgan expect long lines.

Pasta Plus [S] 23 | 13 | 22 | $23
Center Plaza, 209 Gorman Ave. (bet. Rtes. 1 & 198E), Laurel, MD, 301-498-5100
■ "Everything's delicious" at this "hidden" Italian "treat" in Laurel, from the "fresh homemade pastas" (notably the "fabulous lasagna") to the "authentic, homestyle" entrées; plus, the "supernice owner" makes it a "happy" "*Cheers*"-like place, so locals don't really want to let their "secret" out as this "small" eatery already guarantees a prime-time "wait."

Patisserie Poupon S 23 | 17 | 15 | $15 |
1645 Wisconsin Ave., NW (bet. Q & Reservoir Sts.), 202-342-3248
■ Picture-"perfect pastries", coffees and fresh-squeezed fruit juices at this "civilized" Upper Georgetown French cafe promise to induce Parisian reveries ("attitude included"), as do the savory salads, sandwiches and light lunches served on the "relaxing" patio; but devotees ask "who needs a square meal" with such tempting sweets on display?

Paul Kee ●S ▽ 21 | 8 | 14 | $17 |
11305B Georgia Ave. (University Blvd.), Wheaton, MD, 301-933-6886
◪ One of Wheaton's no-decor eateries (unless you count the hanging BBQ ducks), this bare-bones Chinese caters to local Asians with its "great" roasted meats, Cantonese seafood specialties and noodle soups; expect "indifferent service", but persevere because there's a bilingual menu.

Paya Thai S ▽ 18 | 17 | 20 | $20 |
8417 Old Courthouse Rd. (Chain Bridge Rd.), Tysons Corner, VA, 703-883-3881
■ "A welcome alternative to the chaos at Busara and Tara Thai", this "pristine" Tysons Corner Thai is less trendy and well known, but it offers "good-quality" standards and some unusual appetizers in subdued surroundings that allow high-techies a chance to download.

Peacock Cafe S 19 | 18 | 18 | $19 |
3251 Prospect St., NW (bet. 32nd & Wisconsin Sts.), 202-625-2740
◪ "Affordable and fashionable", this "sunny" Georgetown bistro is a "too-popular" option for "everyday" American-Eclectic dining; it's a "favorite" brunch and lunch stop and at night it's filled with an attractive, young clientele that doesn't mind "killing an evening waiting" for dinner.

Peking Gourmet Inn S 24 | 15 | 20 | $27 |
Culmore Shopping Ctr., 6029 Leesburg Pike (Glen Carlyn Rd.), Falls Church, VA, 703-671-8088
◪ "Stick to the Peking duck" and homegrown garlic sprouts and you'll understand why the region's top Chinese needs little decor, why celebrity photos line the walls and why its many "loyal fans" "trek" to its "crowded" Northern Virginia site; the tableside carving show is an attraction in itself, even if some shrug "famous but not great" overall.

Perry's S 18 | 22 | 15 | $29 |
1811 Columbia Rd., NW (18th St.), 202-234-6218
■ If you're "young", "hip" and patient, the summertime "sushi-under-the-stars" rooftop "scene" at this Asian fusion spot is the way "to start an Adams Morgan night" ("come with an attitude" to match theirs); inside is also a "cool" place to sample "clever fusion" cuisine and the Sunday drag queen brunch is "unforgettable."

PERSIMMON
25 | 19 | 23 | $41

7003 Wisconsin Ave. (bet. Leland & Walsh Sts.), Bethesda, MD, 301-654-9860

■ Among "Bethesda's best restaurants", this young New American "palate-pleaser's" "talented kitchen", backed by "knowledgeable servers", manages to turn a "small" setting into a "fine-dining" destination with "creative" dishes that get "better each time"; the only drawbacks: those "waiting" for tables wish there were more space and less din.

Pesce S
24 | 15 | 19 | $35

2016 P St., NW (bet. Hopkins & 20th Sts.), 202-466-3474

☑ At this "intimate" Dupont Circle seafood bistro, the chefs may change, but the market-driven fish dishes always remain "creative" and "delicious"; while its "simple" format of cutting-edge" fare without "luxury" trappings is a winner for most, the "challenge" of a no-reservation policy (except for groups of six or more) and "stark", tight premises is the sinker for a minority.

Peter's Passion
– | – | – | E

1732 Connecticut Ave., NW (bet. S & R Sts.), 202-332-7900

At this Contemporary American above Dupont Circle, chef-owner Peter Pryor (ex Lansdowne Resort, Va.) shares his passion for fresh ingredients and lively flavors with a cosmopolitan clientele; everything, from its stylish digs, au courant martini list and personable black-clad servers to its Asian-, Southwestern- and Southern-influenced menu (bourbon-sauced pork with pepper-jack grits) reflects a Big City sensibility – if you can't get in for dinner, try it for a sophisticated lunch (Monday-Friday).

Petits Plats S
– | – | – | M

2653 Connecticut Ave., NW (Calvert St.), 202-518-0018

One almost expects to see Maurice Chevalier sipping an aperitif at the sidewalk cafe of this Woodley Park French bistro; in the charmingly accented pale yellow dining rooms inside the townhouse, serious eaters order classics such as coquilles St. Jacques and beef medallions with wine-glazed shallots, while a cordial staff completes the picture.

P.F. Chang's China Bistro S
21 | 21 | 18 | $25

White Flint Mall, 11301 Rockville Pike (Nicholson Ln.), Rockville, MD, 301-230-6933
Tysons II Galleria, 1716M International Dr. (Rte. 123), Tysons Corner, VA, 703-734-8996

■ Thanks to their dramatic Disneyesque staging, "hearty" Chinese fare and sense of "fun", these high-"glam" bistros have everyone from "new-tech money"-bags and "wanna-bes" to the "in-laws" scrambling to get in; any complaints about the "terrible waits" and "madhouse" ambiance vanish once the addictive "lettuce wraps" reach the table.

Phillips S
15 | 15 | 15 | $28

900 Water St., SW (9th St.), 202-488-8515
American Ctr., 8330 Boone Blvd. (bet. Rtes. 7 & 23),
Tysons Corner, VA, 703-442-0400

☒ Waterfront views and "extensive" seafood spreads lure hordes of tourists to these franchises where the dishes can be "good", if "not exciting"; Chesapeake critics, however, carp about the "Soviet-style" eats and "hustle-bustle" atmosphere, and find the crab cakes so "embarrassing" that "they should be exiled for crab abuse"; N.B. the Tysons Corner branch is landlocked and offers an à la carte menu.

Pho 75 S⊄
22 | 9 | 15 | $14

1510 University Blvd. E. (New Hampshire Ave.), Langley Park, MD, 301-434-7844
771 Hungerford Dr. (Jefferson St.), Rockville, MD, 301-309-8873
1721 Wilson Blvd. (Quinn St.), Arlington, VA, 703-525-7355
3103 Graham Rd. (Rte. 50), Falls Church, VA, 703-204-1490
382 Elden St. (Herndon Pkwy.), Herndon, VA, 703-471-4145

■ Vietnamese "belly warmers" whose "cheap", "tasty" *pho* is a "steaming" meal in a bowl, these "spartan" "cafeteria-like" venues are a weekly "obsession" for many because the chow is "good pho you and good pho your wallet."

PIZZERIA PARADISO S
25 | 16 | 18 | $20

2029 P St., NW (bet. 20th & 21st Sts.), 202-223-1245

■ "Perfectly" named, the "eternal winner" of this *Survey*'s top pizza honors gets it just right – a "flavorful", "crisp" "wood-smoked" crust judiciously applied with "top-notch ingredients" (some regulars think the sandwiches are "even better"); it's a "charming little place" off Dupont Circle filled with "happy clatter" even if its "paramount" pies and "well-chosen" wines often lead to peak-hour "waits."

Planet Hollywood S
12 | 18 | 14 | $21

1101 Pennsylvania Ave., NW (11th St.), 202-783-7827

☒ An "amusement park" that "entertains Midwestern visitors and kids" with "movie stuff", sound tracks and hopes of "celebrity" sightings, this franchise is way too "loud" to chat, so be grateful that there's "something to look at"; if you go, the "Cap'n Crunch chicken fingers" from the "generic" American menu is pretty popular.

Planet Wayside ⊄
_ | _ | _ | I

420 West Colonial Hwy. (1 mi. west of Rte. 704), Hamilton, VA, 540-338-4315

"You can smell the BBQ all over town", thus inspiring many an impromptu pit stop at this "quaint" roadside retreat in Hamilton on old Route 7; dig into "classic" 'cue, "amazing" soups, hefty sandwiches and other "homemade" Traditional American eats, but save room for the old-fashioned pies and ice cream sundaes; eat in the teeny, "funky" room inside or out under the trees and stars on one of the area's nicest, most unspoiled patios.

Polly's Cafe ◐ [S] 19 | 19 | 17 | $19
1342 U St., NW (bet. 13th & 14th Sts.), 202-265-8385
■ Artsy types have made this New U American their "neighborhood watering hole", enjoying "good burgers" (along with some more "interesting" dishes) and a "rockin' jukebox"; in the wintertime the "cozy" fireplace will help nurse hangovers at a "yummy" brunch, so just "get used to the poor service" – it adds to the laid-back appeal.

Potowmack Landing [S] 15 | 22 | 16 | $30
Washington Sailing Marina, George Washington Pkwy. (½ mi. south of Nat'l Airport), Alexandria, VA, 703-548-0001
◪ "Panoramic" Potomac River vistas and "great" plane-spotting provide "so much to see" at this Alexandria American near National Airport; to enthusiasts it doesn't matter that the "uninspired" food doesn't "measure up to the view" or that service could be "improved", because drinks and sunsets on the outdoor deck are enough.

PRIME RIB 26 | 25 | 25 | $53
2020 K St., NW (bet. 20th & 21st Sts.), 202-466-8811
■ Rated the top steakhouse in DC and the "classiest of the power meateries", this gilt-edged Downtown American attracts lawyers and lovelies who "dress up" to feast on the "finest" prime rib, accompanied by a "wonderful wine list"; the elegant surroundings exude a "coat-and-tie" "dignity" that "can't be duplicated", making all diners "feel important."

Primi Piatti 21 | 20 | 20 | $38
2013 I St., NW (bet. 20th & 21st Sts.), 202-223-3600
■ The "let's do lunch" pick of many World Bankers who work near its Foggy Bottom headquarters is this "stylish", "upscale" Italian trattoria; frequent guests are showered with *primo* care, but newcomers notice that the staff can be "indifferent" to the rest of the crowd.

PRINCE MICHEL [S] 26 | 22 | 26 | $59
Rte. 29 S. HCR4, Box 77, Leon, VA, 540-547-9720
■ High scores signal the "excellence" of this posh haute French in Leon, where the kitchen's "exquisite" updated classics and the staff's "subtle" pampering leave patrons wishing it weren't "so far out" of town; the elegant new bistro and the Jefferson dining rooms offer prix fixe tasting menus, as well as à la carte courses, and the extravagant midday Sunday repast makes for a "fun getaway."

Queen Bee [S] 21 | 12 | 18 | $20
3181 Wilson Blvd. (Washington Blvd.), Arlington, VA, 703-527-3444
◪ "Saigon hands meet, greet and eat" at this Clarendon Vietnamese whose varied menu and "bargain prices" have kept it popular with foodies, despite its homely decor and "hurried" pace; claims that it's "declining" are rebutted by fans addicted to the "out-of-this-world" spring rolls.

Raaga 🄂   ▽ 24 | 21 | 24 | $23

5872 Leesburg Pike (bet. Payne St. & Washington Dr.),
Bailey's Crossroads, VA, 703-998-7000

■ This subcontinental foray into Thai territory in Bailey's
Crossroads has captured a healthy flow of lunch traffic with
its "great" buffet starring "creative" Northern Indian dishes
that are "properly spiced" and "not greasy"; "gracious"
service and "comfortable, appealing" surroundings further
help recruit novices and native troops alike.

RABIENG 🄂   25 | 17 | 20 | $24

Glen Forest Shopping Ctr., 5892 Leesburg Pike (Glen Forest Dr.),
Bailey's Crossroads, VA, 703-671-4222

■ "Incredible Thai country food from the owners of
Duangrat's" earns this "reserved" Bailey's Crossroads
favorite "top" honors; in a "smaller" space with a "more
down-to-earth" atmosphere than its citified sibling, diners
will find gutsy, "spicy" "peasant" dishes infused with a
"wonderful blend of flavors"; P.S. you "must try" the "novel"
Thai-style dim sum at the weekend brunch.

Rail Stop 🄂   22 | 18 | 20 | $29

6478 Main St. (Halfway Rd.), The Plains, VA,
540-253-5644

■ Join the "horsey gentry" at this Hunt Country Traditional
American set in The Plains; it's always been "charming",
but now it's definitely more "fun" since the "country" menu
was updated with "refreshingly simple" renditions; whether
you dine in the "attractive" room or out on the "romantic"
terrace, you'll be surrounded by a "homey, small-town
feel"; P.S. better "reserve early."

Raku 🄂   17 | 18 | 15 | $23

1900 Q St., NW (19th St.), 202-265-7258
7240 Woodmont Ave. (Elm St.), Bethesda, MD, 301-718-8681

◪ In Bethesda, this new wave Asian street cafe has
"evolved" into a "modern" fusion restaurant where dining
can be a "real adventure" ("totally different than before"),
while its Dupont Circle "hipster" sibling remains more
casual, "toying" with small plates (noodles, sushi rolls and
satays); detractors, though, think the food doesn't "live up"
to the "intriguing" decor at either branch and complain
about service slips.

Red Fox Inn 🄂   18 | 23 | 19 | $40

2 E. Washington St. (Madison St.), Middleburg, VA,
540-687-6301

◪ Be "chic" and "arrive in your hunt 'pink'" for drinks and
dinner "after the races" at this "historic" Middleburg inn,
or drop by for a lunch respite while antiquing; its horse-
country ambiance ("request fireside seating") is the main
draw, but the "classic" American food is pretty "good"
too (just "don't order fancy"); critics, however, yawn
"ordinary" yet "pretentious."

Red Hot & Blue S
20 | 15 | 17 | $19

16811 Crabbs Branch Way (Shady Grove Rd.), Gaithersburg, MD, 301-948-7333
6482 Landsdowne Ctr. (Beulah St.), Alexandria, VA, 703-550-6465
3014 Wilson Blvd. (Highland St.), Arlington, VA, 703-243-1510
1600 Wilson Blvd. (Pierce St.), Rosslyn, VA, 703-276-7427
4150 Chain Bridge Rd. (Rte. 123), Fairfax, VA, 703-218-6989
■ "DC isn't a BBQ town" we're often told, but transplanted Southerners swear that the "messy" ribs, pulled pork and banana pudding at these "Memphis-on-the-Potomac" pits are "tasty" "reminders" of home; a meal adds up to a "good value" and even pig purists concede they're "ok for a fix."

Red Sage S
21 | 24 | 20 | $38

605 14th St., NW (F St.), 202-638-4444
◪ A big tourist attraction, this "eye-popping" Southwestern "original" lassoes in Downtown lawyers and lobbyists for "short orders" and "fantastic happy hours" in the frenetic upstairs chile bar; for "real food", expense-account types entertain downstairs where the kitchen, which has a "way with chiles", keeps "reinventing" its dishes; if a few feel it has "fallen off some", at least it's now easier to "get a table."

Red Tomato Cafe S
19 | 19 | 18 | $26

4910 St. Elmo Ave. (bet. Norfolk & Old Georgetown Rds.), Bethesda, MD, 301-652-4499
◪ This "cute" suburban pizza and pasta place is popular for "quick", "kid-friendly" eating; grown-ups hit the wine bar for a companionable sip and a light nibble, but "inconsistent" service is its Achilles' heel.

Renato S
20 | 18 | 20 | $32

10120 River Rd. (Potomac Pl.), Potomac, MD, 301-365-1900
◪ "Potomac neighbors" cozy up at their local Italian where they find Downtown quality in gently lit surroundings; but keep in mind that management "knows the regulars" well and charges "what the [tony] traffic will bear."

Rhodeside Grill ●S
16 | 14 | 16 | $22

1836 Wilson Blvd. (Rhodes St.), Arlington, VA, 703-243-0145
◪ Ignore the "frat-house" scene at the "boisterous" bar at this "great Arlington gathering place" and instead concentrate on the kitchen's "eclectic" American fare prepared with some "flair"; on a "good day", you can find "surprisingly" tasty dishes, though critics shrug "merely ok."

Ricciuti's S
▽ 17 | 12 | 17 | $17

3308 Olney-Sandy Spring Rd. (Georgia Ave.), Olney, MD, 301-570-3388
◪ "Skip the chains" in Olney and go for a "good" pizza at this "friendly", lovable old Olney House venue popular among many locals for its "dependable" brick-oven pies, as well as "ok" pastas, salads and subs; it's all dished up in "homey" surroundings that give off a "hometown" feel.

Rico y Rico [S] – | – | – | E

Rio Entertainment Ctr., 9811 Washingtonian Blvd. (Sam Eig Way), Gaithersburg, MD, 301-330-6611

A striving Contemporary American in Gaithersburg's Rio Entertainment Center tempts suburban shoppers with an upscale, internationally-accented menu, served in a fine dining milieu; wine buffs and curious beginners appreciate the sampler 'flights' of its interesting pours, while romantics go for alfresco dining overlooking a man-made lake.

Rio Grande Cafe [S] 21 | 17 | 18 | $22

4919 Fairmont Ave. (Old Georgetown Rd.), Bethesda, MD, 301-656-2981

4301 N. Fairfax Dr. (Glebe Rd.), Arlington, VA, 703-528-3131

Reston Town Ctr., 1827 Library St. (Reston Pkwy.), Reston, VA, 703-904-0703

231 Rio Blvd. (Washingtonian Blvd.), Gaithersburg, MD, 240-632-2150

◪ Long "lines" and crowds are preludes to the "enjoyable" fajitas and other Tex-Mex standards at these "picturesque" cafes; but foes dismiss them as "corrals" with "cookie-cutter" eats and warn the staff gets "stretched too thin."

RITZ-CARLTON, THE GRILL [S] 24 | 27 | 24 | $49

Pentagon City, 1250 S. Hayes St. (bet. Army Navy Dr. & 15th St.), Arlington, VA, 703-412-2760

■ The "unsurpassed" old-style "elegance" of this Pentagon City grill room is exactly what diners expect from such a "prestigious" name; smoothly executing the "perfect formula for hotel dining", a "gracious" staff brings to table "first-rate" New American–Continental fare in a manner that lends distinction to a "special occasion"; just as "excellent" are the brunch buffet and sybaritic afternoon tea.

Rock Bottom Brewery [S] 15 | 16 | 16 | $20

7900 Norfolk Ave. (St. Elmo Ave.), Bethesda, MD, 301-652-1311 ◑

Ballston Commons, 4238 Wilson Blvd. (Glebe St.), Arlington, VA, 703-516-7688

◪ "Beer trumps the food" while "socializing" and sports-viewing rule at these "young and energetic" (or deafening) brewpubs in Bethesda and Ballston; while some defend the "decent burgers", more advise "just drink and be merry."

Rockland's [S] 22 | 11 | 15 | $16

2418 Wisconsin Ave., NW (Calvert St.), 202-333-2558

4000 Fairfax Dr. (Quincy St.), Arlington, VA, 703-528-9663

■ Upper Georgetown's own "Pied Piper" is this wonderful-smelling joint that slow-smokes some of DC's "best" BBQ – "superb" meats, fish and veggies, teamed with down-home sides (check out its legendary lineup of hot sauces); the Arlington offshoot is tucked inside the "yuppie" billiards parlor Carpool (another kind of "meat market") and offers the same "succulent" ribs 'n' stuff, along with table seating.

Rocky's Cafe ▽ 23 | 17 | 19 | $23

1817 Columbia Rd., NW (bet. Biltmore & Mintwood Sts.), 202-387-2580

■ In Adams Morgan, this young "NYC–style bistro" is essentially a dark, smoky bar with a few tables, but the eclectic kitchen cooks up such "wildly creative" Cajun-Creole (and some Caribbean) dishes that it's getting way too popular for its 40-seat digs; while these "super" eats have "attitude", the "friendly" types that work there surely don't.

Roof Terrace Kennedy Center [S] 17 | 21 | 18 | $42

Kennedy Ctr., 2700 F St., NW (bet. New Hampshire & Virginia Aves.), 202-416-8555

◪ "Thrilling" sunset views "set the stage" for a "hassle-free" evening at this "spacious" rooftop dining room at the Kennedy Center, where the convenient one-stop parking and curtain-time certainty are, alas, more appealing than the New American food; one exception, though, is the "over-the-top" kitchen brunch, which provides a seemingly endless "sampling" of goodies from stoveside food stations.

Rosemary's Thyme Bistro [S] 18 | 16 | 18 | $24

1801 18th St., NW (S St.), 202-332-3200

Colonnade, 5762 Union Mill Rd. (Compton Rd.), Clifton, VA, 703-502-1084

■ Over in Dupont Circle East, this "eager" bistro "retains the charm of old Lauriol Plaza" (whose former digs it occupies) while offering its own "pleasant novelty" with a "nice selection" of Turkish, Mediterranean and several other types of cooking; it's the offshoot of a Clifton cutie where "lots of families with little kids" go for "inexpensive" pizzas, wraps and "interesting" "combos."

R.T.'s [S] 22 | 13 | 20 | $30

3804 Mt. Vernon Ave. (Glebe Rd.), Alexandria, VA, 703-684-6010

◪ Kick back and "feel right at home" at this bright, lively Arlandria bar whose "scrumptious New Orleans cooking" (notably "fabulous crabs" and Jack Daniels shrimp) may set back your diet for years; while most think that this period piece is "wonderful" as is, especially when local seafood like "shad roe is in season", some say the "tired" menu, like the neighborhood, needs reviving.

R.T.'s Seafood Kitchen [S] 17 | 15 | 18 | $28

Courthouse Plaza, 2300 Clarendon Blvd. (bet. Barton St. & Courthouse Rd.), Arlington, VA, 703-841-0100

◪ "Convenient" to movie theaters, office suites and residential dwellings, R.T.'s Arlington relative may lack the original's "zing", but a loyal contingent lauds the "sense of New Orleans in its food", exemplified by its catfish and étouffée; skeptics, however, who find it "hit-or-miss", advise "keep fishing."

Ruan Thai [S] ▽ 25 10 20 $18

11407 Amherst Ave. (University Blvd.), Silver Spring, MD, 301-942-0075

■ "Thai the way it used to be" is the reason why expats and local foodies swoon over this "unpretentious and homey" family-run spot in Wheaton; the small kitchen ("Mama" sometimes still cooks) turns out "spectacular, distinctively tasty dishes" that are "authentic, authentic, authentic", not to mention "cheap", which is why followers swear it "doesn't get much better than this."

Rupperts 24 19 23 $50

1017 Seventh St., NW (bet. L St. & New York Ave.), 202-783-0699

◪ The "off-the-charts" originality of this Downtown New American wakes up sophisticated palates, which are enamored by the "wonderful", "innovative seasonal cooking" (especially "inventive veggies and beautiful desserts") brought out by "very special friends" in a "feels-like-NYC" atmosphere; doubters, though, note that while "they really care" they're also too "self-impressed", adding that "austere purity can be carried too far."

RUTH'S CHRIS STEAK HOUSE [S] 25 23 23 $47

1801 Connecticut Ave., NW (S St.), 202-797-0033
7315 Wisconsin Ave. (Elm St.), Bethesda, MD, 301-652-7877
2231 Crystal Dr. (23rd St.), Crystal City, VA, 703-979-7275

■ No "need to ask where's the beef" at this "clubby", Big Easy–style steakhouse chain – it's drenched in butter and sizzling on your plate, hauled out by "courteous" servers; but while these "top-drawer" "guy" havens are beacons for travelers elsewhere, they rank just below the Prime Rib and Morton's of Chicago in the DC region's power stakes; P.S. make sure you "get a window seat" at the Crystal City branch to best take advantage of its awesome view.

Sabang [S] – – – M

2504 Ennalls Ave. (Georgia Ave.), Wheaton, MD, 301-942-7859

Reminding some Far East travelers of the artifact-bedecked dining room of the Bali Hilton, this spacious Indonesian staple in Wheaton features a varied selection of spicy, "different" specialties from that far-flung archipelago; bring friends and sample the multidish rijsttafel tasting table (there's an à la carte menu too).

Saigon Gourmet [S] ▽ 20 14 19 $22

2635 Connecticut Ave., NW (Calvert St.), 202-265-1360

■ Located on Woodley Park's restaurant row, this "modest" Vietnamese "treasure" provides a wonderful introduction (or refresher course) to a "fresh, healthy" cuisine; its "delicious" cooking combines Chinese techniques with sophisticated seasoning and visual appeal and what's more, the "kind" people who run the place really want you to love their country's food.

Saigon Inn S ▽ | 18 | 13 | 17 | $20 |
2928 M St., NW (bet. 29th & 30th Sts.), 202-337-5588
◪ At this cheapie just-drop-in kind of joint in Georgetown, if the Vietnamese meal deals on the posted menu don't grab you, its casual coziness just might; it's one of M Street's more wallet-friendly choices, so even if the chow is perhaps not so "authentic", a lunch tab of only $4.50 for four dishes makes it a pretty fine standby for many locals.

Saigonnais S | 21 | 14 | 19 | $21 |
2307 18th St., NW (bet. Belmont & Columbia Rds.), 202-232-5300
◪ Recreating an array of the North Vietnamese, Indian and Chinese-influenced dishes found in Saigon, this "intimate", "personable" Indochine alternative in Adams Morgan appeals to admirers with its subtle and aromatic cooking, although those less impressed with the kitchen find the execution "lacks punch."

Saint Basil | – | – | – | M |
12050A N. Shore Dr. (Wiehle Ave.), Reston, VA, 703-742-6466
Despite its sequestered mall location, this modish New American–Mediterranean bistro has been discovered by Reston techies and families who praise its lunchtime brick-oven pizzas, panini and pastas; at night, it goes Downtown with trendy selections like pan-roasted Chilean sea bass over portobello mushrooms with thyme essence, along with its popular, crisp-skin, free-range chicken and garlic-mashed spuds; N.B. Tuesday night is pizza night (if you can't get there at lunch).

Sakana | – | – | – | M |
2026 P St., NW (bet. 20th & 21st Sts.), 202-887-0900
Sometimes "overlooked" by outsiders, this Japanese off Dupont Circle is certainly well known to sushi lovers in the neighborhood for its skillful chefs who prepare a variety of "fresh" fish, "wonderful" udon and traditional tempura dishes; as it offers a "perfect" hideaway atmosphere, keep it in mind for a date.

Sakoontra S | – | – | – | I |
Costco Plaza, 12300 Price Club Plz. (W. Ox Rd.), Fairfax, VA, 703-818-8886
This Cinderella Thai charms Fairfax Price Club shoppers and worker bees with her vibrant good looks, warm manners and customized curries, noodles and stir fries (add veggies, chicken, seafood or meat to suit); inspired by a namesake folktale, her savvy fairy godparent–owners transformed a former California Pizza Kitchen into a tasteful, colorful dining room with an inviting bar; it's suitable for anything from a quick pit stop to a business meeting or dinner out with friends.

Sala Thai 🛇
19 | 15 | 19 | $20

2016 P St., NW (bet. 20th & 21st Sts.), 202-872-1144
2900 N. 10th St. (Washington Blvd.), Arlington, VA,
703-465-2900

☑ Dupont Circle denizens go "underground" for red-"hot" curries and interesting specials at this dark basement Thai; its "solid" "traditional" dishes (including "amazing pad Thai") have proven so appealing that the owners have opened a larger, "prettier" offshoot in Arlington; dissenters, however, sigh "adequate" but "used to be better."

Samadi Sweets 🛇
20 | 11 | 16 | $14

5916 Leesburg Pike (bet. Seven Corners & Skyline St.),
Falls Church, VA, 703-578-0606

■ The tempting assortment of "crispy", honeyed Middle Eastern pastries on display at this "too-small" Falls Church bakery is just part of the story; the cafe also serves "well-prepared" Lebanese food, which can be best sampled at the $11.95 weekend buffet – everything from hummus, falafel and meat pies to lentils and chicken and rice (plus some "unusual dishes"), but be sure to leave room for the "all-you-can-eat sweets – they make the meal."

SAM & HARRY'S ➊
24 | 22 | 24 | $49

1200 19th St., NW (bet. M & N Sts.), 202-296-4333
8240 Leesburg Pike (Rte. 123), Tysons Corner, VA,
703-448-0088

■ "Dark" and "decadent", these clubby Golden Triangle and Tysons Corner meat palaces will make "you want to smoke a cigar the moment you arrive", but first carve into a "dynamite steak", paired with a wonderful wine; the staff's democratic "celebrity" treatment helps make them "quintessential client lunch and dinner" haunts, plus there's less formal bar and tap room dining options; sure, it's "pricey", but you get a *primo* experience.

San Marco
▽ 21 | 17 | 23 | $31

2305 18th St., NW (Kalorama Rd.), 202-483-9300

☑ Small wonder that the "delightful" original owner of this "comfortable" Italian trattoria has been warmly "welcomed back" to Adams Morgan – he and his staff "make everyone feel like a regular" by feeding them "thoroughly satisfying" pastas, pouring good vino and paying "great attention to every detail"; maybe best of all is the highly "reasonable" bill.

San Marzano 🛇
– | – | – | M

3282 M St., NW (33rd St.), 202-965-7007

Mediterranean gourmet pizza expressed from London is the selling point of this very Euro cafe smack in Georgetown's tourist territory; the Neapolitan-style pies, perfected at the popular Pizza Express chain in Britain, are delivered *con brio* in sleek digs appointed with exposed brick and polished marble, along with a few salads and pastas.

Satay Sarinah ⬛   – | – | – | M

*Van Dorn Station, 512A S. Van Dorn St. (Duke St.), Alexandria,
VA, 703-370-4313*

Not too many admirers of the former Sarinah Satay in
Georgetown seem to have followed this "charming"
Indonesian transplant to this newish off-the-beaten-track
site in an Alexandria mall; that's a shame because in a
"simple" setting brightened by colorful puppets and
plants, a "helpful" staff serves complex and assertively
seasoned cuisine that fast makes fans out of even novices.

Saveur ⬛   22 | 18 | 20 | $39

2218 Wisconsin Ave., NW (Calvert St.), 202-333-5885

◪ Chef-owner Keo Kountakoun's "spirited" mix of New
French and American cuisines (with Asian accents) at his
"romantic" Glover Park bistro is earning plenty of plaudits
from devotees who regard him as a "master of sauces and
tastes" who's also adept at "attractive" presentations;
skeptics, however, feel that this "weird hybrid" is "on its
way up but needs more time."

Savory ⬛   ▽ 17 | 16 | 15 | $14

*7071 Carroll Ave. (Columbia Ave.), Takoma Park, MD,
301-270-2233*

◼ A "Berkeley"-in-the-'60s spirit pervades this "oh-so-
Takoma Park" coffeehouse, which attracts boosters with its
vegan-friendly "concoctions" (precooked and reheated),
"better-than-average salads and sandwiches" and "tasty
desserts"; order at the counter, then wait to have your
plates brought to your table by "relaxed" (to put it kindly)
servers; it's such a "nice place to linger" that it "makes
me wish it were a real restaurant."

Sea Catch   22 | 22 | 21 | $40

Canal Sq., 1054 31st St., NW (M St.), 202-337-8855

◪ Catch this Georgetown seafood house for "great crab
cakes" on the summertime deck overlooking the C&O
canal or for a warming, "romantic" "fireside" meal in the
winter; the modern American fare (including some truly
authentic Louisiana bayou dishes) is mostly "good",
sometimes even "noteworthy", but penny-pinchers
object to paying a "premium" for the location.

SEASONS ⬛   26 | 26 | 26 | $55

*Four Seasons Hotel, 2800 Pennsylvania Ave., NW (28th St.),
202-944-2000*

◼ The morning limo lineup outside this major "breakfast
player" in Georgetown attests to the "reliably elegant"
pampering and near-"perfect" orchestration of "classy"
special events at this "serene" New American showcase
with a "gorgeous" garden terrace; overlooking the C&O
canal, it's also a "first-rate" site for afternoon tea or Sunday
brunch; N.B. longtime chef Doug McNeill's gone, but that
shouldn't affect this highly professional operation.

Sen5es [S] | 22 | 19 | 19 | $31 |

3206 Grace St., NW (Wisconsin Ave.), 202-342-9083

■ Taking aim at diners' five senses, this "petite" New French bistro turns out "savory" "gourmet" appetizers and entrées that the sweet of tooth consider mere preludes to its bakery's "superb", jewel-like desserts; though just steps away from Georgetown's Wisconsin Avenue "throngs", its "understated", hidden space provides a "peaceful" "oasis."

Sequoia ◐[S] | 16 | 23 | 16 | $33 |

Washington Harbour, 3000 K St., NW (30th St.), 202-944-4200

◪ The view from this dry-docked ship in Georgetown's Washington Harbour is "unbeatable", but, alas, the same can't be said for its "lackluster" American grub; still, the terrace teems with twentysomethings "desperately seeking someone" and its brunch continues to please "tourists."

Serbian Crown [S] | 19 | 19 | 19 | $44 |

1141 Walker Rd. (Colvin Run Rd.), Great Falls, VA, 703-759-4150

◪ Vodka and caviar, "roving" musicians and flickering candlelight lend an aura of rich "romance" to this old-world Great Falls valentine, while its luxury Russo-Continental (and some French) dishes please local "residents ready to pay" for their pleasures; faultfinders, however, gripe "dated", "pretentious" and "not worth the trip."

Sesto Senso | 20 | 17 | 18 | $32 |

1214 18th St., NW (bet. Jefferson Pl. & M St.), 202-785-9525

◪ At lunchtime and early in the evening, the "talented" kitchen at this cosmopolitan Dupont Circle South hot spot dishes up "honest", "really good" tastes of Northern Italy to the business set; later, its "cafe-style" space morphs into a "sexy" "night scene" where Euros can be found dancing on the balcony and in the downstairs Andalou club.

701 [S] | 23 | 23 | 23 | $43 |

701 Pennsylvania Ave., NW (7th St.), 202-393-0701

■ "Across-the-board excellence" distinguishes this "classy" Penn Quarter New American that "makes you feel special" with its "polished" service, "swank" vodka and caviar bar, and state-of-the-art wine room; expect lots of "eye appeal on the plate", "insider"-spotting from the terrace and live jazz and classical piano music; regulars swear you "can't do better for the quality, service and price."

Seven Seas ◐[S] | 21 | 12 | 17 | $22 |

Federal Plaza, 1776 E. Jefferson St. (bet. Montrose & Rollins Aves.), Rockville, MD, 301-770-5020

◪ "Remarkable" seafood plus other Chinese fare (and sushi) "packs" lots of Asians and foodies into this "don't-look"-too-closely spot in Rockville; order right (ask for the red menu) and you'll get "superb" Taiwanese specialties; N.B. the weekend Northern Chinese–style dim sum is worth a try.

1789 S　　　　26 | 26 | 25 | $53

1226 36th St., NW (Prospect St.), 202-965-1789

■ Open the door of this historic Federal townhouse in Georgetown and "enter the world of blue blazers" and patrons celebrating a "dressy occasion", all warmed by wintertime "fires burning" in "private"-feeling period dining rooms; chef Ris Lacoste's "wonderful" seasonal American cooking, "imaginative but not over the top", is served in "classically" "elegant" surroundings, making it "a place you can take both your mother and your daughter and love yourself."

Shanghai Cafe S　　　▽ 21 | 11 | 19 | $20

7026 Wisconsin Ave. (bet. Leland & Walsh Sts.), Bethesda, MD, 301-986-5140

☑ "No first-year chefs here" boasts this drab Bethesda Chinese storefront whose extensive menu ranges from daily dim sum and Shanghai-style specialties to dishes from other regions; even if detractors find the chow "disappointing", enthusiasts whisper "don't tell anybody about this place."

Shiney's Sweets S　　　– | – | – | I

Seoul Plaza, 4231D Markham St. (Little River Tpke.), Annandale, VA, 703-642-0460

Pakistanis, who know their naan, pilgrimage to this teeny self-serve storefront in Annandale for tandoor-blistered breads that remind them of home; the cheap all-you-can-eat lunch ($4.95) and dinner ($5.95) buffets offer "excellent", carefully spiced curries and Indian dishes as well, and the staff loves to introduce newcomers to their exotic sweets.

Shula's Steak House S　　　– | – | – | VE

1143 New Hampshire Ave., NW (M St.), 202-828-7762

When the waiter passes the menu (literally, it's printed on a football) at this macho Dupont Circle South steakhouse, with a 48-ounce Angus steak, a 32-ounce prime rib or a three-to-five-pound lobster, you realize that ex–Miami Dolphins coach Don Shula's enterprise runs a serious training table; its dark wood, deep armchairs and crisp white tablecloths provide a familiar backdrop for meaty indulgence, and if you're looking for a sporty souvenir, you can always bring an autographed pigskin home.

Silverado S　　　20 | 18 | 19 | $23

Magruder's Shopping Ctr., 7052 Columbia Pike (Gallows Rd.), Annandale, VA, 703-354-4560

☑ Suburban singles belly up to the bar at Great American Restaurants, Inc.'s "Southwestern outpost" in Annandale, while "once-a-week" diners dig into American food prepared with a regional flair (like blackened prime rib); here, as at the group's other success stories (Artie's, Carlyle Grand Cafe, Mike's American Grill, Sweetwater Tavern), the savvy menu, "aim-to-please" "team service" and "great value" trump the "noise" and "waits."

Silver Diner [S] 13 | 14 | 14 | $15

Mid-Pike Plaza, 11806 Rockville Pike (bet. Montrose & Old Georgetown Rds.), Rockville, MD, 301-770-2828 ◐
3200 Wilson Blvd. (bet. Clarendon & Washington Blvds.), Arlington, VA, 703-812-8600 ◐
12250 Fair Lakes Pkwy. (W. Ox Rd.), Fairfax, VA, 703-359-5999
11951 Killingsworth Ave. (Baron Cameron/Reston Pkwy.), Reston, VA, 703-742-0801 ◐
8101 Fletcher St. (International Dr.), Tysons Corner, VA, 703-821-5666 ◐

◪ "Retro" and "low-budget", this chain of '50s-style diners provides "campy" entertainment, along with "plain, hearty" eats from morning through late at night; but despite its wide popularity, many foes slam it as a "slapdash" imitation that merely "makes you wish for the real" thing.

Simply Grill [S] ▽ 18 | 6 | 13 | $12

Spectrum Ctr., 1835 Fountain Dr. (New Dominion Rd.), Reston, VA, 703-471-1410

◪ "Bargain eating" in the tony Reston Town Center area is hard to find (literally), but one option is this shopping center Persian kebab house serving "delicious and healthy" Middle Eastern meze and carefully grilled meats; order at the counter, "sit down" and let the "nice people" bring you your food; P.S. don't miss "the bread, the best part of the meal."

Skewers/Cafe Luna [S] 20 | 15 | 18 | $19

1633 P St., NW (bet. 16th & 17th Sts.), 202-387-7400

■ At these Dupont Circle East neighborhood favorites, choose between the Middle Eastern kebab eatery upstairs (starring "excellent and filling meze" and "good veggie skewers") or the casual Italian alternative downstairs; you "can't beat the food/price ratio" or the "great crowd" at either venue, but note that service improves if you're "cute."

Smith & Wollensky's ◐ [S] 22 | 21 | 21 | $46

1112 19th St., NW (bet. L & M Sts.), 202-466-1100

◪ "Come with clients, not a date", to this "masculine" NYC-in-DC "big meat" haven set on Dupont Circle South's premier "steak block", where its "quality" beef and extensive wine cellar face "Big Competition"; while many welcome the "attentive" service, critics find the room "cold " and add that it's no "match" for the Manhattan "mother ship"; P.S. the adjacent grill cooks a "fabulous burger."

Sole [S] – | – | – | E

Washington Harbor, 3050 K St., NW (30th St.), 202-625-7653

It's not port side in Marrakech or Marseille, but this new Washington Harbor dining spot with sporty boat and people-watching from umbrella-shaded tables brings the Mediterranean a bit closer to home; ditto its menu traveling from sunny Spanish tapas to North African tagines and its airy modernity (complete with a trendy lounge); on balmy days, its tourist-magnet terrace is SRO.

Stardust Restaurant & Lounge S   22 20 21 $33
608 Montgomery St. (bet. N. Washington & St. Asaph Sts.),
Alexandria, VA, 703-548-9864
■ A North Old Town "plus", this amusingly starstruck
"neighborhood place" presents an "original", "ambitious"
Eurasian roster that highlights "interesting" seafood, pasta
and meat dishes (think chicken won tons with smoked ham
and crispy whole fish with a chile-basil sauce), served by
an "accommodating" staff; "eclectic" appetizers are half-
priced at the bar (weekdays from 5–7 PM) for sampling on
the cheap should the menu seem "too tricky."

Starland Cafe S   17 17 18 $29
5125 MacArthur Blvd., NW (Arizona Ave.), 202-244-9396
■ "Secretly good", this New American in the Palisades
fills a niche with "easy" yet serious multipurpose dining,
providing a "limited" but "affordable" menu and a modern
space that's suitable for a casual bite or a celebratory
meal; it's an "evening delight" on the balcony with all
those "twinkly lights", though "when too many people
come" (there's not much else around) it can get "noisy."

Stella's S   ─ ─ ─ M
1725 Duke St. (Diagonal Rd.), Alexandria, VA,
703-519-1946
Forties-era photos and jazz recordings draw bright, young
things to the bar and upscale business types to this buzzing
Old Town dining room, and in the summertime the scene
spreads out to the "beautiful" outdoor terrace replete with a
fountain; not least of its attractions is the "well-prepared",
"seasonally influenced" New American cuisine given a
Southern accent via Virginian influences.

Stone Manor S   ▽ 23 26 25 $59
5820 Carroll Boyer Rd. (Sumantown Rd.), Middletown, MD,
301-473-5454
■ Getting away to this "lovely" "historic" "country" manor
near Frederick is "unbelievably relaxing"; the antique-filled
dining rooms are "quaint" backdrops for "first-rate",
"beautifully presented" New American cuisine and even the
between-course "waits" make smitten guests hark back to
more leisurely times; though it's a "long ride" from town,
it's "worth" it for such a "romantic" "special occasion."

Sushi-Ko S   25 17 20 $32
2309 Wisconsin Ave., NW (south of Calvert St.), 202-333-4187
◪ While this Upper Georgetown Japanese scores high
marks for its "fresh, flavorful" and "inventive" sushi, insiders
enthuse that its "unique" East-West dinner entrées taste
"even better"; Gen X-ers are delighted by the pairing of
Asian foods with fine French wines ("sushi with a Burgundy
is genius"), but the minimalist decor gets very mixed
reactions, as does the occasionally "lacking" service.

Sushi Taro S | 24 | 20 | 21 | $30 |
1507 17th St., NW (P St.), 202-462-8999
■ Evoking an "authentic" Tokyo feel, this second-story Japanese wows knowledgeable Asians with its "first-rate" sushi and "extensive" selection of cooked fish dishes; its Adams Morgan East digs are unpretentious, but that shouldn't keep you away from "speedy satisfaction" and fine lunch deals.

Sweet Basil S | – | – | – | M |
4910 Fairmont Ave. (bet. Norfolk Ave. & Old Georgetown Rd.), Bethesda, MD, 301-657-7997
Everything from the decor – exotic musical instruments on pale yellow walls, a glimpse of blue sky and clouds painted on a cutaway ceiling – to this Bethesda Asian's menu of uncommon dishes (turkey sausage and cucumbers in lemongrass dressing) to its low-key atmosphere, explains why its owners call it a 'new' Thai; freshness and healthy eating are its mantras, and there's a separate menu listing for vegetarians.

Sweetwater Tavern S | 21 | 19 | 20 | $23 |
14250 Sweetwater Ln. (Multiplex Dr.), Centreville, VA, 703-449-1100
3066 Gatehouse Plaza Dr. (bet. Gallows Rd. & Rte. 50), Merrifield, VA, 703-645-8100
◪ "Consistently enjoyable everyday" places, this tandem of ranch-sized, Southwestern-themed brewpubs fits the Great American Restaurants, Inc. template with its "wide" choice of American eats (given some cowboy-country tweaks), attractive setting, energetic "tag-team" service and midrange tabs; of course, like its kin, it's way "too popular" so prepare for a "wait."

Tabard Inn S | 22 | 22 | 20 | $36 |
1739 N St., NW (bet. 17th & 18th Sts.), 202-833-2668
■ The "fireplace is great on a cold day" and the "lovely patio is a summertime treat" at this "romantic" Dupont Circle institution with a "quaint" ambiance that "exudes warmth"; though opponents object to the "inconsistent" fare and occasional "rough" service, advocates "applaud" the "innovative", seasonal New American menu.

TABERNA DEL ALABARDERO | 25 | 25 | 24 | $50 |
1776 I St., NW (18th St.), 202-429-2200
■ As "sensuous" as Spain itself, this pricey Downtown Basque classic "transports" guests to the "old world" "in grand style" with "world-class" cooking, an "exhaustive" wine list and "impeccable service"; the "extravagant" setting is apt for "entertaining clients" or "someone you really like", thus it's not hard to see why "the King of Spain" once dined here; P.S. "strolling serenaders" play classical Spanish music Friday–Saturday nights.

Tachibana [S] 24 | 18 | 20 | $30

6715 Lowell Ave. (Emerson Ave.), McLean, VA, 703-847-1771

■ A warren of sushi bars, semiprivate alcoves and still other dining areas, McLean's pet Japanese customarily draws a "full house", testament to its skillful chefs who execute "consistently fresh" dishes (including "delicious" seaweed salad); while insiders relish items they "can't find" elsewhere, skeptics carp "overrated", "pricey and dated."

Tahoga [S] 22 | 20 | 21 | $44

2815 M St., NW (bet. 28th & 29th Sts.), 202-338-5380

◪ There's a California feel to this Georgetown Contemporary American where the "minimalist decor", "chic" ambiance and "romantic" courtyard form the backdrop for "creative" seasonal cuisine; foes who fault "inconsistent cooking" hope that a new chef will even out the kitchen.

Taipei/Tokyo Cafe [S] 22 | 7 | 15 | $14

1596 Rockville Pike (Halpine Rd.), Rockville, MD, 301-881-8533
Metro Ctr. Plaza, 11510A Rockville Pike (Nicholson Ln.), Rockville, MD, 301-881-8388 💳

■ Sure, they're plain Janes, but these Sino-Japanese twins are Rockville "cult favorites" for dishing out "the fastest sushi in town", as well as "hearty homemade noodle bowls"; their "fast, furious and fearless" attitude ("eat fast to avoid dirty looks") and "no-atmosphere" rooms make them "no great gourmet experience, but somehow" a meal is "really fun."

Tako Grill [S] 22 | 16 | 19 | $26

7756 Wisconsin Ave. (Cheltenham Rd.), Bethesda, MD, 301-652-7030

■ Bethesda's "comfortable" Japanese serves up "diverse", "dependable" fare that's "not challenging" to some; rough patches, including a main room that's "lost some character" and a staff that seems "overextended when busy", are smoothed over by the "excellent" *robatayaki* (tapas-like grilled dishes), noodle bowls and "fresh" sushi; N.B. its new black-and-red sake bar feels very up-to-date.

Taqueria Poblano [S] – | – | – | I

2400B Mt. Vernon Ave. (Oxford St.), Alexandria, VA, 703-548-8226

At his colorful Del Ray cafe, chef-owner Glenn Adams recreates the *cucina Mexicano* of his Southern California youth – LA-style crispy tacos with charcoal-grilled pork, soft tacos al 'pastor' from the rotisserie and 'real' burritos, plus vegetarian versions; the casual vibe and low prices belie the serious cooking here (he buys tortillas from several sources, each suited to a particular dish); P.S. in nice weather, locals swarm the sidewalk cafe for a 'wake-up-your-mouth' Sunday brunch.

TARA THAI 🏠   22 | 21 | 19 | $23
12071 Rockville Pike (Montrose St.), Rockville, MD, 301-231-9899
7501E Leesburg Pike (Pimmit Dr.), Falls Church, VA, 703-506-9788
226 Maple Ave. (bet. Lawyer's Rd. & Nutley St.), Vienna, VA,
703-255-2467
4828 Bethesda Ave. (bet. Arlington Rd. & Wisconsin Ave.),
Bethesda, MD, 301-657-0488

■ At this "snazzy" suburban Thai chainlet, the underwater
decor makes a "tasty" meal an "adventure" that's equally
suitable for kids, "cheap" dates and business lunches;
while landlubbers may ask "why the hype", the "aquatic"
setting, "consistent" fare and "quick" service are "obvious
reasons" why they're often "crowded."

Taste of Saigon 🏠   24 | 18 | 21 | $25
8201 Greensboro Dr. (International Dr.), Tysons Corner, VA,
703-790-0700
410 Hungerford Dr. (Beall Ave.), Rockville, MD, 301-424-7222

■ Order "black pepper anything" at this *Survey*'s top
Vietnamese and you'll "come away feeling happy"; the duo's
"excellent combination" of "fine", "authentic" cooking,
"attractive" suburban settings and "appropriate pricing"
makes them perennial "winners."

Taste of the World   – | – | – | M
283 Sunset Park Dr. (Spring St.), Herndon, VA, 703-471-2017

Herndon techies surf the food world at this suburban
"bargain" where the International kitchen's Filipino,
Southeast Asian, Indian and Latin American dishes are hits
("all the soups are excellent"); sunny, sponged walls and a
shelf full of icons are further interesting attractions.

Taverna Cretekou 🏠   21 | 21 | 20 | $32
818 King St. (bet. Alfred & Columbus Sts.), Alexandria, VA,
703-548-8688

■ Join in on the festivities at this Old Town taverna where
festive Thursday nights featuring dancing, waiters "busting
plates" in traditional style and "summer dining in the arbor"
transport diners to Greece; the "reliable" menu and "warm"
service are "100 percent Greek", and though a few prefer
the "atmosphere" over the food, most feel it's a "good bet."

Teaism   18 | 17 | 14 | $15
800 Connecticut Ave., NW (H St.), 202-835-2233
400 Eighth St., NW (D St.), 202-638-6010 🏠
2009 R St., NW (Connecticut Ave.), 202-667-3827 🏠

☑ Even if you don't "take tea seriously", this trio of "*chai*
heavens" offers a "soothing" ambiance in settings that
range from "funky" to Tibetan-accented formality; admirers
"unwind" over interesting brews and "healthy" Pan-Asian
fusion fare, but critics find the food "disappointing" and
warn that the service, "wonderful at off-hours", may tax
the most "Zen-like" patience when it's busy.

TEATRO GOLDONI 24 | 26 | 21 | $51
1909 K St., NW (bet. 19th & 20th Sts.), 202-955-9494
◪ With its "dramatic" commedia dell'arte inspirations and "wonderful lighting", this "exciting" K Street player "sets out to dazzle" and it succeeds; its "cutting-edge" Italian menu is "playful", "innovative" and mostly "very good", and the chef's "enthusiasm" is evident "on every plate"; detractors, however, feel the total effect is "too contrived" and hint that the staff "needs to fly as a team."

Tel Aviv Cafe ◐ [S] 17 | 16 | 16 | $24
4869 Cordell Ave. (Norfolk Ave.), Bethesda, MD, 301-718-9068
◪ Pilgrims swear that this Bethesda sidewalk cafe, where families and "trendy" "singles" alike gather to people-watch, buzzes with the "spirit and energy of Israel"; though many find the falafel "excellent", foes kvetch about "bland", "overpriced" Mediterranean fare, as well as "noisy" "crowds" and "slow" service; your call.

Temel [S] – | – | – | M
3232 Old Pickett Rd. (Old Lee Hwy.), Fairfax, VA, 703-352-5477
This lovely, modern restaurant in a nondescript Fairfax mall is full of surprises – from the handsome wood-and-glass interior and soothing waterfalls to the professional hospitality and, best of all, the Mediterranean cooking; standouts on the Turkish, Greek and Israeli menu are the Middle Eastern 'pizzas', meze, doner kebab (weekends) and irresistible, warm bread.

Tempo [S] 24 | 18 | 22 | $32
4231 Duke St. (N. Gordon St.), Alexandria, VA, 703-370-7900
■ A "delightful" surprise awaits at this converted Alexandria gas station where chef-owners Wendy and Serge Albert turn out "wonderful standards and creative" renditions of "inspired" French and Italian fare (notably seafood) in an "art-filled" interior; though a few find the "old garage" "noisy" and the staff's tempo too "leisurely", they're a beat behind the majority that lauds this "suburban find" as a "class act."

Ten Pehn – | – | – | E
1001 Pennsylvania Ave., NW (10th St.), 202-393-4500
Au courant Asian fusion eats vie with the eye candy and high glam surroundings at this hot Downtown address where Jeff Tunks (DC Coast) and his crew's riffs on popular Far East dishes look as spiffy as its clientele; few spots offer such a sophisticated backdrop for everything from a barroom meeting or a casual bite to a full-fledged celebration, although solo diners may have the best of it, with no conversation to distract them from the scene.

Terrazza 22 | 21 | 22 | $40

2 Wisconsin Circle (bet. Western & Wisconsin Aves.), Chevy Chase, MD, 301-951-9292

■ Among the high-end Northern Italians in the area, this "spacious" terrace-level Chevy Chase spot is an "underrated match" with its "sophisticated" pastas and "great fish" dishes served in a "contemporary" setting; drowning out the gripes about the chronically "noisy" "acoustics" are cheers for its "welcoming" ambiance and "warm" service.

T.H.A.I. [S] 23 | 22 | 22 | $22

Village at Shirlington, 4029 S. 28th St. (Randolph St.), Arlington, VA, 703-931-3203

■ Outdoor seating on Shirlington's prime "people-watching" thoroughfare, a dramatic "modern" interior and "artistic" plates attract locals to this "nouveau" Thai; while it's "not cheap", most find the "imaginative presentations" of "creative cuisine", "stylish ambiance" and "wonderful staff" "worth the asking price."

Thai Basil [S] – | – | – | M

14511 Lee Jackson Hwy. (Airline Pkwy.), Chantilly, VA, 703-631-8277

At this Thai venue in Chantilly, the "kitchen is personally run by the proprietor", who delights in providing "menu guidance" to novices; the selections are "completely authentic" and "inexpensive for what you get", making it a fine ethnic addition to the neighborhood.

Thai Derm ▽ 21 | 9 | 21 | $17

939 Bonifant St. (Georgia Ave.), Silver Spring, MD, 301-589-5341

■ Savvy surveyors certify that Silver Spring's "hidden gem" of a Thai is a "real best buy"; though it scores low marks for decor, "the nicest owners" and "personal" service create a "relaxing atmosphere" that makes diners "feel like part of the family" as they sample the "authentic" cuisine.

Thai Kingdom [S] 19 | 15 | 18 | $23

2021 K St., NW (bet. 20th & 21st Sts.), 202-835-1700

◪ Tongue-tingling spices rule at this longstanding K Street realm where family photos lord over the room; loyalists pay tribute to the "reliable", "authentic" Thai fare at "reasonable prices", but rebels rate the food "dull" and "unsatisfying."

Thaiphoon [S] – | – | – | M

2011 S St., NW (20th St.), 202-667-3505

Taste bud–tingling seafood and vegetable dishes are well represented on the menu of this modish Thai, although timid palates can find plenty of milder choices too; located above DuPont Circle, not far from the Visions art-house cinema, (assuring good people-watching), its warm colors and smart design provide an appealing backdrop for its patrons, and its glassed-in front terrace is a draw.

Thanh Thanh S   – | – | – | I

11423 Georgia Ave. (University Blvd.), Wheaton, MD, 301-962-3530

In Wheaton, where a United Nations of inexpensive ethnics caters to knowledgeable eaters, this affordable Vietnamese is making a mark with fresh versions of Indochine standards (try the quail appetizer and one of its whole fresh fish dishes, as well as its meal-in-a-bowl pho) that live up to its name, which means 'clear and pure' back home; its prettied-up premises accommodate family parties and groups as comfortably as twosomes.

That's Amore S   18 | 16 | 18 | $25

15201 Shady Grove Rd. (Research Blvd.), Rockville, MD, 301-670-9666
Potomac Run Shopping Ctr., 46300 Potomac Run Plaza (Cascades Pkwy. & Leesburg Pike), Sterling, VA, 703-406-4900
Danor Plaza, 150 Branch Rd. (Rte. 123), Vienna, VA, 703-281-7777
◪ "Big groups" and "hungry mouths" sing the praises of these family-style trattorias, which dish up "humongous", table-sized portions of "garlicky" Italian food; the gregarious like the "upbeat atmosphere", but critics say the "industrial" eats and "crowded, noisy" settings are "a *boré*"; you'll have to choose your own tune.

Thyme Square S   19 | 19 | 18 | $27

4735 Bethesda Ave. (Woodmont Ave.), Bethesda, MD, 301-657-9077
◪ At this "funky" Bethesda Eclectic, the meatless menu travels "all over the map", offering "hearty", health-conscious veggie, fish and chicken dishes as "bold" as its color-splashed walls; but while it's a "mecca" for many vegetarians, not all are moved by its "higher alternative" mission, as skeptics scowl at "dull", "erratic" cooking and service that "breaks down" when busy.

Timothy Dean S   – | – | – | E

St. Regis Hotel, 923 16th St., NW (K St.), 202-879-6900
Hometown hero Timothy Dean (ex NYC's Palladin) brings his acclaimed French-accented New American cooking to the palatial site near the White House once occupied by Lespinasse; amid updated decor that's as opulent as ever, diners savor fresh, light dishes from changing menus based on local products (e.g. corn soup with bone-marrow flan) at prices not quite as luxe as its predecessor's.

Timpano S   18 | 19 | 18 | $31

12021 Rockville Pike (Montrose Rd.), Rockville, MD, 301-881-6939
◪ Sinatra music, dry martinis and a "dark" supper-clubby setting set the tone at this Italian-accented chophouse on Rockville Pike, where the "meet 'n' greet" bar scene, Thursday swing nights and live music on Fridays and Saturdays add to its "big-city feel"; cynics sneer that the "image can't carry" the "chain-type" cooking.

Tivoli 21 19 21 $37

1700 N. Moore St. (19th St.), Rosslyn, VA, 703-524-8900

◪ Boosters insist that this "elegant" "unheralded gem" in Rosslyn "belongs Downtown" due to its sophisticated, "expertly served" Continental–Northern Italian fare, "super" wine list, and desserts that nobody can "get enough of"; critics say it "needs to be revamped", but to devotees this "consistent" "favorite" only "gets better with age."

Tono Sushi [S] 20 14 18 $25

2605 Connecticut Ave., NW (Calvert St.), 202-332-7300

◪ There's a "cool jazzy feel" to this Woodley Park Japanese thanks to its "fun new approaches that include, but go beyond, sushi", as well as its "friendly" staff; while there may be "better" choices around, it hits enough high notes (the "Mexican roll and miso soup are all I need to live") "at fair prices" to make it a "neighborhood favorite."

Tony & Joe's Seafood Place [S] 16 19 17 $31

Washington Harbour, 3000 K St., NW (30th St.), 202-944-4545

◪ "Beautiful" views of the Potomac and Washington Harbour make this a "great waterfront setting for casual dining" and happy-hour action; the "food may not be top-notch, but who cares" when there's live jazz, adding to the "convivial atmosphere" out on the "terrace by the river."

Tony Cheng's Mongolian/Seafood [S] 20 13 18 $22

619 H St., NW (bet. 6th & 7th Sts.), 202-842-8669

◪ A "Chinatown adventure" in all-you-can-eat dining, this standby lets customers "pick out" their own ingredients for on-site cooking at the "efficient", "entertaining" Mongolian BBQ downstairs; meanwhile, daily dim sum and some of the "best seafood" in C-town are served in the venerable (or "threadbare") multiregional Chinese eatery upstairs.

Toro Tapas & Grill [S] 16 16 16 $23

4053 S. 28th St. (S. Randolph St.), Arlington, VA, 703-379-0502

◪ This tapas joint is a "nice addition" to Shirlington, offering snack-sized Spanish and Latino dishes and sangria in a "bright" setting; though "hit-or-miss" cooking and "spotty" service are red flags to bullish types, its "great location by the movie theater" keeps it lively.

Tosca [S] – – – E

1112 F. St., NW (bet. 11th & 12th Sts.), 202-367-1990

It didn't take long for cucina cognoscenti to sing about this Downtown diva's debut; its contemporary Northern Italian menu features locally farmed and imported ingredients, and spotlights dishes from chef/co-owner Cesare Lanfranconi's (ex Galileo) native Lombardy; its sophisticated design has curtained alcoves, sliding glass walls and serious, sound-dampening acoustics to insure privacy, with a chef's table in the open kitchen for behind-the-scenes buffs.

Tragara 🅂　　　20 | 20 | 20 | $44
4935 Cordell Ave. (bet. Norfolk Ave. & Old Georgetown Rd.),
Bethesda, MD, 301-951-4935
◪ At its best for "intimate" dining and "classy" functions,
when "elegant" fare, "lovely" presentations and "serene"
surroundings matter most, this Bethesda Northern Italian
cultivates stalwarts who rely on the "marvelous" food
to give them the "strength to handle" service lapses;
belittlers, however, knock the "sometimes wonderful,
sometimes mediocre" cooking, as well as the "stiff" staff
and "expensive" tabs.

Tryst 🅂　　　16 | 22 | 15 | $13
2459 18th St., NW (bet. Belmont & Columbia Rds.),
202-232-5500
◼ The "cute, comfy couches" at this Adams Morgan
"coffee and conversation spot" make it a "wonderful place
to chill with friends"; it's a hit among "the twentysomething
set", which excuses the "so-so" light American bites and
service flaws because the owners are so "sincere" and
the "people-watching" so good; P.S. there's quite a "nite"
scene at the bar.

Turning Point Inn 🅂　　　22 | 23 | 23 | $42
3406 Urbana Pike (Rte. 80), Frederick, MD, 301-831-8232
◼ A "good place for celebrating" life's "turning points",
this "charming" country inn near Frederick successfully
blends "delicious" New American dishes with a British
accent and updated classics (including "wonderful lobster
bisque") with "attentive" service that recalls "days past"
in "pleasant" surroundings; especially "lovely for ladies
who lunch", it's "well worth the drive" from DC.

Tuscarora Mill 🅂　　　21 | 20 | 21 | $33
Market Station, 203 Harrison St. SE (Loudoun St.), Leesburg, VA,
703-771-9300
◼ Set in a handsomely restored century-old building, this
clubby spot is "where important Leesburg denizens meet"
for casual bites, "after-work" drinks or power dinners; the
"dependable", "interesting" American menu is based on
"local, seasonal" ingredients, while a "superb wine list",
"warm atmosphere" and "accommodating staff" provide
yet more grist for this "busy" mill.

219 🅂　　　19 | 20 | 19 | $36
219 King St. (Fairfax St.), Alexandria, VA, 703-549-1141
◪ While its New Orleans front may be a "tourist" magnet,
that doesn't keep locals from also enjoying this Old Town
staple's "decent Creole" cooking; even if cynics sneer about
"tired" food, the "marvelous" settings – from the heated
porch and the "romantic" dining rooms to the "jazz lounge"
upstairs and the lower-priced basement bar – offer
something for everyone.

Two Quail S   21 23 21 $35
320 Massachusetts Ave., NE (bet. 3rd & 4th Sts.),
202-543-8030

◪ Whether for a "quaint" Mother's Day brunch, a political lunch or foodie "foreplay" ("seduce your love in a curtained booth with rich food"), this "adorable" Capitol Hill American attracts with its "quirky" (or "absurd") decor (think your "old aunt's sitting room" or "Delmonico's in *Hello Dolly*"); the "rainy-day comfort food" is "yummy" but it "ain't gourmet", leaving a few lonely hearts "disappointed."

Udupi Palace S   24 13 19 $16
1329 University Blvd. E. (New Hampshire Ave.), Langley Park,
MD, 301-434-1531

■ "Wonderful" *dosas* (filled savory pancakes), *pakoras* (fritters) and vegetable curries at this "bare-bones" Langley Park Indian show how "delicious" and "varied" vegetarian fare can be; the "fantastic" choices and "charming" staff combine to make the experience "authentic", as well as an "excellent value."

Uni S   – – – M
2122 P St., NW (bet. 21st & 22nd Sts.), 202-833-8038

A second-story new wave Japanese where DuPont Circle singles and convivial small groups sip sake-tinis (martinis made with sake) and sample sushi, innovative seasonal small dishes (scallops with sea urchin butter) and hip entrées in a minimalist setting that's enlivened by clever touches (faux windows with purposefully cracked glass); its hip neighborhood appeal is boosted by $1 happy-hour sushi, all-day Saturday dining and window tables perfect for scoping the sidewalk scene.

Union Street Public House S   17 18 17 $23
121 S. Union St. (bet. King & Prince Sts.), Alexandria, VA,
703-548-1785

■ "Convenient and affordable", this atmospheric Old Town watering hole with its "please-everyone" American menu and two-story space (singles in the downstairs bar, families upstairs) works for groups of all ages and sizes; the "better-than-average" chow goes "great with the microbrews", but service can be "slow" when it gets "crowded."

Upper Crust Bakery S⊄   – – – I
2 Pendleton St. (Rte. 50), Middleburg, VA,
540-687-5666

For Middleburg neighbors, a trip to this bakery/cafe is a "social occasion", so expect a delicious glimpse of small-town life on display at this "old-time happy place"; bring your goodies – "yummy breakfast treats", "quality" sandwiches, signature mutton buttons (chocolate on shortbread) and "divine" butterscotch 'cowpies' – to tables in the Toll House or out on the deck, or ask for a picnic to go.

U-topia [S] 19 | 20 | 17 | $22

1418 U St., NW (bet. 14th & 15th Sts.), 202-483-7669

◪ "Hip, festive" and "handy" for taking in New U galleries and clubs, this International eatery pulses with live jazz Thursdays–Sundays; in addition to serving up pastas, seafood and "lovely" veggie fare, it's something of an art space itself, which leads jaded types to judge the "walls more interesting" than the "average" dishes.

Vegetable Garden [S] 20 | 14 | 18 | $18

11618 Rockville Pike (bet. Nicholson Ln. & Old Georgetown Rd.), Rockville, MD, 301-468-9301

◪ "Great if you're really a vegetarian" or just looking for a "healthy" meal, this Rockville strip mall Chinese does "interesting" things with soy (e.g. "fake" meats and "tofu you'd swear is chicken"), as well as Western veggie burgers and pastas; but the unconvinced wonder "where's the flavor?", insisting that "better dishes" can be found at conventional Sino spots and without the "tense" service.

VIDALIA [S] 26 | 23 | 24 | $49

1990 M St., NW (bet. 19th & 20th Sts.), 202-659-1990

■ The "luscious" Southern-accented New American comfort food turned out at this Dupont Circle South expense-account "treat" has nouveau and native Southerners alike cheering the "great" kitchen that "performs magic" with seasonal local and Dixie ingredients; though claustrophobes clamor about the "basement" location and not everyone cottons to the staff's "Deep South" tempo, the "warm" ambiance, "nice lighting", and "personable" staff convey a stylish "hospitality" that's "classy in every way."

Vienna Inn [S] 15 | 10 | 12 | $13

120 E. Maple Ave. (bet. Center & Park Sts.), Vienna, VA, 703-938-9548

■ When Vienna residents crave "classic chili dogs", a cold beer and good-humored sass, they head for this authentic "dive"; always a "delight" but a "must-see at lunch", it's one of the last bastions of "quintessential Old Virginny"; N.B. though it recently changed hands, its fans hope the new owners will keep this landmark as it's been since 1960.

Vignola [S] 18 | 11 | 15 | $18

113A N. Washington St. (bet. Beall Ave. & Middle Ln.), Rockville, MD, 301-340-2350

■ "Old" Rockville's Italian "gem", this counter-service deli offers "delicious rice balls", subs and a few pastas at lunch, for takeout or eating in; at night the "modest" dining area becomes a full-service restaurant, featuring "homestyle cooking" that evokes memories of Capri, even if hardcores dismiss it as "Italian lite"; N.B. there's live music Friday–Sunday nights.

Vigorelli, The 🅂
18 | 16 | 18 | $33

*3421 Connecticut Ave., NW (bet. Macomb & Porter Sts.),
202-244-6437*

◪ "Immensely appealing", this Cleveland Park Italian uses its wood-burning ovens to execute "creative" plays on Ligurian recipes; its "lively" informality draws an attractive crowd, though grumbles of too "pricey", "noisy" and "inconsistent" can be heard amid the "buzzy" vibe; N.B. Arenella, its rooftop adjunct, presents its own menu of uncommon open-hearth items.

Village Bistro 🅂
22 | 14 | 19 | $30

*Colonial Village, 1723 Wilson Blvd. (Quinn St.), Arlington, VA,
703-522-0284*

◪ No, this Continental "treasure" housed in a "nondescript" Arlington strip mall hasn't closed or moved, but a touch-up did add warm tones and cheery accents to the "intimate" setting; the "reasonably priced" fare highlights seafood specials that might "surprise" you, which is why locals would like to keep it a "secret", albeit the occasional "crazy scene" suggests that the word's already out.

Vivo 🅂
– | – | – | M

1509 17th St., NW (bet. P & Q Sts.), 202-986-2627

Fresh mozzarella made daily (get there early and watch), homemade pastas and sausages, and wood-burning oven specialties attest to this DuPont Circle East trattoria's Italian roots; it's one of Roberto Donna's eateries, with a seasoned staff, a cool modern setting and prices commensurate with the quality ingredients and preparations (albeit a bit above the neighborhood norm); considering that its sib Galileo supplies it with choice foodstuffs, such as its notable cheese plate, it's a deal.

Warehouse Bar & Grill 🅂
19 | 19 | 20 | $31

*214 King St. (bet. Fairfax & Lee Sts.), Alexandria, VA,
703-683-6868*

◪ In Old Town "everyone eats here", amid the "caricatures" of local bigwigs that give this spot its "character"; tourists love to "pick out the diners" from their mugs on display, while regulars vie for choice "people-watching" seats near the "front window"; but reactions to the Cajun-Creole surf 'n' turf ranges from "outstanding" to "just ok."

West End Cafe 🅂
17 | 17 | 18 | $33

*Washington Circle Hotel, 1 Washington Circle
(New Hampshire Ave.), 202-293-5390*

◪ A fixture for Kennedy Center ticket-holders, this West End New American supper club wins applause for its "excellent-value" pre-theater menu, easy parking, "free" "shuttle" and lively post-performance scene (with jazz piano Tuesday–Saturday); it's also a "nice spot" for a business lunch, but signs that it's becoming a bit "worn" leave critics sitting on their hands.

West 24 🅂   – | – | – | M

World Wildlife Fund Bldg., 1250 24th St., NW (bet. M & N Sts.),
202-331-1100

At Democrat James Carville and Republican Mary Matalan's
bipartisan American bistro, cause crusaders, convention-
goers and biz-savvy West Enders find common ground in
the comfy couch-filled bar or at nicely-spaced booths and
banquettes; its reasonably priced seasonal menu moves
from the likes of sturdy Midwestern meat dishes to southern-
accented catfish and black-eyed peas, with the blues in the
background adding to its something-for-everyone appeal.

White Tiger 🅂   21 | 17 | 19 | $23

146 Maple Ave. (bet. Center & Park Sts.), Vienna, VA,
703-255-0800
301 Massachusetts Ave., NE (3rd St.), 202-546-5900

■ These "attentive", "atmospheric" Indian twins occupy
two very different spaces – a Capitol Hill sidewalk cafe
and restaurant and a former supper club in Vienna – but
they both serve the same "authentic", "heavenly" fare;
"Hill staffers favor" the "generous" buffet, while VA's
townsfolk hope the younger suburban sib is "here to stay."

WILLARD ROOM   24 | 28 | 26 | $56

Willard Intercontinental Hotel, 1401 Pennsylvania Ave., NW
(14th St.), 202-637-7440

■ Since 1851, this "drop-dead" gorgeous Downtown hotel
institution has "defined elegance" and privilege; chef Gerard
Mandani's "refined and elegant platings" of "extraordinary"
New American–French fare, accompanied by a lovely wine
list, complement the "majestic" (and recently spiffed-up)
setting and "old-world service" (the staff "treats you
like a Vanderbilt" here), even if a few find it predictably
"stuffy" and "pricey."

Willie & Reed's 🅂   17 | 18 | 18 | $19

4901A Fairmont Ave. (Norfolk Ave.), Bethesda, MD,
301-951-1100

■ "If you like ESPN", you'll root for this Bethesda "sports
bar" where state-of-the-art viewing (including booths
with private TVs) rules; while hecklers hoot at "too many
televisions", fans cheer not only the score of screens
and interesting "collectibles" on display, but also the
American food, especially the "amazing" make-your-
own chopped salad.

Willow Grove Inn 🅂   ▽ 23 | 25 | 20 | $53

14079 Plantation Way (Rte. 15), Orange, VA, 540-672-5982

■ "Southern elegance", genuine warmth and an "inspired"
regional American menu make this "lovely" historic mansion
in Orange a "wonderful" stop when visiting Charlottesville
and Monticello; the "beautiful" setting makes the dining
experience even more "outstanding" so patrons gladly
excuse any "occasional goofs."

Woo Lae Oak S   23 | 16 | 17 | $29
River House, 1500 S. Joyce St. (15th St.), Arlington, VA, 703-521-3706

◼ Though many Westerners are content with the "best" *bulgogi* (cook-your-own BBQ), hot pots and other "standard" fare available at this dated Korean in Arlington, it also offers a wider range of "serious", "authentic" choices, as the largely Asian clientele can attest.

Wrap Works S   16 | 12 | 13 | $11
1601 Connecticut Ave., NW (Q St.), 202-265-4200
1079 Wisconsin Ave. (bet. K & M Sts.), 202-333-0220
Reston Town Ctr., 1820 Discovery St. (Reston Pkwy.), Reston, VA, 703-318-5200

◼ The internationally flavored "overstuffed" wraps, salads and "refreshing" fruit shakes at these high-traffic "people-watching" posts remain popular, despite raps on the service and the consistency of the eats; still, for "a quick, light meal", many find this chainlet a "fresh" and "filling" option.

Wurzburg-Haus S   18 | 15 | 17 | $25
Red Mill Shopping Ctr., 7236 Muncaster Mill Rd. (Shady Grove Rd.), Rockville, MD, 301-330-0402

◼ "Cravings" for sauerbraten, Wiener schnitzel, potato pancakes and other "heavy" Deutsche treats send plenty of hungry mouths to this "strip mall" Rockville Bavarian where costumed servers and an "oom pah pah" atmosphere contribute to a "pleasant", if sometimes "slow", meal; but while the cooking is "lighter and more veggie-friendly than in the past", it's still "not for dieters."

Yama Japanese S   ▽ 21 | 17 | 19 | $28
328 Maple Ave. W. (bet. Center St. & Lawyers Rd.), Vienna, VA, 703-242-7703

◾ Vienna raw-fish fanciers tell us that the chef at this unassuming Japanese creates "good" rolls with unusual ingredients and slices sushi so "fresh" it's "like butter"; one or two demur, though, it "promises more than it delivers."

Yanyu S   24 | 25 | 20 | $44
3433 Connecticut Ave., NW (Newark St.), 202-686-6968

◾ Possibly DC's "best and most original Asian cuisine" is served at this Cleveland Park boutique where everything – from the dramatic Far East–inspired decor to the "beautiful" tableware to the "meticulous" presentations – is a "work of art"; but the service, while "attentive", lags a bit behind and a few diners find the effort "pretentious."

Yosaku S   21 | 14 | 19 | $27
4712 Wisconsin Ave., NW (Davenport St.), 202-363-4453

◾ Don't sell short this "tried-and-true", "reasonable" Japanese family spot near the shops of Friendship Heights, because friendly people here deliver "top-notch" sushi and soul-warming noodle soups amid old-shoe comforts.

Zed's 🅂   19 | 15 | 18 | $21
1201 28th St., NW (M St.), 202-333-4710

◪ "Mainstream" Ethiopian is what you'll find at this "bargain" staple, now quartered in more attractive Georgetown digs (not yet fully reflected in the above decor rating); the dining "experience" – scoop up your choice of "fantastic" spicy dishes with spongy bread, sans utensils – remains the same, though a handful feel the "food has lost some of its flavor."

Zuki Moon 🅂   20 | 17 | 18 | $26
824 New Hampshire Ave., NW (bet. H & I Sts.), 202-333-3312

▪ Acclaimed as a "wonderful dining option near the Kennedy Center", the "inventive" Asian cuisine at this "unique" spot makes for an "ideal light" meal that reflects Mary Richter's "excellence-in-simplicity" sensibility; her many admirers cheer the new chairs, which should lift the decor rating.

Washington, DC
Indexes

CUISINES
LOCATIONS
SPECIAL FEATURES

CUISINES

Afghan

Faryab Afghan
Kabul Caravan
Panjshir
Paradise

American (New)

Addie's
Arbor
Ardeo
Ashby Inn
Bistro
Bistro Bistro
Black's Bar & Kitchen
Bleu Rock Inn
Blue Stone Cafe
Broad St. Grill
Butterfield 9
Cafe Bethesda
Carlyle Grand Cafe
Cashion's
Chardonnay
Coeur De Lion
DC Coast
Dean & DeLuca
eCiti Cafe & Bar
Elysium
Equinox
Evening Star
4 & 20 Blackbirds
Garden Cafe
Gordon Biersch
Grapeseed
Greenwood
Inn at Little Washington
Iota
Jasmine Cafe
Jefferson Rest.
Kinkead's
Kobalt
Lafayette
Majestic Cafe
Mark
Market St. B&G

Melrose
Mendocino
Metro Ctr. Grille
Morrison-Clark Inn
Mrs. Simpson's
New Heights
Nora
Occidental
Old Angler's Inn
Oval Room
Palena
Palm Court
Palomino
Peacock Cafe
Persimmon
Peter's Passion
Rhodeside Grill
Rico y Rico
Ritz-Carlton/Grill
Roof Terrace Kennedy Ctr.
Rupperts
Saint Basil
Saveur
Seasons
701
1789
Starland Cafe
Stella's
Stone Manor
Tabard Inn
Tahoga
Timothy Dean
Turning Point Inn
Vidalia
West End Cafe
West 24
Willard Room

American (Regional)

Black's Bar & Kitchen
B. Smith's
Crisfield
Crisfield at Lee Plaza
Jeffrey's/Watergate

Silverado
Stella's
Vidalia
Willow Grove Inn

American (Traditional)

America
Artie's
Ben's Chili Bowl
Bob & Edith's Diner
Cafe Deluxe
Calvert Grille
Capitol City Brewing
Caucus Room
C.F. Folks
Cheesecake Factory
Christopher Marks
Clyde's
Daily Grill
Diner
District ChopHse.
ESPN Zone
Fairmont Bar
Gaffney's
Hard Rock Cafe
Hard Times Cafe
Hogate's
Houston's
Inn at Glen Echo
John Harvard's
J. Paul's
Kramerbooks & Afterwords
Luna Grill
M & S Grill
Martin's Tavern
Mike's American
Monocle
Montgomery's Grille
Nathan's
Oceanaire
Old Ebbitt Grill
Old Hickory Grill
Original Pancake Hse.
Palm
Planet Hollywood
Planet Wayside
Polly's Cafe

Potowmack Landing
Rail Stop
Red Fox Inn
Rock Bottom Brewery
Sequoia
1789
Silver Diner
Sweetwater Tavern
Tryst
Tuscarora Mill
Two Quail
Union St. Public Hse.
Upper Crust Bakery
Vienna Inn
Willie & Reed's

Asian

Asia Nora
Big Bowl
Cafe Asia
Ching Ching Cha
Flat Top
Lotte Plaza Market
Malaysia Kopitiam
Oodles Noodles
Perry's
Raku
Saigonnais
Stardust
Sweet Basil
Teaism
Ten Pehn
Yanyu
Zuki Moon

Bakery

Bread Line
Cafe Marianna
Così
Firehook
La Madeleine
Panera Bread
Samadi Sweets
Sen5es
Shiney's Sweets
Upper Crust Bakery

Barbecue

BD's Mongolian BBQ
Greenfield Churrascaria
Hee Been
Ilmee
King St. Blues
Old Glory BBQ
Old Hickory Grill
Planet Wayside
Red Hot & Blue
Rockland's
Tony Cheng's
Woo Lae Oak

Belgian

Le Mannequin Pis
Marcel's

Brazilian

Coco Loco
Greenfield Churrascaria
Grill from Ipanema
Malibu Grill

Burmese

Burma

Cajun/Creole

Black's Bar & Kitchen
Cafe Marianna
Cajun Bangkok
Louisiana Express
Rocky's Cafe
R.T.'s
R.T.'s Seafood
219
Warehouse B&G

Californian

Paolo's

Caribbean

Mango Mike's
Negril
Rocky's Cafe

Chinese

A&J Rest.
China Garden
City Lights of China
Foong Lin
Fortune
Full Kee
Full Key
Good Fortune
Hollywood East
Hope Key
Hunan Chinatown
Hunan Lion
Hunan Number One
Hunan Palace
Mark's Duck Hse.
Maxim Palace
Meiweh
Miu Kee
Mr. K's
New Fortune
Oriental East
Paul Kee
Peking Gourmet Inn
P.F. Chang's
Seven Seas
Shanghai Cafe
Taipei/Tokyo Cafe
Tony Cheng's
Vegetable Garden

Coffeehouse/Dessert

Così
Dean & DeLuca
Donna's Coffee Bar
Espresso Bar
Firehook
Kramerbooks & Afterwords
Patisserie Poupon
Savory

Coffee Shop/Diner

Bob & Edith's Diner
Diner
Florida Ave. Grill
Luna Grill
Metro 29
Original Pancake Hse.
Silver Diner

Continental

Bailiwick Inn
Dominique's
It's About Thyme
Palm Court
Ritz-Carlton/Grill
Serbian Crown
Tivoli
Village Bistro

Cuban

Banana Cafe
Havana Breeze

Deli/Sandwich Shop

Chutzpah
Krupin's
Panera Bread
Parkway Deli

Dim Sum

A&J Rest.
China Garden
Fortune
Good Fortune
Hunan Number One
Mark's Duck Hse.
Maxim Palace
New Fortune
Oriental East
Seven Seas

Eclectic/International

Bilbo Baggins
Blue Iguana
Cafe Marianna
Cities
Così
Felix
Ice House Cafe
Iota
Lightfoot Cafe
Peacock Cafe
Rosemary's Thyme
Stardust
Taste of the World
Thyme Square

U-topia
Wrap Works

Eritrean

Harambe African

Ethiopian

Meskerem
Zed's

European

Bistro Bernoise

French

Dominique's
Eiffel Tower Cafe
Hermitage Inn
Jean-Michel
La Bergerie
La Chaumiere
La Colline
La Cote d'Or Cafe
La Ferme
La Miche
La Provence
L'Auberge Chez François
L'Auberge Provencale
Le Gaulois
Le Refuge
Le Relais
L'Etoile
Le Vieux Logis
Marcel's
Matisse
Mediterranee
Prince Michel
Tempo
Willard Room

French (Bistro)

Bis
Bistro Francais
Bistro 123
Bistrot du Coin
Bistrot Lepic
Cafe Parisien Express
Cafe Roval

Dominique's
Frogs & Friends
La Brasserie
La Chaumiere
La Cote d'Or Cafe
La Fourchette
La Provence
Lavandou
Le Gaulois
Le Petit Mistral
Le Refuge
Les Halles
Marcel's
Patisserie Poupon
Petits Plats
Sen5es
Willard Room

French (New)

Blackie's
Citronelle
Gerard's Place
Japoné
Le Jardin
Le Relais
Le Rivage
Marcel's
Saveur
Sen5es
Willard Room

German

Old Europe
Wurzburg-Haus

Greek

Taverna Cretekou

Hamburgers

Addie's
Carlyle Grand Cafe
Clyde's
District ChopHse.
Five Guys
Hard Rock Cafe
Houston's
Martin's Tavern

Mike's American
Occidental
Polly's Cafe
Rock Bottom Brewery

Indian

Aaranthi
Aditi
Bombay Bistro
Bombay Club
Bombay Curry
Bombay Gaylord
Bombay Palace
Bombay Tandoor
Cafe New Delhi
Cafe Taj
Connaught Place
Delhi Dhaba
Haandi
Heritage India
Madras Palace
Mehak
Raaga
Shiney's Sweets
Udupi Palace
White Tiger

Indonesian

Sabang
Satay Sarinah

Irish

Fadó Irish Pub

Italian

(N=Northern; S=Southern;
N&S=Includes both)

Agrodolce (N&S)
Al Tiramisu (N&S)
Argia (N&S)
Arucola (N&S)
Barolo (N)
Bella Luna (N&S)
Bertucci's (N&S)
Buca di Beppo (S)
Buon Giorno (N&S)
Cafe Milano (N&S)

Cafe Mileto (N&S)
Cafe Oggi (N&S)
California Pizza Kit. (N&S)
Centro (N)
Cesco (N)
Coppi's (N&S)
Da Domenico (N&S)
Dante (N)
Dolce Vita (N&S)
Donatello (N&S)
Ecco Cafe (N&S)
Espresso Bar (N&S)
Etrusco (N&S)
Faccia Luna (N&S)
Filomena (N&S)
Galileo (N&S)
Generous George's (N&S)
Geranio (N&S)
Giovanni's Trattu (N&S)
Il Borgo (N&S)
Il Cigno (N&S)
Il Lupo (N&S)
Il Pizzico (N&S)
Il Radicchio (N&S)
I Matti (N&S)
I Ricchi (N)
Joe's Place (N&S)
Landini Brothers (N)
Luigino (N)
Maestro (N&S)
Maggiano's (S)
Mama Lucia (N&S)
Mare e Monti (N&S)
Michael's (N&S)
Obelisk (N)
Osteria Goldoni (N)
Paolo's (N&S)
Pasta Mia (N&S)
Pasta Plus (N&S)
Primi Piatti (N&S)
Red Tomato Cafe (N&S)
Renato (N&S)
Ricciuti's (N&S)
San Marco (N&S)
San Marzano (N&S)
Sesto Senso (N)

Skewers/Cafe Luna (N&S)
Teatro Goldoni (N)
Tempo (N&S)
Terrazza (N)
That's Amore (N&S)
Timpano (N&S)
Tivoli (N)
Tosca (N)
Tragara (N)
Vignola (N&S)
Vigorelli (N)
Vivo (N)

Japanese
Akasaka
Arigato
Bonsai
Cafe Asia
Cafe Japoné
Hakuba
Hama Sushi
Hinode
Japoné
Kawasaki
Kaz Sushi
Konami
Makoto
Matuba
Niwano Hana
Sakana
Sushi-Ko
Sushi Taro
Tachibana
Taipei/Tokyo Cafe
Tako Grill
Tono Sushi
Uni
Yama Japanese
Yosaku

Jewish
Felix
Krupin's
Parkway Deli

Korean
Hee Been
Ilmee

Lotte Plaza Market
Woo Lae Oak

Kosher

L'Etoile
Neyla

Latin American

Cafe Atlantico
Crisp & Juicy
El Gavilan
El Pollo Rico
Grill from Ipanema
Lauriol Plaza
Toro

Lebanese

Bacchus
Lebanese Taverna
Samadi Sweets

Malaysian

Malaysia Kopitiam

Mediterranean

Bambulé
BeDuCi
Cafe Midi
Cafe Ole
Cafe Promenade
Levante's
Matisse
Medaterra
Mediterranee
Mezza 9
Mimi's American
Olives
Palomino
Rosemary's Thyme
Saint Basil
Skewers/Cafe Luna
Sole
Tel Aviv Cafe
Temel

Mexican/Tex-Mex

Austin Grill
Burrito Brothers

Burro
Cactus Cantina
California Tortilla
Lauriol Plaza
Los Chorros
Mexicali Blues
Mi Rancho
Neyla
Rio Grande Cafe
Taqueria Poblano

Middle Eastern

Bacchus
Faryab Afghan
Food Factory
Hautam Kebobs
Kazan
Lebanese Taverna
Le Tarbouche
Mimi's American
Paradise
Pasha Cafe
Samadi Sweets
Simply Grill
Skewers/Cafe Luna
Temel

Mongolian

BD's Mongolian BBQ

Moroccan

L'Etoile

Pakistani

Food Factory
Shiney's Sweets

Persian

Caravan Grill
Hautam Kebobs
Moby Dick
Paradise
Simply Grill

Peruvian

Crisp & Juicy
El Pollo Rico
Nibbler

Pizza

Bertucci's
California Pizza Kit.
Coppi's
Dolce Vita
Ecco Cafe
Faccia Luna
Generous George's
Il Lupo
Il Radicchio
Joe's Place
Luigino
Maggiano's
Mama Lucia
Paolo's
Pasta Plus
Pizzeria Paradiso
Red Tomato Cafe
Ricciuti's
Saint Basil
San Marzano

Russian

Serbian Crown

Salvadoran

El Tamarindo
Los Chorros
Mexicali Blues

Seafood

Black's Bar & Kitchen
Blue Point Grill
Capital Grille
Crisfield
Crisfield at Lee Plaza
DC Coast
Georgetown Seafood
Grillfish
Hogate's
Horace & Dickie's
Hunter's Inn
Jerry Seafood
Johnny's Half Shell
J. Paul's
Kinkead's
Legal Sea Foods

Le Rivage
McCormick & Schmick's
Oceanaire
Palm
Pesce
Phillips
Prime Rib
R.T.'s
R.T.'s Seafood
Sea Catch
Seven Seas
Shula's Steak House
Stardust
Tony & Joe's
Tony Cheng's
Village Bistro
Warehouse B&G

Southern/Soul

B. Smith's
Florida Ave. Grill
Georgia Brown's
Heart In Hand
Horace & Dickie's
King St. Blues
Old Hickory Grill
Vidalia

Southwestern

Cottonwood Cafe
Gabriel
Red Sage
Silverado
Sweetwater Tavern

Spanish

Andalucia
Gabriel
Jaleo
Lauriol Plaza
Taberna del Alabardero
Toro

Steakhouse

Angelo & Maxie's
Blackie's
Bobby Van's

Capital Grille
Caucus Room
District ChopHse.
Hunter's Inn
Malibu Grill
Morton's of Chicago
Nick & Stef's
Outback Steakhse.
Palm
Prime Rib
Ruth's Chris
Sam & Harry's
Shula's Steak House
Smith & Wollensky's
Timpano

Tapas

Grapeseed
Jaleo
Toro

Tearoom

Ching Ching Cha
Teaism

Thai

Andaman
Bangkok Bistro
Bangkok Garden
Benjarong
Bua
Busara
Cajun Bangkok
Crystal Thai
Duangrat's
Dusit
Haad Thai
Neisha Thai
Paya Thai
Rabieng
Ruan Thai
Sakoontra
Sala Thai

Sweet Basil
Tara Thai
T.H.A.I.
Thai Basil
Thai Derm
Thai Kingdom
Thaiphoon

Turkish

Kazan
Nizam's
Rosemary's Thyme

Vegetarian

(* Vegetarian-friendly)

Aditi
Madras Palace
New Heights*
Nora*
Savory
Thyme Square*
Udupi Palace
Vegetable Garden
Vigorelli*

Vietnamese

Cafe Dalat
Del Ray Garden
Green Papaya
Huong Que
Little Saigon
Little Viet Garden
Miss Saigon
Nam's of Bethesda
Nam Viet
Pho 75
Queen Bee
Saigon Gourmet
Saigon Inn
Saigonnais
Taste of Saigon
Thanh Thanh

LOCATIONS

WASHINGTON, D.C.

Capitol Hill

America
Angelo & Maxie's
Banana Cafe
Barolo
Bis
Blue Stone Cafe
B. Smith's
Burrito Brothers
Capitol City Brewing
Caucus Room
Così
Gordon Biersch
Horace & Dickie's
Il Radicchio
La Brasserie
La Colline
Monocle
Nick & Stef's
Oceanaire
Tosca
Two Quail
White Tiger

Chinatown/Convention Center/Penn Quarter

Austin Grill
Bertucci's
Burma
Cafe Atlantico
Capital Grille
Capitol City Brewing
Coco Loco
Coeur De Lion
Dean & DeLuca
District ChopHse.
ESPN Zone
Fadó Irish Pub
Full Kee
Haad Thai
Hunan Chinatown

Jaleo
Les Halles
Luigino
M & S Grill
Mark
Mehak
Metro Ctr. Grille
Morrison-Clark Inn
Planet Hollywood
Rupp128s
701
Teaism
Tony Cheng's

Downtown/Dupont Circle South

Bobby Van's
Bombay Club
Bread Line
Burrito Brothers
Butterfield 9
Cafe Promenade
C.F. Folks
Chardonnay
Christopher Marks
Così
Daily Grill
DC Coast
Donna's Coffee Bar
Equinox
Espresso Bar
Firehook
Galileo
Georgetown Seafood
Georgia Brown's
Gerard's Place
Giovanni's Trattu
Hard Rock Cafe
Havana Breeze
Il Laboratorio
I Ricchi

Bambulé
Bistro Bernoise
Cactus Cantina
Cafe Deluxe
Cafe Ole
Cheesecake Factory
El Tamarindo
Greenwood
Krupin's
Lavandou
Lebanese Taverna
Maggiano's
Makoto
Matisse
Medaterra
Mrs. Simpson's
Nam Viet
Negril
New Heights

Old Europe
Palena
Peter's Passion
Petits Plats
Rockland's
Saigon Gourmet
Starland Cafe
Sushi-Ko
Tono Sushi
Vigorelli
Yanyu
Yosaku

West End

Bistro
Donatello
Marcel's
Melrose
West End Cafe

NEARBY MARYLAND

**Bethesda/
Chevy Chase**

Andalucia
Andaman
Austin Grill
Bacchus
Bangkok Garden
BD's Mongolian BBQ
Black's Bar & Kitchen
Buon Giorno
Cafe Bethesda
Cafe Deluxe
California Pizza Kit.
California Tortilla
Centro
Cesco
Clyde's
Cottonwood Cafe
Delhi Dhaba
Del Ray Garden
Fairmont Bar
Faryab Afghan
Foong Lin

Grapeseed
Green Papaya
Grillfish
Haandi
Hard Times Cafe
Hinode
Houston's
Jaleo
Jean-Michel
La Ferme
La Madeleine
La Miche
Legal Sea Foods
Levante's
Le Vieux Logis
Louisiana Express
Matuba
McCormick & Schmick's
Moby Dick
Montgomery's Grille
Nam's of Bethesda
Oodles Noodles
Original Pancake Hse.

Outback Steakhse.
Paradise
Persimmon
Raku
Red Tomato Cafe
Rio Grande Cafe
Rock Bottom Brewery
Ruth's Chris
Shanghai Cafe
Sweet Basil
Tako Grill
Tara Thai
Tel Aviv Cafe
Terrazza
Thyme Square
Tragara
Willie & Reed's

Gaithersburg/ Shady Grove/Olney

Agrodolce
Buca di Beppo
Cafe Mileto
Hakuba
Hunan Palace
Hunter's Inn
Joe's Place
Le Mannequin Pis
Madras Palace
Mama Lucia
Mi Rancho
Moby Dick
Negril
New Fortune
Nibbler
Outback Steakhse.
Red Hot & Blue
Ricciuti's
Rico y Rico
Rio Grande Cafe
Turning Point Inn

Langley Park/ Laurel/Landover

Food Factory
Hard Times Cafe

Jerry Seafood
Mare e Monti
Negril
Pasta Plus
Pho 75
Udupi Palace

Middletown/Urbana

Stone Manor

Potomac/Glen Echo

Cafe Roval
Hunter's Inn
Inn at Glen Echo
Old Angler's Inn
Renato

Rockville/ White Flint

A&J Rest.
Addie's
Andalucia
Benjarong
Bombay Bistro
California Tortilla
Cheesecake Factory
Crisp & Juicy
Greenfield Churrascaria
Hard Times Cafe
Hautam Kebobs
Hinode
Houston's
Il Pizzico
La Madeleine
Lebanese Taverna
Mama Lucia
Niwano Hana
Original Pancake Hse.
P.F. Chang's
Pho 75
Seven Seas
Silver Diner
Taipei/Tokyo Cafe
Tara Thai
Taste of Saigon

NEARBY VIRGINIA

El Pollo Rico
Faccia Luna
Flat Top
Food Factory
Gaffney's
Hard Times Cafe
Hope Key
Hunan Number One
Il Radicchio
Iota
Joe's Place
Kabul Caravan
Lebanese Taverna
Legal Sea Foods
Little Viet Garden
Luna Grill
Matuba
Mediterranee
Metro 29
Mexicali Blues
Nam Viet
Outback Steakhse.
Pasha Cafe
Pho 75
Queen Bee
Rhodeside Grill
Rio Grande Cafe
Ritz-Carlton/Grill
Rock Bottom Brewery
Rockland's
R.T.'s Seafood
Ruth's Chris
Sala Thai
Silver Diner
Village Bistro
Woo Lae Oak

Falls Church/ Baileys Crossroads/ Shirlington

Argia
Bonsai
Broad St. Grill
Capitol City Brewing
Carlyle Grand Cafe
Crisp & Juicy
Duangrat's

Fortune
Full Kee
Haandi
Huong Que
Joe's Place
La Cote d'Or Cafe
La Madeleine
Little Saigon
Malibu Grill
Maxim Palace
Mehak
Miu Kee
Neisha Thai
Old Hickory Grill
Panjshir
Peking Gourmet Inn
Pho 75
Raaga
Rabieng
Samadi Sweets
Tara Thai
T.H.A.I.
Toro

Great Falls

Dante
L'Auberge Chez François
Le Relais
Serbian Crown

Leesburg/Middleburg/ The Plains

Eiffel Tower Cafe
Frogs & Friends
It's About Thyme
Lightfoot Cafe
Planet Wayside
Prince Michel
Rail Stop
Red Fox Inn
Tuscarora Mill
Upper Crust Bakery

McLean

Cafe Oggi
Cafe Taj
Il Borgo

Kazan
Le Petit Mistral
Michael's
Tachibana

Reston/Herndon/Chantilly

Angelo & Maxie's
Big Bowl
Bistro Bistro
Burrito Brothers
Clyde's
Delhi Dhaba
Fortune
Hama Sushi
Hard Times Cafe
Ice House Cafe
Il Cigno
Ilmee
Jasmine Cafe
La Madeleine
Market St. B&G
McCormick & Schmick's
Palm Court
Panera Bread
Paolo's
Pho 75
Rio Grande Cafe
Saint Basil
Silver Diner
Simply Grill
Taste of the World
Thai Basil
Wrap Works

Rosslyn/Courthouse

Cafe Asia
China Garden
Mezza 9
Red Hot & Blue
Tivoli

Springfield/Fairfax/ Annandale/Centreville

A&J Rest.
Arigato
Artie's
Austin Grill

Bailiwick Inn
Bella Luna
Bertucci's
Blue Iguana
Bombay Bistro
Chutzpah
Connaught Place
Dolce Vita
Five Guys
Hard Times Cafe
Heart In Hand
Hee Been
Hermitage Inn
Il Lupo
Joe's Place
King St. Blues
Lotte Plaza Market
Malibu Grill
Mark's Duck Hse.
Mike's American
Moby Dick
Original Pancake Hse.
Outback Steakhse.
Panera Bread
Red Hot & Blue
Rosemary's Thyme
Sakoontra
Shiney's Sweets
Silverado
Silver Diner
Sweetwater Tavern
Temel
That's Amore

Tysons Corner/ Vienna

Aaranthi
Amma Veg. Kit.
Bertucci's
Bistro 123
Bombay Tandoor
Burrito Brothers
Busara
California Pizza Kit.
Capital Grille
Da Domenico
Daily Grill
eCiti Cafe & Bar

Washington, VA/ Flint Hill/White Post/ Orange/Manassus

SPECIAL FEATURES

Additions

Andaman
Angelo & Maxie's
Arbor
Bailiwick Inn
Benjarong
Big Bowl
Bistro Bernoise
Blackie's
Bombay Tandoor
Cafe Japoné
Caucus Room
Chutzpah
Diner
Flat Top
Gaffney's
Gordon Biersch
Green Papaya
Greenwood
Hakuba
Il Lupo
Japoné
Jeffrey's/Watergate
Kobalt
Le Jardin
Madras Palace
Maestro
Majestic Cafe
Mama Lucia
Michael's
Mimi's American
Nick & Stef's
Oceanaire
Palena
Peter's Passion
Rico y Rico
Sakoontra
Shula's Steak House
Sole
Sweet Basil
Taqueria Poblano
Temel
Ten Pehn
Thaiphoon

Thanh Thanh
Tosca
Uni
Vivo
West 24

Breakfast

(Best of many;
see also Hotel Dining)

Ben's Chili Bowl
Bob & Edith's Diner
Bread Line
Diner
Florida Ave. Grill
La Colline
Louisiana Express
Martin's Tavern
Old Ebbitt Grill
Original Pancake Hse.
Teaism
Upper Crust Bakery

Brunch

(Best of many)

A&J Rest.
Arbor
Ashby Inn
Banana Cafe
Bella Luna
Bilbo Baggins
Bistro
Bleu Rock Inn
Blue Stone Cafe
Bombay Club
B. Smith's
Cafe Atlantico
Cafe Marianna
Cafe Promenade
Carlyle Grand Cafe
Cashion's
Elysium
4 & 20 Blackbirds
Gabriel
Georgia Brown's
Hermitage Inn

Inn at Glen Echo
Kinkead's
Kramerbooks & Afterwords
Le Relais
Maestro
Majestic Cafe
Mango Mike's
Market St. B&G
Mark's Duck Hse.
Melrose
Morrison-Clark Inn
Mrs. Simpson's
Parkway Deli
Perry's
Phillips
Potowmack Landing
Rabieng
Rail Stop
Red Fox Inn
Ritz-Carlton/Grill
Roof Terrace Kennedy Ctr.
Samadi Sweets
Seasons
Sen5es
Stone Manor
Tabard Inn
Taqueria Poblano
Thyme Square
Turning Point Inn
Willow Grove Inn

Buffet Served
(Check prices, days
and times)
Aaranthi
Banana Cafe
BD's Mongolian BBQ
Bella Luna
Bistro
Bombay Bistro
Bombay Gaylord
Bombay Tandoor
Cafe Mileto
Cafe Promenade
Cafe Taj
Caravan Grill
Coco Loco

Connaught Place
Delhi Dhaba
Food Factory
Gabriel
Greenfield Churrascaria
Madras Palace
Malibu Grill
Mehak
Metro Ctr. Grille
Paradise
Phillips
Ritz-Carlton/Grill
Shiney's Sweets
Tony Cheng's
White Tiger

Business Dining
(Best of many)
Addie's
Angelo & Maxie's
Ardeo
Artie's
Barolo
Benjarong
Bis
Blackie's
Bobby Van's
Bombay Club
Bombay Tandoor
Butterfield 9
Cafe Promenade
Capital Grille
Caucus Room
Cesco
Citronelle
Daily Grill
DC Coast
Equinox
Etrusco
Gaffney's
Galileo
Garden Cafe
Georgia Brown's
Gerard's Place
Gordon Biersch
Hakuba
Hunan Lion

I Ricchi
Jefferson Rest.
Jeffrey's/Watergate
Kaz Sushi
Kinkead's
Kobalt
Konami
Lafayette
Le Relais
Maestro
M & S Grill
Marcel's
Mark
Market St. B&G
Matisse
Melrose
Michael's
Monocle
Morrison-Clark Inn
Morton's of Chicago
Nick & Stef's
Occidental
Oceanaire
Old Ebbitt Grill
Olives
Osteria Goldoni
Oval Room
Palena
Palm
Palm Court
Prime Rib
Primi Piatti
Red Sage
Red Tomato Cafe
Ritz-Carlton/Grill
Ruth's Chris
Sam & Harry's
Seasons
701
1789
Shula's Steak House
Smith & Wollensky's
Sushi-Ko
Taberna del Alabardero
Tahoga
Taste of Saigon

Teatro Goldoni
Temel
Terrazza
Timothy Dean
Tivoli
Tosca
Tragara
Vidalia
Vivo
Warehouse B&G
West End Cafe
West 24
Willard Room

Catering
(Best of many)
Al Tiramisu
Bacchus
Bistro Bernoise
Bombay Tandoor
Bread Line
B. Smith's
Cafe Japoné
Caravan Grill
Caucus Room
China Garden
Chutzpah
Citronelle
Dean & DeLuca
Dominique's
Flat Top
Hakuba
Jasmine Cafe
La Madeleine
Lebanese Taverna
Legal Sea Foods
Louisiana Express
Malaysia Kopitiam
Mama Lucia
Michael's
Mimi's American
Neyla
Nick & Stef's
Old Hickory Grill
Panera Bread
Phillips
Raku

Red Hot & Blue
Rico y Rico
Rockland's
Sakoontra
Silver Diner
Sole
Taste of Saigon
Temel
Thanh Thanh
Tosca
Uni
Vidalia
Zed's
Zuki Moon

Chef's Table
(Best of many)
Citronelle
Fairmont Bar
Galileo
Marcel's
Matisse
Melrose
Primi Piatti
Teatro Goldoni
Tosca

Child Friendly
(Besides the normal fast-food places; *children's menu)
Arucola
Austin Grill
Bertucci's*
Big Bowl
Cactus Cantina
Clyde's
Flat Top
Generous George's
Hard Rock Cafe
Hard Times Cafe
Lebanese Taverna
Los Chorros
Mama Lucia
Matuba
Original Pancake Hse.
Planet Hollywood
Ricciuti's

Rio Grande Cafe
Silver Diner
Tara Thai
T.H.A.I.

Delivery/Takeout
(Best of many; D=delivery, T=takeout)
A&J Rest. (T)
Addie's (T)
Al Tiramisu (T)
Andalucia (T)
Andaman (T)
Ardeo (T)
Argia (T)
Arucola (D,T)
Asia Nora (T)
BeDuCi (T)
Benjarong (T)
Bistro Bernoise (T)
Bombay Tandoor (T)
Bread Line (T)
Cafe Atlantico (T)
Cafe Japoné (T)
Cafe Midi (T)
Capital Grille (T)
Cesco (T)
C.F. Folks (D,T)
Chutzpah (T)
Clyde's (T)
Dean & DeLuca (D,T)
Diner (T)
Dolce Vita (T)
El Pollo Rico (T)
Firehook (D,T)
Flat Top (T)
Galileo (D)
Georgia Brown's (T)
Hakuba (T)
Horace & Dickie's (T)
Il Lupo (T)
Jaleo (T)
Kaz Sushi (T)
Konami (T)
La Brasserie (T)
L'Etoile (T)
Louisiana Express (D,T)

Luigino (T)
Madras Palace (T)
Mark (T)
Old Ebbitt Grill (T)
Old Hickory Grill (D,T)
Osteria Goldoni (T)
Palm (T)
Pesce (T)
Rico y Rico (T)
Rockland's (D,T)
Sakoontra (D,T)
Samadi Sweets (T)
Sesto Senso (T)
Sole (T)
Sushi-Ko (T)
Sweet Basil (T)
Taqueria Poblano (T)
Teaism (D,T)
Temel (T)
Uni (D,T)
Upper Crust Bakery (T)
Vidalia (T)
Vigorelli (T)

Dessert

Bread Line
Cafe Marianna
Carlyle Grand Cafe
Cashion's
Citronelle
Dean & DeLuca
Espresso Bar
Fairmont Bar
Firehook
Galileo
Inn at Little Washington
Kinkead's
Kramerbooks & Afterwords
Majestic Cafe
Morrison-Clark Inn
Obelisk
Palena
Samadi Sweets
Sen5es
1789
Shiney's Sweets
Thyme Square

Tivoli
Tragara

Dining Alone
(Other than hotels, coffee
shops, sushi bars and places
with counter service)

Bread Line
Clyde's
Daily Grill
DC Coast
Dean & DeLuca
Diner
Gaffney's
Johnny's Half Shell
Kinkead's
Mama Lucia
Marcel's
Old Ebbitt Grill
Olives
Patisserie Poupon
Pizzeria Paradiso
Rockland's
Teaism
Uni

Entertainment
(Call for days and times of
performances; best of many)

Andalucia (guitar/Spanish)
Bistro Bistro (jazz)
Bombay Club (piano)
Broad St. Grill (blues/jazz)
B. Smith's (jazz)
Clyde's (guitar/jazz)
Coco Loco (Brazilian jazz)
Coeur De Lion (piano/jazz)
Connaught Place (guitar/sitar)
Dolce Vita (strolling musician)
Elysium (piano)
Evening Star (bands)
Fadó Irish Pub (Celtic)
Felix (DJ/jazz/piano)
Georgia Brown's (blues)
Hakuba (bands)
Ice House Cafe (jazz)
Inn at Glen Echo (jazz)

Iota (varies)
Jefferson Rest. (jazz/piano)
Kinkead's (jazz)
Kobalt (harp/jazz/piano)
Kramerbooks/Afterwords (jazz)
Mango Mike's (steel drums)
Old Europe (piano)
Old Glory BBQ (blues)
Perry's (varies)
Prime Rib (piano)
Rhodeside Grill (varies)
Rock Bottom Brewery (varies)
Serbian Crown (Russian)
701 (jazz/piano)
Starland Cafe (varies)
Taberna/Alabardero (Spanish)
219 (jazz)
U-topia (jazz)
West End Cafe (piano)
Willard Room (piano)
Wurzburg-Haus (accordion)

Family Style

Arucola
Buca di Beppo
Maggiano's
Malibu Grill
Mama Lucia
That's Amore

Fireplace

Al Tiramisu
Bilbo Baggins
Fadó Irish Pub
4 & 20 Blackbirds
Green Papaya
Hermitage Inn
La Chaumiere
La Ferme
Matisse
Old Angler's Inn
Polly's Cafe
Sea Catch
1789
Sole
Tabard Inn

Historic Interest

(Year opened; *building)

1753 L'Auberge Provencale
1778 Willow Grove Inn
1800 Bilbo Baggins
1851 Willard Room
1860 Old Angler's Inn
1860 1789*
1865 Morrison-Clark Inn*
1867 Martin's Tavern*
1869 Hermitage Inn
1887 Tabard Inn
1890 Nora
1890 Rupperts
1893 Gordon Biersch*
1904 Two Quail
1908 B. Smith's*
1910 4 & 20 Blackbirds

Hotel Dining

Ashby Inn
   Ashby Inn
Bleu Rock Inn
   Bleu Rock Inn
Clarion Hampshire Hotel
   L'Etoile
Doubletree Park Terrace
   Chardonnay
Four Seasons Hotel
   Seasons
Hay Adams Hotel
   Lafayette
Henley Park Hotel
   Coeur De Lion
Hotel George
   Bis
Hyatt Arlington
   Mezza 9
Hyatt Hotel
   Market St. B&G
Inn at Little Washington
   Inn at Little Washington
Jefferson Hotel
   Jefferson Rest.
Latham Hotel
   Citronelle

Marriott at Metro Ctr.
  Metro Ctr. Grille
Mayflower Hotel
  Cafe Promenade
Morrison-Clark Inn
  Morrison-Clark Inn
Morrison House Hotel
  Elysium
Park Hyatt Hotel
  Melrose
Radisson-Barcelo
  Gabriel
Reston Hyatt
  Panera Bread
Ritz-Carlton
  Kobalt
Ritz-Carlton/Pentagon City
  Ritz-Carlton/Grill
Ritz-Carlton/Tysons Corner
  Maestro
State Plaza Hotel
  Garden Cafe
St. Gregory Hotel
  Donna's Coffee Bar
St. Regis Hotel
  Timothy Dean
Tabard Inn
  Tabard Inn
Washington Circle Hotel
  West End Cafe
Washington Monarch
  Bistro
Watergate Hotel
  Jeffrey's/Watergate
Westfield Marriott Hotel
  Palm Court
Willard Intercontinental
  Willard Room
Willow Grove Inn
  Willow Grove Inn

"In" Places

Addie's
Ardeo
Asia Nora
Big Bowl
Bis
Bistrot Lepic
Black's Bar & Kitchen
Butterfield 9
Cafe Japoné
Cafe Milano
Carlyle Grand Cafe
Cashion's
Caucus Room
Cities
Diner
Equinox
Etrusco
Full Kee
Galileo
Georgia Brown's
Grapeseed
Hakuba
Inn at Little Washington
Jaleo
Johnny's Half Shell
Kaz Sushi
Konami
Kramerbooks & Afterwords
La Chaumiere
La Fourchette
Lauriol Plaza
Majestic Cafe
Mimi's American
Monocle
Nathan's
Nora
Obelisk
Old Ebbitt Grill
Olives
Oval Room
Palena
Palm
Pesce
Peter's Passion
Pizzeria Paradiso
Red Sage
Red Tomato Cafe
Rio Grande Cafe
Rocky's Cafe
R.T.'s
Rupperts

Sam & Harry's
Sesto Senso
701
Stella's
Sushi-Ko
Tabard Inn
Tahoga
Teatro Goldoni
Tel Aviv Cafe
Ten Pehn
Vidalia
West 24
Yanyu

Late Late – After 12:30

(All hours are AM)

Ben's Chili Bowl (2)
Bistro Francais (3)
Bob & Edith's Diner (24 hrs.)
Cafe Japoné (1:30)
Coppi's (1)
Così (1)
Diner (24 hrs.)
El Tamarindo (3)
Full Kee (1)
Full Key (1)
Good Fortune (1)
Hard Times Cafe (2)
Hollywood East (1)
Hope Key (1)
Horace & Dickie's (2)
Hunan Number One (1:45)
Metro 29 (1)
New Fortune (1)
Old Ebbitt Grill (1)
Paul Kee (1)
Polly's Cafe (1)
Seven Seas (1)
Smith & Wollensky's (1:30)

Meet for a Drink

America
Andaman
Angelo & Maxie's
Artie's
Big Bowl
Black's Bar & Kitchen

Cafe Japoné
Capitol City Brewing
Caucus Room
Cities
Clyde's
Coco Loco
Fadó Irish Pub
Gaffney's
Georgia Brown's
Gordon Biersch
Jaleo
John Harvard's
J. Paul's
Konami
Kramerbooks & Afterwords
La Brasserie
Les Halles
Le Tarbouche
Levante's
M & S Grill
Marcel's
Market St. B&G
McCormick & Schmick's
Mike's American
Mimi's American
Nathan's
Old Ebbitt Grill
Palomino
Red Sage
Red Tomato Cafe
Rocky's Cafe
701
Tahoga
Teaism
That's Amore
Tryst
Vienna Inn
West 24

Offbeat

Ben's Chili Bowl
Bob & Edith's Diner
Ching Ching Cha
Five Guys
Florida Ave. Grill
Greenwood
Johnny's Half Shell

Matuba
Meskerem
Mimi's American
Perry's
Planet Wayside
Rupperts
Tabard Inn
Teaism
U-topia

Outdoor Dining

(G=garden; P=patio;
S=sidewalk; T=terrace;
W=waterside; best of many)

Addie's (P)
America (P)
Arbor (S)
Arucola (P)
Austin Grill (P)
Bacchus (P)
Bailiwick Inn (G)
Bambulé (T)
Banana Cafe (S)
Bangkok Bistro (P)
BeDuCi (S)
Big Bowl (S)
Bistro (P)
Bistro Bernoise (S)
Bistro Bistro (P,S)
Bistro 123 (T)
Black's Bar & Kitchen (P)
Bleu Rock Inn (T)
Blue Point Grill (P)
Bombay Club (S)
Bread Line (S)
Bua (P)
Busara (P)
Cactus Cantina (S)
Cafe Atlantico (P,S)
Cafe Bethesda (P)
Cafe Deluxe (S)
Cafe Japoné (S)
Cafe Marianna (G)
Cafe Milano (P,S)
Cafe Mileto (P)
Cafe New Delhi (P)
Cafe Oggi (P)

Cafe Ole (P)
Cafe Parisien Express (S)
Cafe Roval (P)
Cafe Taj (P)
California Tortilla (P)
Capitol City Brewing (P)
Carlyle Grand Cafe (P)
Cashion's (S)
Cesco (P,S)
C.F. Folks (P)
Chardonnay (G)
Clyde's (T)
Coco Loco (G)
Così (P,S)
Cottonwood Cafe (P)
Crystal Thai (T)
Dean & DeLuca (P)
Diner (S)
Duangrat's (S)
El Tamarindo (S)
Equinox (S)
Etrusco (S)
Faccia Luna (P)
Firehook (G,S)
Flat Top (S)
Gabriel (P)
Gaffney's (P)
Galileo (P)
Garden Cafe (P)
Georgetown Seafood (P)
Gerard's Place (S)
Gordon Biersch (S)
Hakuba (P)
Heart In Hand (T)
Hermitage Inn (P)
Hogate's (P,W)
Hunter's Inn (P)
Il Cigno (T)
Il Lupo (S)
Inn at Glen Echo (T)
Inn at Little Washington (G,P)
It's About Thyme (P)
Jasmine Cafe (T)
Jeffrey's/Watergate (T)
Konami (G)
Kramerbooks & Afterwords (P,S)

La Brasserie (S)
La Colline (S)
La Cote d'Or Cafe (P)
La Ferme (G)
La Fourchette (S)
La Madeleine (P,S)
L'Auberge Chez François (G)
Lauriol Plaza (S)
Lebanese Taverna (P,S)
Le Gaulois (P)
Le Jardin (P)
Le Petit Mistral (T)
Le Rivage (T,W)
Les Halles (P,S)
Levante's (P)
Le Vieux Logis (P)
Little Viet Garden (P)
Luna Grill (P)
Mama Lucia (S)
Marcel's (P)
Martin's Tavern (S)
McCormick & Schmick's (P,S)
Melrose (P)
Michael's (P)
Mimi's American (S)
Mi Rancho (P)
Montgomery's Grille (P)
Morton's of Chicago (P)
New Heights (S)
Nick & Stef's (P)
Old Angler's Inn (T)
Oodles Noodles (S)
Oval Room (S)
Paya Thai (S)
Peacock Cafe (S)
Perry's (T)
Phillips (G)
Planet Wayside (P)
Polly's Cafe (S)
Potowmack Landing (P,W)
Primi Piatti (S)
Rail Stop (P)
Raku (S)
Red Tomato Cafe (S)
Rhodeside Grill (S)
Rico y Rico (P)

Rio Grande Cafe (P,S)
Rock Bottom Brewery (P,S)
Roof Terrace Kennedy Ctr. (T)
Saigon Gourmet (S)
Savory (P)
Sea Catch (P,T,W)
Sequoia (T)
701 (P)
Skewers/Cafe Luna (T)
Smith & Wollensky's (S)
Sole (P,T,W)
Stardust (P)
Starland Cafe (P)
Stone Manor (P)
Sweet Basil (G)
Sweetwater Tavern (P,T)
Tabard Inn (G)
Tahoga (G)
Taqueria Poblano (S)
Taverna Cretekou (P)
Tel Aviv Cafe (S)
Temel (P)
Tempo (P)
Ten Pehn (P)
Terrazza (T)
Tivoli (P)
Tony & Joe's (P,W)
Tuscarora Mill (P)
219 (T)
Upper Crust Bakery (P)
West 24 (P)
Willow Grove Inn (T)
Wrap Works (S)

Parking
(L=parking lot;
V=valet parking;
*=validated parking)

A&J Rest. (L)
Aaranthi (L)
Addie's (L)
Agrodolce (L)
Akasaka (L,V)
Al Tiramisu (V)
America*
Andalucia (L)
Ardeo (V)

Argia (L)
Arigato (L)
Artie's (L)
Arucola (L)
Asia Nora (V)
Austin Grill (L)
Bacchus (V)
Bailiwick Inn (L)
Bambulé (L)
Barolo (V)
BeDuCi (V)
Bella Luna (L)
Benjarong (L)
Bilbo Baggins*
Bis (V)
Bistro (L)
Bistro Bistro (L)
Bistro Francais (V)
Bistro 123 (L)
Blackie's (L,V)
Black's Bar & Kitchen*
Bleu Rock Inn (L)
Blue Point Grill (L)
Bob & Edith's Diner (L)
Bobby Van's (V)
Bombay Bistro (L)
Bombay Palace (V)
Bombay Tandoor (L)
Bonsai (L)
Broad St. Grill (L)
B. Smith's*
Buca di Beppo (V)
Buon Giorno (V)
Cafe Atlantico (V)
Cafe Bethesda (V)
Cafe Marianna (L)
Cafe Milano (L)
Cafe Mileto (L)
Cafe New Delhi (V)
Cafe Oggi (L)
Cafe Ole*
Cafe Parisien Express (L)
Cafe Promenade (V)
Cafe Roval (L)
Cafe Taj (L)
California Pizza Kit. (L)

Calvert Grille (L)
Capital Grille*
Carlyle Grand Cafe (L)
Cashion's (V)
Cesco (V)
Chardonnay (L)
Cheesecake Factory (L)
Christopher Marks (V)
Chutzpah (L)
Cities (V)
Clyde's (L)*
Coco Loco (V)
Coeur De Lion (L,V)
Connaught Place (L)
Crisfield (L)
Crisfield at Lee Plaza (L)
Crisp & Juicy (L)
Crystal Thai (L)
Da Domenico (L)
Daily Grill (L,V)
Dante (L)
DC Coast (V)
Dean & DeLuca (L)
Delhi Dhaba (L)
Dolce Vita (L)
Donatello (V)
Duangrat's (L)
Dusit (L)
Eiffel Tower Cafe (L)
El Gavilan (L)
Equinox (V)
Fadó Irish Pub (V)
Fairmont Bar (V)
Fortune (L,V)
4 & 20 Blackbirds (L)
Frogs & Friends (L)
Gabriel (L)*
Galileo (V)
Garden Cafe (L)
Generous George's (L)
Georgia Brown's (V)
Gerard's Place (V)
Gordon Biersch (V)
Greenfield Churrascaria (L)
Greenwood (V)
Haandi (L)

New Heights (V)
Nibbler (L)
Nick & Stef's (V)
Niwano Hana (L)
Nizam's (L)
Nora (V)
Obelisk (V)
Occidental*
Oceanaire (V)
Old Angler's Inn (L)
Old Ebbitt Grill (V)
Old Hickory Grill (L)
Olives (V)
Oriental East (L)
Original Pancake Hse. (L)
Osteria Goldoni (L,V)
Oval Room*
Palena (L)
Palm (L,V)
Palomino (V)
Panjshir (L)
Pasha Cafe (L)
Pasta Plus (L)
Paul Kee (L)
Paya Thai (L)
Peking Gourmet Inn (L)
Pesce (V)
P.F. Chang's (L)
Phillips (L)
Potowmack Landing (L)
Prime Rib (V)
Primi Piatti (L,V)
Prince Michel (L)
Raaga (L)
Rabieng (L)
Red Fox Inn (L)
Red Sage*
Renato (L)
Ricciuti's (L)
Rico y Rico (L)
Rio Grande Cafe (L)
Ritz-Carlton/Grill (V)
Rock Bottom Brewery (L)
Roof Terrace Kennedy Ctr. (L)
R.T.'s (L)
R.T.'s Seafood (L)

Ruppers (L,V)
Ruth's Chris (V)*
Saigon Gourmet (L)
Sakoontra (L)
Samadi Sweets (L)
Sam & Harry's (L,V)
Satay Sarinah (L)
Saveur (V)
Savory (L)
Sea Catch (L,V)
Seasons (L,V)
Sequoia (L)
Serbian Crown (L)
Sesto Senso (V)
701 (V)
Seven Seas (L)
1789 (V)
Shula's Steak House (V)
Silverado (L)
Simply Grill (L)
Smith & Wollensky's (V)
Sole (L)
Sushi-Ko (V)
Sweetwater Tavern (L)
Taberna del Alabardero (L)
Tachibana (L)
Tahoga (V)
Taipei/Tokyo Cafe (L)
Taqueria Poblano (L)
Tara Thai (L)
Taste of Saigon (L)
Taste of the World (L)
Teatro Goldoni (V)
Tel Aviv Cafe (V)
Tempo (L)
Ten Pehn (V)
Terrazza (V)
T.H.A.I.*
Thai Basil (L)
Thai Kingdom (L)
That's Amore (L)
Timpano (L)
Tivoli (L)
Toro (L)
Tosca (V)
Tragara (V)

Turning Point Inn (L)
Tuscarora Mill (L)
Udupi Palace (L)
Upper Crust Bakery (L)
Vegetable Garden (L)
Vidalia (V)
Vignola (L)
Village Bistro (L)
Warehouse B&G (L)*
West End Cafe (V)
West 24 (V)
White Tiger (L)
Willard Room (L,V)
Willie & Reed's*
Woo Lae Oak (L)
Wurzburg-Haus (L)
Yama Japanese (L)
Yanyu (V)
Zuki Moon (L,V)

Parties & Private Rooms

(Any nightclub or restaurant
charges less at off-times;
* indicates private rooms
available; best of many)

Addie's*
America*
Andaman*
Arucola*
Bis*
Bistrot Lepic*
Blackie's*
Bobby Van's*
Bombay Tandoor*
B. Smith's*
Busara*
Cafe Milano*
Capital Grille*
Caucus Room*
Cesco*
Cities*
Clyde's*
Duangrat's*
Fortune*
Gaffney's*
Galileo*
Generous George's*

Gordon Biersch*
Greenwood*
I Matti*
Japoné*
Kobalt*
L'Auberge Chez François*
Le Jardin*
Le Vieux Logis*
Luigino*
Maestro*
Maggiano's*
McCormick & Schmick's*
New Fortune*
Nick & Stef's*
Oceanaire*
Old Ebbitt Grill*
Palm*
Petits Plats
Prime Rib*
Primi Piatti*
Red Fox Inn*
Shula's Steak House*
Sole*
Tabard Inn*
Taberna del Alabardero*
Tahoga*
Teatro Goldoni*
Temel*
Tivoli*
Tragara*
Two Quail*
Uni*
West 24*

People-Watching

America
Andaman
Arbor
Big Bowl
Bis
Bistro Francais
Black's Bar & Kitchen
Bob & Edith's Diner
Bread Line
B. Smith's
Butterfield 9
Cafe Japoné

Cafe Milano
Cafe Promenade
Carlyle Grand Cafe
Cashion's
Caucus Room
Cities
Clyde's
Dean & DeLuca
Diner
Dominique's
Galileo
Georgia Brown's
Gordon Biersch
Grapeseed
Inn at Little Washington
Jaleo
Johnny's Half Shell
Kinkead's
La Brasserie
La Colline
La Fourchette
Lauriol Plaza
Levante's
Monocle
New Fortune
Nora
Old Ebbitt Grill
Olives
Oval Room
Palm
Peter's Passion
Primi Piatti
Seasons
Sequoia
701
Stella's
Tahoga
Teatro Goldoni
Ten Pehn
T.H.A.I.
Thaiphoon
Tryst

Bombay Club
Bombay Tandoor
Butterfield 9
Capital Grille
Caucus Room
Citronelle
Daily Grill
Equinox
Etrusco
Galileo
Inn at Little Washington
Jeffrey's/Watergate
Kaz Sushi
Kinkead's
La Colline
Le Relais
Maestro
Marcel's
Monocle
Morton's of Chicago
Nick & Stef's
Nora
Occidental
Old Ebbitt Grill
Osteria Goldoni
Oval Room
Palena
Palm
Prime Rib
Sam & Harry's
Seasons
701
Taberna del Alabardero
Taste of Saigon
Teatro Goldoni
Timothy Dean
Tosca
Vidalia
West 24
Willard Room

Power Scenes

Ardeo
Bis
Bobby Van's

Pre/Post-Theater Dining
(Call to check prices,
days and times; best of many)
Bambulé
Bistro Francais
Carlyle Grand Cafe

Christopher Marks
Dominique's
Donatello
Fairmont Bar
Gabriel
Garden Cafe
Lafayette
Le Rivage
Marcel's
Oval Room
Roof Terrace Kennedy Ctr.
701
1789
Tivoli
West End Cafe

Prix Fixe Menus/ Tasting Menus
(Call to check prices, days and times; best of many)
Bailiwick Inn
BeDuCi
Blue Stone Cafe
Citronelle
Elysium
Equinox
Fairmont Bar
Gabriel
Gerard's Place
Hermitage Inn
L'Auberge Chez François
Lavandou
Le Petit Mistral
Le Rivage
Maestro
Marcel's
Obelisk
Palena
Prince Michel
Stone Manor
Tosca
Willard Room

Pub/Bar/Microbrewery
Clyde's
District ChopHse.
Fadó Irish Pub

Gaffney's
Houston's
Ice House Cafe
Inn at Glen Echo
John Harvard's
J. Paul's
King St. Blues
Martin's Tavern
Nathan's
Old Ebbitt Grill
Polly's Cafe
Rock Bottom Brewery
R.T.'s
1789
Sweetwater Tavern
Union St. Public Hse.

Quiet Conversation
Asia Nora
Bailiwick Inn
Bangkok Garden
Bombay Club
Bonsai
Butterfield 9
Cafe Bethesda
Caucus Room
Chardonnay
Ching Ching Cha
Citronelle
Coeur De Lion
Elysium
Equinox
Gabriel
Garden Cafe
Gerard's Place
Heritage India
Inn at Little Washington
Japoné
Jefferson Rest.
La Ferme
Maestro
Majestic Cafe
Makoto
Melrose
Morrison-Clark Inn
Mrs. Simpson's
New Heights

Obelisk
Oceanaire
Palena
Palm Court
Ritz-Carlton/Grill
Sea Catch
Seasons
Sen5es
1789
Taberna del Alabardero
Temel
Tosca
Willard Room

Raw Bar

Black's Bar & Kitchen
Blue Point Grill
Clyde's
Crisfield
Crisfield at Lee Plaza
Gaffney's
Georgetown Seafood
Johnny's Half Shell
J. Paul's
Kinkead's
Legal Sea Foods
McCormick & Schmick's
Metro Ctr. Grille
Old Ebbitt Grill
Phillips
Sea Catch
Tony & Joe's

Reservations Advised

Bleu Rock Inn
Caucus Room
Citronelle
DC Coast
Dominique's
Elysium
Hermitage Inn
Inn at Little Washington
Kinkead's
L'Auberge Provencale
Maestro
Nora
Obelisk

Palena
Prince Michel
Ritz-Carlton/Grill
Ruppers
Sole
Stone Manor
Taberna del Alabardero
Thaiphoon
Vegetable Garden

Romantic

Bombay Club
Citronelle
Coeur De Lion
Green Papaya
Inn at Little Washington
Japoné
L'Auberge Chez François
Le Jardin
Le Refuge
Majestic Cafe
Melrose
Mrs. Simpson's
New Heights
Nora
Obelisk
Old Angler's Inn
Palena
Seasons
701
1789
Tabard Inn
Taberna del Alabardero
Tahoga
Two Quail
Vignola

Senior Appeal

Blackie's
Caucus Room
Dante
Jean-Michel
Jeffrey's/Watergate
Kobalt
Krupin's
La Chaumiere
La Ferme

L'Auberge Chez François
Le Gaulois
Le Petit Mistral
Le Rivage
Le Vieux Logis
Madras Palace
Matisse
Michael's
Morton's of Chicago
Oceanaire
Phillips
Prime Rib
Ruth's Chris
Tako Grill
Tivoli
Tragara
Willard Room

Montgomery's Grille
Nathan's
Old Ebbitt Grill
Perry's
Red Sage
Rock Bottom Brewery
Rocky's Cafe
Sequoia
Sesto Senso
Ten Pehn
Timpano
Tony & Joe's
Tryst
Uni
Union St. Public Hse.
U-topia
Willie & Reed's

Singles Scenes

America
Andaman
Angelo & Maxie's
Arbor
Artie's
Austin Grill
Bambulé
Banana Cafe
Big Bowl
Cafe Atlantico
Cafe Deluxe
Cafe Japoné
Cafe Milano
Christopher Marks
Coco Loco
Diner
District ChopHse.
Felix
Gordon Biersch
John Harvard's
J. Paul's
King St. Blues
Kramerbooks & Afterwords
Le Tarbouche
M & S Grill
Mango Mike's
McCormick & Schmick's
Mike's American

Sleepers
(Good to excellent food, but little known)

Agrodolce
Akasaka
Argia
Bombay Gaylord
Bonsai
Cafe New Delhi
Chardonnay
Ching Ching Cha
El Gavilan
Hama Sushi
Hee Been
Hermitage Inn
Huong Que
Kabul Caravan
Konami
Le Mannequin Pis
Mare e Monti
Mehak
Neisha Thai
New Fortune
Niwano Hana
Oriental East
Paul Kee
Raaga
Rocky's Cafe
Ruan Thai

Saigon Gourmet
San Marco
Thai Derm
Willow Grove Inn

Spa Menus
Asia Nora
Burro
California Tortilla
La Ferme
Melrose
Morrison-Clark Inn
Nora
Seasons
Sen5es
Tako Grill
Thyme Square

Tea
(Check days & times)
Bailiwick Inn
Ching Ching Cha
Elysium
Jefferson Rest.
Kobalt
Ritz-Carlton/Grill
Seasons
Stone Manor
Teaism

Teflons
(Get lots of business, despite so-so food, i.e. they have other attractions that prevent criticism from sticking)
America
Bambulé
California Pizza Kit.
Capitol City Brewing
Così
Fadó Irish Pub
Hard Rock Cafe
Hogate's
Hunter's Inn
Montgomery's Grille

Phillips
Planet Hollywood
Rock Bottom Brewery
Silver Diner
Vienna Inn

Theme Restaurants
Bistrot Lepic
Buca di Beppo
Cities
Coco Loco
ESPN Zone
Greenfield Churrascaria
Hard Rock Cafe
Kabul Caravan
L'Etoile
Maggiano's
Malibu Grill
Mimi's American
Planet Hollywood
Sweetwater Tavern
Teatro Goldoni
That's Amore
Toro

Transporting Experience
Andaman
Bombay Club
Caucus Room
Ching Ching Cha
Green Papaya
Inn at Little Washington
Japoné
L'Auberge Chez François
Makoto
Nizam's
Palena
Red Sage
Stone Manor
Tara Thai
Taverna Cretekou

View
America
Bleu Rock Inn

Visitors on Expense Accounts

Winning Wine Lists

Maestro
M & S Grill
Marcel's
Melrose
Mendocino
Mezza 9
Nathan's
New Heights
Nick & Stef's
Nora
Obelisk
Old Ebbitt Grill
Osteria Goldoni
Oval Room
Palena
Palm
Prime Rib
Prince Michel
Rico y Rico
Rupperts
Sam & Harry's
Seasons
Smith & Wollensky's
Stone Manor
Sushi-Ko
Taberna del Alabardero
Tahoga
Tivoli
Tosca
Vidalia
Willard Room

Worth a Trip

MARYLAND
Middletown
   Stone Manor
Urbana
   Turning Point Inn
VIRGINIA
Culpeper
   It's About Thyme
Flint Hill
   4 & 20 Blackbirds
Hamilton
   Planet Wayside
Leon
   Prince Michel
Marshall
   Frogs & Friends
Middleburg
   Red Fox Inn
   Upper Crust Bakery
Orange
   Willow Grove Inn
Paris
   Ashby Inn
The Plains
   Rail Stop
Washington
   Bleu Rock Inn
   Inn at Little Washington
White Post
   L'Auberge Provencale

Baltimore, Annapolis and the Eastern Shore

Baltimore's Most Popular

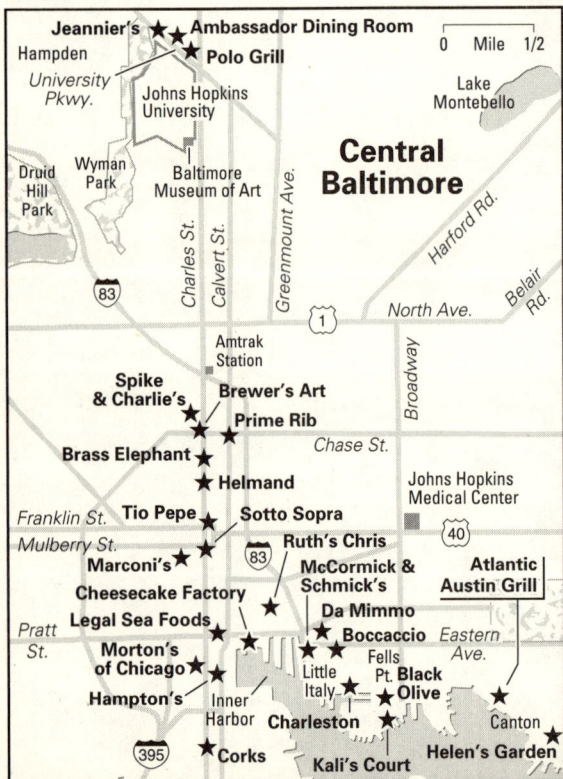

140 — Antrim 1844 Country Inn ★
Taneytown

83 ★ Milton Inn
Sparks

Rudys' 2900 ★ Oregon Grille ★
Finksburg
Hunt Valley

Outback ★ Steakhouse*
Bel Air
95

Due Linwood's ★
Owings Mills

Cafe Troia
Orchard Market Cafe ★
Towson

795

Ruth's Chris ★
Pikesville

Baltimore
Detail below →

695

70

Tersiguel's ★
Ellicott City

MARYLAND

King's Contrivance ★
Columbia

Chesapeake Bay

29

Miles
0   5

95 295

Baltimore-Washington Int'l Airport

Washington, D.C.

Northwoods
Red Hot & Blue ★
50

208 Talbot
St. Michaels

Annapolis ★

Jeannier's ★★ Ambassador Dining Room
Hampden   ★ Polo Grill

University Pkwy.

Johns Hopkins University

0   Mile   1/2

Lake Montebello

Druid Hill Park

Wyman Park

Baltimore Museum of Art

Central Baltimore

83

Charles St.
Calvert St.
Greenmount Ave.

Harford Rd.

Belair Rd.

1 North Ave.

Amtrak Station

Broadway

Spike & Charlie's ★   ★ Brewer's Art
                      ★ Prime Rib

Chase St.

Brass Elephant ★

Johns Hopkins Medical Center

★ Helmand

Franklin St.   Tio Pepe ★   ★ Sotto Sopra
Mulberry St.   40

Marconi's ★★   83   Ruth's Chris ★
                     McCormick & Schmick's ★
Cheesecake Factory ★   Atlantic
                         Da Mimmo ★   Austin Grill
Pratt   Legal Sea Foods ★   Boccaccio ★   Eastern Ave.

Morton's ★   Fells
of Chicago ★   Little   Pt. Black
Hampton's ★   Italy   Olive ★   ★ Canton
         Inner   Helen's Garden
         Harbor   Charleston ★
395
     ★ Corks   Kali's Court ★

Baltimore's Most Popular

Each of our reviewers has been asked to name his or her five favorite restaurants. The 40 spots most frequently named, in order of their popularity, are:

1. Prime Rib
2. Tio Pepe
3. Charleston
4. Linwood's
5. Ruth's Chris
6. McCormick & Schmick's
7. Polo Grill
8. Hampton's
9. Cheesecake Factory
10. Helmand
11. Morton's of Chicago
12. Brass Elephant
13. Boccaccio
14. Oregon Grille
15. Milton Inn
16. Tersiguel's
17. Black Olive
18. Rudys' 2900*
19. Atlantic
20. Outback Steakhouse/A
21. Antrim 1844
22. Ambassador Din. Rm.
23. Orchard Market Cafe
24. Cafe Troia
25. Due
26. Jeannier's
27. Austin Grill
28. Kali's Court
29. Helen's Garden
30. Spike & Charlie's
31. Sotto Sopra
32. Corks
33. Marconi's
34. Legal Sea Foods
35. 208 Talbot/A
36. Brewer's Art
37. Da Mimmo
38. King's Contrivance/C*
39. Red Hot & Blue/A
40. Northwoods/A

It's obvious that many of the restaurants on the above list are among the most expensive, but if popularity were calibrated to price, we suspect that a number of other restaurants would join the above ranks. Thus, for frugal gourmets, we have listed 80 Best Buys on page 166.

A=Annapolis/Eastern Shore, C=Columbia
* Tied with the restaurant listed directly above it

Top Ratings

Top lists exclude restaurants with low voting.

Top Food Ranking

28 Lewnes' Steakhouse/A
Prime Rib
Hampton's
27 Antrim 1844
Inn at Perry Cabin/A
Charleston
Rudys' 2900
26 Linwood's
208 Talbot/A
Boccaccio
Helmand
Trattoria Alberto
Joss Cafe Sushi Bar/A
Polo Grill
Northwoods/A
Peter's Inn
Tersiguel's
25 Morton's of Chicago
Brighton's
Tio Pepe

Milton Inn
Matsuri
Pisces
Ruth's Chris
Brass Elephant
Samos
Orchard Market Cafe
Oregon Grille
Thai
Black Olive
Josef's Country Inn*
Edo Sushi
24 Narrows/A
Kawasaki
Pierpoint
Piccola Roma/A
Henninger's Tavern
Due
Da Mimmo
Harry Browne's/A

Top Food by Cuisine

American
27 Charleston
26 Polo Grill
25 Milton Inn
Brass Elephant
Oregon Grille

American (New)
28 Hampton's
27 Antrim 1844
26 Linwood's
208 Talbot/A
25 Brighton's

Asian
24 Asean Bistro/C
23 Noodles Corner/C
22 Olive & Sesame
20 Minato
Hoang's

Chinese
23 Hunan Manor/C
Szechuan Best
22 Szechuan House
21 Szechuan
20 Jumbo Seafood

Continental
27 Inn at Perry Cabin/A
Rudys' 2900
26 Northwood's/A
25 Josef's Country Inn
24 King's Contrivance/C

Crab House
22 Obrycki's
Cantler's/A
21 Bo Brooks
Harris/A
20 Crab Claw/A

French
26 Tersiguel's
24 Jeannier's
22 Martick's
21 Cafe Normandie/A
18 La Madeleine/C

Greek
25 Samos
Black Olive
23 Kali's Court
20 Ikaros
19 Opa!

A=Annapolis/Eastern Shore, C=Columbia
* Tied with the restaurant listed directly above it

Indian
23 Ambassador Din. Rm.
   Banjara
22 Mughal Garden
21 Bombay Grill
20 Akbar

Italian
26 Boccaccio
   Trattoria Alberto
24 Due
   Da Mimmo
23 Cafe Troia

Japanese
26 Joss Cafe Sushi Bar/A
25 Matsuri
   Edo Sushi
24 Sushi Hana
22 San Sushi

Seafood
25 Pisces
   Black Olive
24 Narrows/A
   O'Leary's/A
23 Kali's Court

Steakhouse
28 Lewnes' Steakhouse/A
   Prime Rib
25 Morton's of Chicago
   Ruth's Chris
   Oregon Grille

Vegetarian
22 Helen's Garden
   Golden West Cafe
21 Genevieve's
20 Cafe Zen
17 One World Cafe

Top Food by Special Feature

Breakfast*
23 Morning Edition
21 Blue Moon
18 Donna's
   Woman's Ind. Exch.
17 One World Cafe

Brunch
28 Hampton's
27 Inn at Perry Cabin/A
26 Polo Grill
24 Pierpoint
23 Morning Edition

Business Lunch
26 Linwood's
   Boccaccio
   Polo Grill
25 Brighton's
   Milton Inn

Hotel Dining
28 Hampton's
   Harbor Court
27 Inn at Perry Cabin/A
   Inn at Perry Cabin
26 Polo Grill
   Doubletree Inn
25 Morton's of Chicago
   Sheraton Inner Harbor
   Pisces
   Hyatt Regency

Newcomers/Unrated
   Blue Agave
   Eurasian Harbor
   Manley's Bistro
   Tapas Teatro
   Towne Hall

Worth a Trip
27 Antrim 1844
   Taneytown
   Inn at Perry Cabin/A
   St. Michaels
26 208 Talbot/A
   St. Michaels
25 Milton Inn
   Sparks
22 Robert Morris Inn/A
   Oxford

---

* Other than hotels

Top Decor Ranking

29 Inn at Perry Cabin/A
Hampton's
28 Antrim 1844
27 Brighton's
Milton Inn
Brass Elephant
26 Prime Rib
Elkridge Furnace Inn
Linwood's
Aldo's
Oregon Grille
Charleston
25 Windows
Pisces
Polo Grill
King's Contrivance/C
Robert Morris Inn/A
24 Joy America Cafe
Kali's Court
Boccaccio

Treaty of Paris/A
Tersiguel's
An Poitin Stil
23 Ambassador Din. Rm.
Gertrude's
Brewer's Art
Sotto Sopra
Corinthian/A
Asean Bistro/C
Ruth's Chris
208 Talbot/A
Atlantic
Lewnes' Steakhouse/A
Due
22 Henninger's Tavern
Harry Browne's/A
Hamilton's
Morton's of Chicago
Carrol's Creek Cafe/A
Tio Pepe

Outdoor

Ambassador Din. Rm.
Bo Brooks
Cantler's Riverside Inn/A
Carrol's Creek Cafe/A
Cheesecake Factory
Crab Claw/A
Gertrude's

Helen's Garden
Inn at Perry Cabin/A
Mason's/A
River Watch
Rusty Scupper
Tapas Teatro
Tomato Palace

Rooms

Aldo's
Antrim 1844
Brass Elephant
Charleston
Columbia/A
Eurasian Harbor

Hampton's
Inn at Perry Cabin/A
Milton Inn
Oregon Grille
Petit Louis
Prime Rib

Views

Baldwin's Station
Bay Cafe
Bo Brooks
Hampton's
Hemingway's/A
Inn at Perry Cabin/A

Joy America Cafe
Michael Rork's/A
Pisces
Rusty Scupper
Sander's Corner
Windows

Top Service Ranking

27 Hampton's
Prime Rib
Antrim 1844
26 Inn at Perry Cabin/A
Lewnes' Steakhouse/A
Charleston
25 Brighton's
Linwood's
Rudys' 2900
24 208 Talbot/A
Tersiguel's
Harry Browne's/A
Northwoods/A
Boccaccio
Milton Inn
Polo Grill
Brass Elephant
Banjara
Piccola Roma/A
23 Morton's of Chicago

Oregon Grille
Marconi's
Ruth's Chris
Ambassador Din. Rm.
Trattoria Alberto
King's Contrivance/C
Helmand
Cafe Madrid
Josef's Country Inn
Robert Morris Inn/A
Due
Elkridge Furnace Inn
Tio Pepe
Narrows/A
22 Jeannier's
O'Learys/A
Orchard Market Cafe
Pisces
Sushi Hana
Hamilton's

Best Buys

Top Bangs for the Buck

List derived by dividing the cost of a meal into its ratings.

1. Panera Bread
2. Golden West Cafe
3. Woman's Ind. Exch.
4. Noodles Corner/C
5. Chick & Ruth's Delly/A
6. Blue Moon Cafe
7. Holy Frijoles
8. Attman's Deli.
9. Jimmy's
10. One World Cafe
11. Faidley's
12. Rallo's
13. Papermoon Diner
14. Baugher's
15. Samos
16. Morning Edition
17. Cafe Zen
18. Genevieve's
19. Double T Diner
20. SoBo Cafe
21. Peter's Inn
22. Desert Cafe
23. Banjara
24. Garry's Grill/A
25. Ze Mean Bean Cafe
26. Nick's Inner Harbor
27. Hunan Manor/C
28. Thai
29. Duda's Tavern
30. Ding How
31. La Madeleine/C
32. El Azteca
33. Szechuan
34. Helmand
35. Szechuan Best
36. Szechuan House
37. Helen's Garden
38. Ban Thai
39. Nacho Mama's
40. Suzie's Soba

Additional Good Values

Acropolis
Ambassador Din. Rm.
An Poitin Stil
Backfin
Bandaloops
Bicycle
Cafe Hon
Cheesecake Factory
Davis' Pub/A
Fazzini's Italian Kitchen
Forest Diner
Friendly Farms
Gibby's
Holly's/A
Ikaros
India Palace
Jalapeño/A
Jennings Cafe
Jilly's
J.J.'s Everyday

Johnny Dee's
Kaufman's Tavern
Kelly's
Mamie's
Mangia Mangia
Olive Grove
Orchard Market Cafe
Peppermill
Perring Place
Petit Louis
Purim Oak
Saigon
Scotto's Cafe
Simon's Pub
Szechuan
Timber Creek Tavern
Timbuktu
Tsunami/A
Wild Orchid Cafe/A
Windows on the Bay

Baltimore, Annapolis and the Eastern Shore Restaurant Directory

Baltimore

	F	D	S	C
Acropolis [S]	17	12	18	$21

4714-4718 Eastern Ave. (Oldham St.), 410-675-3384
■ Hellenic "good times" roll at this "friendly family affair" in Greektown, which "works incredibly hard to please" and serves up "huge portions" of grilled fish and lamb at "can't-believe" affordable prices; you'll get the same "warm" hospitality whether in a suit or "shabby dress" – after all, this unpretentious staple, like its customers, doesn't judge value by appearances.

	F	D	S	C
Adam's Ribs [S]	20	12	18	$19

589 Baltimore-Annapolis Blvd. (McKinsey Rd.), Severna Park, 410-647-5757
See review in Annapolis and the Eastern Shore Directory.

	F	D	S	C
Akbar [S]	20	16	21	$19

823 N. Charles St. (bet. Madison & Read Sts.), 410-539-0944
Columbia Mktpl., 9400 Snowden River Pkwy. (Rte. 175), Columbia, 410-381-3600
3541 Brenbrook Dr. (Liberty Rd.), Randallstown, 410-655-1600
◪ In Mount Vernon, Columbia and Randallstown, this "cozy" trio of "reliable" Indian "stalwarts" satisfies simple cravings for a "tasty curried something" in a "civilized" atmosphere; "bargain" buffets and "well-executed" dishes, backed by "discreet", "prompt" service, make them "a fine place to relax"; still, a few whisper "uneven."

	F	D	S	C
ALDO'S [S]	22	26	21	$43

306 S. High St. (Fawn St.), 410-727-0700
■ Little Italy's most "beautiful space, architecturally", this "upscale" Southern Italian generates swoons with its dramatic atrium ("like walking into a marble courtyard"); the food and tuxedo service are "elegant" too, though some complain they "fail to meet" the "sophisticated" surroundings; nonetheless, many see it "challenging" nearby top-rated Boccaccio on every front.

	F	D	S	C
Alonso's [S]	15	9	14	$16

415 W. Cold Spring Ln. (Keswick Rd.), 410-235-3433
◪ "This burger could fight Godzilla" claim veterans of this Roland Park "time-warp" neighborhood favorite; alas, the monster one-pounders are among the only survivors of the landmark saloon's merger with Tex-Mex neighbor Loco Hombre, as the menu has been Italianized and the decor "upgraded" (some say "ruined"), leaving many lamenting that it has "lost its character."

Ambassador Dining Room 23 | 23 | 23 | $25
3811 Canterbury Rd. (University Pkwy.), 410-366-1484
■ "Elegant Old Baltimore mixed with British Empire–style Indian" scores a "hit" at this Homewood spot housed in the "gracious" dining room of a "'30s-era apartment house"; "white-glove service" enhances the "consistently fine" food, and a terrace with a "beautiful garden" ("dine around the fountain in the summer") is a plus.

Amicci's S 19 | 13 | 17 | $21
231 S. High St. (bet. Fawn & Stiles Sts.), 410-528-1096
◪ "Less fancy" (and cheaper) than many others in Little Italy, this casual "red-sauce" eatery wins friends with its "flavorful" heavy-duty food, despite the "cramped", "low-end" setting and "rushed" service; though one regular complains the "*pane rotundo* [garlicky shrimp in a bread bowl] has made me *rotundo*!", he "can never pass it up."

Angelina's S 18 | 11 | 17 | $25
7135 Harford Rd. (Rosalie Ave.), 410-444-5545
■ The "famous", "bodacious" crab cakes and "sweet" waitresses who call you 'hon' make this Northeast Baltimore Ital-American pub "Bawlmer all the way"; but some warn "don't order anything but the crab cakes."

An Poitin Stil ◕ S 19 | 24 | 18 | $20
2323 York Rd. (bet. Padonia & Timonium Rds.), Timonium, 410-560-7900
■ "Taking the city by storm" ("you can get to Ireland sooner than get seated"), this Irish pub re-creation in Timonium is packing 'em in with its elaborate (or "kitschy") Emerald Isle decor and menu of upscale bar food and reinterpreted Gaelic classics, including a "credible shepherd's pie"; if you like "great beer" and plenty of atmosphere, you'll "have fun" even during the "long wait for a table."

ANTRIM 1844 COUNTRY INN S 27 | 28 | 27 | $55
30 Trevanion Rd. (Rte. 140), Taneytown, 410-756-6812
■ "Perfect in every way" gush visitors to this pre–Civil War mansion near Gettysburg that's graced with "magnificent" gardens; inside, the "opulent" dining rooms filled with "many roaring fires and 19th-century period pieces" set the mood for "superb" prix fixe New American meals; no wonder couples find it ideal for the seduction, the engagement and the wedding itself.

Artful Palate ▽ 21 | 13 | 18 | $19
10517 York Rd. (north of Warren Rd.), Cockeysville, 410-683-3303
■ Sandwiched between a couple of Cockeysville's auto shops, this low-key BYO repairs hungry appetites with casual American lunches and "creative, delicious" dinners; with so few options nearby, most look beyond the "bright" former sub shop's decor to find a certain "hidden beauty."

Asean Bistro 🅂   24   23   21 $24
8775 Centre Park Dr. (Rte. 108), Columbia, 410-772-5300
■ Jesse Wong's Pan-Asian eatery adds a new dimension to Columbia's dining prospects by showcasing "upscale", "fresh, contemporary" fare, paired with a "solid wine list", in a decorative setting complete with a "miniature waterfall"; at the same time, it provides what many expect from a suburban Chinese restaurant (albeit at "higher prices") – "fast delivery" and "real-value carryout."

ATLANTIC 🅂   22   23   21 $36
American Can Co. Bldg., 2400 Boston St. (Hudson St.), 410-675-4565
☑ Some call it "very NYC" and others are reminded of LA or Chicago, but most agree that the "trendy warehouse look" of this "hip" seafood house set in a former Canton cannery is definitely *not* typical Baltimore; one goes here "to be seen" and check out the "beautiful people", but don't miss the "concept food"; be warned, however, of the noise so "don't expect to talk to your companions."

Attman's Delicatessen 🅂   22   8   15 $12
1019 E. Lombard St. (bet. Central Ave. & Fallsway), 410-563-2666
■ "Corned Beef Row's" hardy "survivor" still boasts "great noshing" and world-class "kibitzing" at this "superb" East Baltimore deli with plenty of "character" (instead of decor); "it's the only place [left] where they ask if 12 pounds of hot dogs are for here or to go."

Austin Grill 🅂   18   17   18 $21
American Can Co. Bldg., 2400 Boston St. (Hudson St.), 410-534-0606
See review in Washington, DC Directory.

Backfin 🅂   –   –   –   M
1116 Reisterstown Rd. (Sudbrook Ln.), Pikesville, 410-484-7344
A "neighborhood place" on Pikesville's restaurant row, this "homey", nautically themed spot is "at the top" of many fin fanciers' lists for its "A-plus crab cakes and crab imperial", and daily fish specials; the "pleasant service" further helps to make it a "favorite."

Baldwin's Station 🅂   22   21   21 $33
7618 Main St. (railroad tracks), Sykesville, 410-795-1041
■ "Off the beaten track" in more ways than one, this "quaintly beautiful" restored rail station in Sykesville offers the ageless pleasure of watching "freight trains" go by from a charming "country" setting; "surprising" for such a "little-town" spot is the mostly "excellent" New American cooking (Angus beef is a specialty) and the well-regarded live music (country, bluegrass and folk) on Wednesday nights.

Bamboo House 🇸   20 | 19 | 20 | $24
Yorktowne Plaza, 26 Cranbrook Rd. (York Rd.), Cockeysville,
410-666-9550

Joey Chiu's Greenspring Inn 🇸
10801 Falls Rd. (Greenspring Valley Rd.), Brooklandville,
410-823-1125

☑ "Great host" Joey Chiu knows that his silver-haired suburban clientele wants a dining experience that's "classy without the snobbery" and his two "serene" restaurants in Cockeysville and Brooklandville deliver with "predictable" yet "tasty" Chinese food and sushi; the service is "lovely" and "accommodating", and includes nice touches like "hot towels between courses."

Bandaloops   – | – | – | M
1024 S. Charles St. (bet. Cross & Hamburg Sts.), 410-727-1355
Tom Robbins fans will recognize the name of this "casual, comfortable" Federal Hill Eclectic, but you don't have to be a *litterateur* to appreciate its "perfect" mussels, "good" pastas and "excellent specials" – all "a cut above" the usual pub grub; once past the boisterous bar populated by locals, diners will also appreciate the "nice" staff and "warm, friendly atmosphere."

Banjara 🇸   23 | 19 | 24 | $20
1017 S. Charles St. (bet. Cross & Hamburg Sts.), 410-962-1554
■ Known for its "attentive" service ("bordering on a relationship") as much as for its "spicy, complex flavors", this South Baltimore Indian makes "a great date spot" with its "flattering lighting" and "dark" surroundings; it's also reliable for takeout "curry in a hurry" at a "reasonable price", leading many fans to proclaim that they "can't get enough of this wonderful" "favorite."

Ban Thai   20 | 12 | 20 | $17
340 N. Charles St. (Mulberry St.), 410-727-7971
■ The "nicely seasoned" fare and "knowledgeable" staff at this Downtown Thai will "win your heart" and the "cheap" prices will please your pocketbook – that is if you can "get past" the "unappealing" pink "luncheonette" decor; but bear in mind that this "quick and tasty" "alternative to the Italians and the chains" is a "takeout treat."

Bare Bones 🇸   16 | 13 | 16 | $19
St. John's Plaza, 9150 Baltimore Nat'l Pike (west of Rte. 29),
Ellicott City, 410-461-0770
9811 York Rd. (Padonia Rd.), Timonium, 410-667-9600
☑ "It's good to be a carnivore" sitting down before a heap of "mouthwatering ribs", washed down with a cold "home brew", at these BBQ halls/brewpubs, where the happy-hour "mob" and the "eat-till-I-pop" crowd mingle; foes, however, bemoan the "clueless servers" and "hit-or-miss" chow ("large portions can be a blessing . . . or not").

Barn Restaurant & Crab House S　– – – M
9527 Harford Rd. (Joppa Rd.), Parkville, 410-882-6182
North of the Beltway in Parkville, a big basement beer hall
serves surf 'n' turf and year-round steamed crabs under old
Baltimore Colts photos to happy neighborhood regulars of
all ages; upstairs a young crowd drinks to loud rock and live
sports radio broadcasts; N.B. order your crab cakes broiled.

Baugher's S　16 10 18 $12
289 W. Main St. (Rtes. 31 & 32), Westminster,
410-848-7413
■ A "leisurely drive" to this old-fashioned "Westminster
landmark", a produce stand and Traditional American
restaurant, remains a "pleasant tradition" for "real country
food" ("great fried chicken") served up by "farmers'
daughters"; P.S. regulars always "save room" for the
"delicious" "homemade" ice cream and fruit pies.

Bay Cafe S　14 16 13 $21
2809 Boston St. (Linwood Ave.), 410-522-3377
■ High-energy happy hours and an always thriving "beer
scene" with a "great view of the harbor" define this Canton
marina "meet market" for the twentysomething set; some
elders enjoy the signature shrimp salad and "relaxation
on the water" early, "before the nightlife begins", but others
lament the "mediocre" American eats and service that
"waste" the "terrific location."

Bayou Blues Cafe S　15 17 16 $22
The Avenue at White Marsh, 8133A Honeygo Blvd.
(Perry Hall Blvd.), White Marsh, 410-931-2583
■ On White Marsh's mock main drag (aka the "strip
shopping center"), this busy Big Easy–themed cafe packs
'em in with its red-hot Cajun-Creole and Maryland eats, as
well as the nightly live music; while some quip "better
blues than bayou" and gripe about "sporadic service",
fans insist the "food's really good."

Bertha's S　17 16 16 $20
734 S. Broadway (Lancaster St.), 410-327-5795
■ While it may have "lost some of the quirky edge" of its
"heyday", this "legendary" Fells Point pub still has plenty
of mussel power left to pull in the crowds with its "delicious"
seafood, "unusual" "Scottish high tea" (by reservation),
loads of "local color" and live jazz and blues; but be
forewarned: detractors say its "famous" bivalves are "gritty."

Bertucci's S　17 15 16 $17
12 Bel Air S. Pkwy. (Rte. 24), Bel Air, 410-569-4600
Snowden Sq., 9081 Snowden River Pkwy. (Robert Fulton Dr.),
Columbia, 410-312-4800
1818 York Rd. (Ridgely Rd.), Timonium, 410-561-7000

(continued)

Bertucci's

8130 Corporate Dr. (bet. Honeygo & Perry Hall Blvds.), White Marsh, 410-931-0900

◪ Nearly 1,000 surveyors weighed in on this Italian chain, so there's bound to be disagreement: defenders call them "dependable" "family places" (youngsters "love to play with the dough") for "great" rolls and "cheap" salads, pastas and "tasty" brick-oven pizzas, but bashers find the romper-room atmosphere "too noisy" and the food too "unexciting."

Bicycle – – – E

1444 Light St. (Fort Ave.), 410-234-1900

Tables under the hanging bikes at chef Barry Rumsey's tiny South Baltimore storefront have proven hard to get, so bikeway backups may occur (although a new tented patio out back helps a bit); once seated, the sophisticated city and suburban mix enjoys Eclectic fare like red pepper bisque and crab cakes over sweet corn with wasabi aïoli.

BLACK OLIVE [S] 25 18 21 $41

814 S. Bond St. (bet. Shakespeare & Thames Sts.), 410-276-7141

◪ "*The* place to go for fresh fish" is this "sophisticated" Fells Point Greek taverna where a "charming" family gives a "pick-your-own" "tour" of exotic seafood (including "fish we've never heard of!") that are cooked simply and paired with fine Greek wines; despite the "exceptional" quality, some quip it's "cheaper to cruise Greece" than pay premium prices for what they see as "plain" fare served in a "casual" setting (now expanded next door).

Blue Agave [S] – – – E

1032 Light St. (Cross St.), 410-576-3938

South Baltimore's new Southwestern with high ceilings, exposed pipes and dark-orange stucco has found a following among Beltway types and urbanites for its enchiladas and corn cakes at the buzzing galvanized-steel tequila bar, and for grilled quail with *mole poblano* and leg of lamb steamed in banana leaves in the slightly calmer dining room.

Blue Moon Cafe [S] 21 19 19 $15

1621 Aliceanna St. (bet. Bond St. & Broadway), 410-522-3940

◪ Attention breakfast lovers: the "clever" people who run this "funky" Fells Point cafe "get it", whipping up "excellent omelets", the "best home fries" and "biscuits to die for"; they serve lunch too and stay open overnight Thursday–Saturday; fans say that the only problem is that the spot "has been discovered", which translates to "long waits" for weekend brunches.

Bo Brooks Crab House 🖪　　21 | 9 | 17 | $26

*Baltimore Marine Ctr., 2701 Boston St. (Lakewood Ave.),
410-558-0202*

■ "Show me the crabs, no time for salads and such" say
"hardcore" fans at this relocated institution's waterfront
digs in Canton (not yet reflected in the above decor rating);
while it may have lost some of its "real Baltimore" feel in the
move, a covered porch and new music and dining barge put
you right in the mood for "large crabs seasoned just right."

BOCCACCIO 🖪　　26 | 24 | 24 | $44

925 Eastern Ave. (bet. Exeter & High Sts.), 410-234-1322

■ "It's hard to be the best", especially if you're Baltimore's
top-rated Italian, but this "*primo*" Little Italy "power" place
has proven yet again that it "can't be beat" by continuing
to showcase "first-class" cuisine "impeccably served" in
an "elegant" setting"; if they started "honoring reservation
times", they might win even greater accolades.

Bombay Grill 🖪　　21 | 19 | 20 | $22

*2 E. Madison St. (N. Charles St.), 410-837-2973
11308 Reisterstown Rd. (High Falcon Rd.), Owings Mills,
410-998-9295*

Bombay Peacock Grill 🖪

*10005 Old Columbia Rd. (Eden Brook Dr.), Columbia,
410-381-7111*

Cafe Bombay 🖪

114 E. Lombard St. (Calvert St.), 410-539-2233

■ These "hardworking" subcontinentals please suits and
penny-wise "Indian graduate students" alike with a spice
palette that runs from tame to "actually hot", lunch buffets
that provide "something new and tasty" "at a good price",
and a staff that "offers explanations"; it's all offered in
surroundings that range from "elegant" to "exotic."

BRASS ELEPHANT 🖪　　25 | 27 | 24 | $40

924 N. Charles St. (bet. Eager & Read Sts.), 410-547-8480

■ Housed in a "beautifully restored" Mount Vernon
townhouse, this "plush" Edwardian is perfect for "giving
your wife a piece of jewelry" or "impressing" a client and
the "delicious" American-Continental cooking mostly "lives
up to one of the best rooms in town"; order the "fantastic
tasting menu" or the "bargain" pre-theater prix fixe, or
check out happy hour in the "retro" upstairs bar where
the "over-30" set enjoys "scrumptious small plates."

Brewer's Art 🖪　　20 | 23 | 17 | $26

1106 N. Charles St. (bet. Biddle & Chase Sts.), 410-547-6925

◪ "Young professionals" and the "pierced Baltimore" set
coexist at this "beautiful" old Mount Vernon mansion, writing
a "tale of two floors": in the "elegant", "Europeanesque"
parlor, the former sip house-brewed Belgian-style beers
and sample the Eclectic menu, while the latter "feel hip
hanging" downstairs at the smoky, "funky catacomb" bar.

BRIGHTON'S 🇸 25 | 27 | 25 | $41
*Harbor Court Hotel, 550 Light St. (bet. Conway & Lee Sts.),
410-347-9750*

■ "Sunny and lovely" with a "magnificent view" of the
Inner Harbor, this "jewel" of a hotel restaurant's "classy"
manners and "imaginative" New American menu make it
a "great power breakfast and lunch spot" (it also serves
dinner Monday–Saturday) but with a "lighter feel" than
Hampton's, the property's upscale venue; the "delightful"
"high tea" may brighten your view of hotel canteens forever.

Caesar's Den 🇸 19 | 16 | 20 | $34
223 S. High St. (Stiles St.), 410-547-0820

☑ "Quintessential Little Italy dining" – a "comfortable" place
with "typical" pasta, seafood and veal dishes that improve
(like the service) "if they know you" is the mark of this
longstanding trattoria; though there are certainly "better"
Italian choices, this one captures the enclave's "Old
Baltimore" feel, plus it pours uncommonly interesting wines.

Cafe Bretton ▽ 20 | 21 | 18 | $30
*849 Baltimore-Annapolis Blvd. (McKinsey Rd.),
Severna Park, 410-647-8222*

☑ Visit "the countryside of France in your backyard" at this
Severna Park Franco-Continental where everything from its
"quaint" appearance to the "homegrown, garden-fresh
produce" incorporated in its "homey" dishes establishes
a "European atmosphere"; even if some report "magical
meals but also total duds", it's "worth a try"; dinner only.

Cafe Hon 🇸 15 | 14 | 16 | $15
1002 W. 36th St. (bet. Falls Rd. & Roland Ave.), 410-243-1230

☑ "The name says it all – fun and unpretentious" with
Traditional American "comfort" food, "casual" service, an
old-timey "kitcheny" look and lots of "big hair" sightings;
for many, this "step-up-from-a-diner" in Hampden proves
that "sometimes the imitation's better than the real thing",
but critics retort it "works too hard at being homey."

Cafe Madrid 🇸 22 | 18 | 23 | $34
505 S. Broadway (Eastern Ave.), 410-276-7700

■ If you've never been to Tio Pepe, Downtown's venerable
Spanish institution, you may not understand why this
"hidden Fells Point find" is "trying so hard" to be a "good"
copycat, "without the pretense"; it's doing a pretty nice job,
as many have "added this to our list of favorites" citing a
staff that "couldn't be friendlier" and an "interesting" menu.

Cafe Troia 🇸 23 | 19 | 21 | $35
28 W. Allegheny Ave. (York Rd.), Towson, 410-337-0133

☑ Though dining out at an Italian eatery that's "not in Little
Italy" smacks of blasphemy in Baltimore, the well-heeled
in Towson embrace this "serious" yet "enjoyable" source
of "upscale pastas", "grand osso buco and nice wines."

Cafe Zen S
20 | 14 | 19 | $16

438 E. Belvedere Ave. (York Rd.), 410-532-0022

◪ Sino-Japanese food with a health-oriented "difference" is the "fresh" appeal of this modernly "minimalist" spot ("no fish tanks or red-color scheme" here) near the Senator movie theater; though the place is often "bustling", "in an un-zenlike way", with "too many kids", the food is "plentiful" and "cheap", even if naysayers counter little fat, little flavor, "dull."

California Pizza Kitchen S
15 | 12 | 14 | $17

Harborplace, 201 E. Pratt St. (Light St.), 410-783-9339
See review in Washington, DC Directory.

Candle Light Inn S
19 | 21 | 21 | $31

1835 Frederick Rd. (N. Rolling Rd.), Catonsville, 410-788-6076

◪ A "charming throwback" to a more "formal" era, this "romantic" Catonsville classic seats "nostalgists" out on a "lovely" patio or inside in "quaint" candlelit (of course) rooms, and feeds them "good-sized" American-Continental dishes ("nothing outlandish"); skeptics, however, think this "old-timer" "needs updating."

Capitol City Brewing Co. S
14 | 16 | 16 | $19

Harborplace, 301 Light St., Pavilion #93 (Pratt St.), 410-539-7468
See review in Washington, DC Directory.

Captain Harvey's
– | – | – | E

11510 Reisterstown Rd. (Nicodemus Rd.), Owings Mills, 410-356-7550
Run by the same family since 1935, this Owings Mills American-Continental institution doubles as a clubby, "elegant" "fine-dining" establishment and a casual, brightly lit "crab house"; it's sometimes overlooked amid the area's rapid growth, but those who find it are "pleasantly surprised" and vow "we'll keep it."

CHARLESTON
27 | 26 | 26 | $47

1000 Lancaster St. (bet. Central & Exeter Sts.), 410-332-7373

■ "Baltimore's answer to NYC and SF" (and that's not just local pride talking) is this Inner Harbor East "fabulous" American "gem" owned by chef Cindy Wolf and her hubby, Tony Forman; her "innovative" Southern-accented cuisine is "queen", while his "monumental wine cellar" and expertise is "king"; add on "handsome" surroundings and "pampering" service proffered by an intelligent staff and the result is a dining experience that "wows" just about everyone; it's "worth" the "splurge."

CHEESECAKE FACTORY S
21 | 18 | 17 | $23

Harborplace, Pratt St. Pavilion (Calvert St.), 410-234-3990
See review in Washington, DC Directory.

Chiapparelli's [S] 18 | 16 | 18 | $28
237 S. High St. (Fawn St.), 410-837-0309
◪ Sure, this Little Italy "staple" ladles "heavy red sauce on everything" and "suffers from touristitis" (not to mention that the waiters who try to "rush you out the door" have clearly never been to "charm school"), but still the hordes descend upon this Italian touchstone of Old Baltimore; besides, its salad dressing is as "exceptional" as ever.

Ciao Bella [S] – | – | – | M
236 S. High St. (bet. Fawn & Stiles Sts.), 410-685-7733
Chef-owner Tony Gambino serves up traditional Italian fare with a "homemade feel", including seafood and family-sized pasta platters, at this "customer-friendly" "treasure" in "the heart of Little Italy"; keep in mind that on weekends its two "romantic" dining rooms fill up quickly with harbor visitors and couples.

City Cafe [S] 19 | 18 | 17 | $18
1001 Cathedral St. (Eager St.), 410-539-4252
■ "Eclectic" sums up this "lively" Mount Vernon corner cafe whose "wonderful, spacious, light-filled interior" fronted by "huge" people-watching windows invites passersby to "stay a while and relax" over serious coffee, brunch, "snazzy" snacks and salads or a "perfect plate of pasta"; though it's "busy" at peak meal times, resulting in "sporadic" service, the staff is genuinely "friendly."

Claddagh Pub ◐ [S] 19 | 15 | 17 | $20
Canton Sq., 2918 O'Donnell St. (Curley St.), 410-522-4220
■ Good times and "creative bar food" perfectly suit the "yuppie types" who crowd into this "casual" Canton Irish pub, stretching the servers even thinner (hint: "get more" help) and creating quite a din (sometimes you "can't hear across the table"); no matter say satisfied regulars, because the atmosphere is simply "great."

Clyde's ◐ [S] 17 | 20 | 18 | $25
10221 Wincopin Circle (Little Patuxent Pkwy.), Columbia, 410-730-2829
See review in Washington, DC Directory.

Coburn's Tavern & Grill [S] – | – | – | I
2921 O'Donnell St. (S. Curley St.), 410-342-0999
This former coffee shop is now a real restaurant under George Platis and Maura Smith, and was instantly popular as a seven-day breakfast destination for the revitalized Canton's new and old residents; ambitious Eclectic dinner specials keep them coming back later to the relaxed bar on O'Donnell Square.

Corks 🅂 | 23 | 19 | 21 | $37 |
1026 S. Charles St. (bet. Cross & Hamburg Sts.), 410-752-3810
☑ Cleverly "maximizing" its "minimal" townhouse space in Federal Hill, this New American makes learning about wine "fun", pairing vintages with "creative" but "not overdesigned" dishes; it pleases both "wine snobs" with its expertise and "great values" and novices with the staff's nonintimidating "enthusiasm", but some find it too "uneven" and feel its "potential" has not yet been reached.

Corner Stable 🅂 | 19 | 8 | 15 | $20 |
9942 York Rd. (Church Ln.), Cockeysville, 410-666-8722
☑ Some of "Baltimore's best fries" and ribs is what "all the fuss" is about at this Cockeysville roadhouse; while most carnivores maintain that its "falling-off-the-bones" meats set the "standard", white-glove types gripe about the "too dark" grungy premises; N.B. this is the original CS (others with the same name are separately owned).

Cosmopolitan Bar & Grill 🅂 | – | – | – | M |
2933 O'Donnell St. (S. Potomac St.), 410-563-5000
On happening O'Donnell Square, Canton's stylish perch for cosmo sippers features a downstairs bar scene for twenty- and thirtysomething meetings and an upstairs dining room that provides respite and modern Italian nourishment.

Crab Shanty 🅂 | 18 | 16 | 16 | $25 |
3410 Plumtree Dr. (Rte. 40, 1 mi. west of Rte. 29), Ellicott City, 410-465-9660
☑ Beached "inland" near Ellicott City, this nautically bedecked fish feastery reels 'em in with "stock" fin fare and steamed crabs in season, along with "tender steaks"; though highly popular (and thus "noisy"), the food draws wavy readings ("well-prepared" vs. "mass-produced") and service also swings between "cheerful" and "don't care."

Crazy Lil's | – | – | – | M |
27 E. Cross St. (Light St.), 410-347-9793
By the Cross Street market scene, Tony Guarino recreates the good times of his now-closed Dooby's at this dark, energetic SoBo cave; the downstairs bar has a lit *Animal House* sign and a young crowd downing steamed shrimp and burgers; upstairs there's a slightly more adult dining room and open kitchen, where steak Chesapeake and other Traditional American fare are the order of the day.

Crepe du Jour 🅂 | – | – | – | M |
1609 Sulgrave Ave. (Kelly Ave.), 410-542-9000
Moving up from outdoor crêpe cart to indoor real kitchen, engaging Mustapha Snoussi supplies a quick trip to France for language students, expats and regulars as he schmoozes while cooking dessert crêpes and bistro favorites like croque monsieur and coq au vin in a cozy old Mt. Washington house.

Dalesio's of Little Italy 🅂   21 | 19 | 20 | $35

829 Eastern Ave. (Albemarle St.), 410-539-1965
☑ Proving that "lean cuisine" can be "delicious", this "accommodating" Little Italy spa-fare specialist set in a "romantic" townhouse serves "reliable" Italian "standards" as well, along with good wines and desserts; despite a few grumbles that it's "inconsistent", most leave feeling it's a "neat place."

Da Mimmo ◑🅂   24 | 20 | 21 | $45

217 S. High St. (Stiles St.), 410-727-6876
☑ To its coddled coterie, an "excellent" veal chop as "big as a Buick", a "fancy" low-wattage setting and "kingpin" treatment (including limo service from Downtown hotels) make it "worth the price of admission" to this glitzy Italian; but neither massive portions nor "movie star" sightings can appease frugal foes who gripe about "expensive" tabs and "stuffy" waiters who "steer you" to "overpriced specials", even if it is "one of Little Italy's top" spots.

Della Notte 🅂   19 | 20 | 20 | $27

801 Eastern Ave. (President St.), 410-837-5500
☑ On-site parking and a gang-pleasing menu of "traditional and modern" Italian food are "pluses" at this "festive", "Disney-esque" Little Italy palace that's large enough to accommodate "Roman columns and a large tree", as well as busloads of diners; some call it "noisy" and "too big" (which might explain the occasionally "frazzled" service), but fans give it credit for "trying hard."

Desert Cafe   18 | 14 | 16 | $15

1605-07 Sulgrave Ave. (Newbury St.), 410-367-5808
☑ This "funky", romantic little Mt. Washington Middle Eastern is the place to go when you're looking for a "cheap" alternative to "burgers" ("great" falafel and "dynamite gazpacho" here) or a "cute dessert-and-coffee place"; it's a "quiet", "friendly" oasis that's staffed by people who "treat you well"; N.B. now under new ownership.

Ding How 🅂   19 | 16 | 21 | $17

631 S. Broadway (Fleet St.), 410-327-8888
12234 Tullamore Rd. (Padonia Rd.), Cockeysville,
410-628-0888
■ Though it's been around for years, this "serviceable" Fells Point Chinese is "not well known" outside the neighborhood, where it's a popular pub crawl "pop-in" and "take-out" staple; insiders who've mastered the art of "selectively" ordering here "stay away from the fried stuff", but even novices who can't find anything "special" on the menu appreciate the "calm" ambiance and "friendly" service; N.B. there's another branch in Cockeysville.

DiPasquale's at the Pikes S   16 | 17 | 13 | $21
921 Reisterstown Rd. (Sudbrook Ln.), Pikesville,
410-580-1400
◪ Inspired by its "attractive" redo of the old Pikes Theater,
locals have high hopes for this "long-needed" Pikesville
Italian market where patrons report that the deli and takeout
are the "best" options; new manager Harrey Sugarman
(ex Harvey's) is tweaking both the menu and service.

Donna's   18 | 16 | 15 | $18
Gallery at Harborplace, 200 E. Pratt St. (Calvert St.),
410-752-9040
22 S. Green St. (Baltimore St.), 410-328-1962 S
3101 St. Paul St. (31st St.), 410-889-3410 S
Cross Keys, 40 Village Sq. (Falls Rd.), 410-532-7611 S
2 W. Madison St. (N. Charles St.), 410-385-0180 S
1819 Reisterstown Rd. (Hooks Ln.), Pikesville, 410-653-6939 S
2080 York Rd. (Timonium Rd.), Timonium, 410-308-2041 S
The Avenue at White Marsh, 8145 Honeygo Blvd.
(Campbell Blvd.), White Marsh, 410-931-1026 S
◪ Baltimore's "chi-chi" "homegrown" coffee chain is
notable for its "roasted veggies", "artsy settings" and "hip"
(or "self-impressed"?) help; with its "ubiquitous" presence,
it's "convenient" for everything from a "breakfast meeting"
to a light meal of "creative" Eclectic sandwiches and
salads, but signs of "uneven" quality arouse murmurs that
"Starbucks' little sister" is "getting too big."

Double T Diner ◑S   15 | 13 | 17 | $14
6300 Baltimore Nat'l Pike (N. Rolling Rd.), Catonsville,
410-744-4151
10055 Baltimore Nat'l Pike (Enchanted Forest Dr.), Ellicott City,
410-750-3300
1 Mountain Rd. (Ritchie Hwy.), Pasadena, 410-766-9669
4740 E. Joppa Rd. (Bel Air Rd.), Perry Hall, 410-248-0160
10741 Pulaski Hwy. (Ebenezer Rd.), White Marsh,
410-344-1020
543 Market Place Dr. (Rte. 24), Bel Air, 410-836-5591
◪ When you're "in the mood" for "cheap", "down-home
grub", these "mirror-and-chrome" outposts beckon; they're
"old-fashioned" in spirit and dish up "anything you could
ever want to eat at any time", and service lives up to
"nostalgic" expectations; but folks who don't get it shrug
"a diner is a diner is a diner."

DuClaw Brewing Co. ◑S   17 | 17 | 16 | $20
16 Bel Air S. Pkwy. (Rte. 24), Bel Air, 410-515-3222
◪ Well suited for its "polo-shirted" thirtysomething crowd,
this raucous, "casual" Bel Air brewpub's "consistent"
American chow complements house brews that "can't be
beat"; but foes insist its chief virtue is just being a place
to go to in the "middle of nowhere."

Duda's Tavern ⦿
19 | 14 | 18 | $16

1600 Thames St. (Bond St.), 410-276-9719
■ An exemplar of a "real, mellow Baltimore watering hole", this pocket-sized Fells Point "hangout" provides the neighborhood with "friendly" vibes, "great" bar food (the crab cakes and smoked-fish salad are "winners") and a "wide selection" of beers (16 on tap, 150 by the bottle); what's more, say locals, "you can lose the tourists here."

Due S
24 | 23 | 23 | $35

McDonough Crossroads, 25 Crossroads Dr. (McDonough & Reisterstown Rds.), Owings Mills, 410-356-4147
■ "The less formal side of Linwood's", this "upscale" spot in Owings Mills impresses partisans as "less expensive" and more "comfortable" than its sibling next door but just as "creative" and "delicious"; a range of "tantalizing" Northern Italian choices, along with a willingness to "accommodate" any whim, makes it an "easy place to dine", though a few fuss that it can be "uneven" when busy.

Edo Sushi S
25 | 17 | 22 | $22

53 E. Padonia Rd. (York Rd.), Timonium, 410-667-9200
■ In Timonium, "the best sushi of the moment" shines through the "spartan" "strip mall" setting of this Japanese BYO, inspiring raw fish fanciers to swear that its "excellent", "fresh" selections are as "good as it gets in Charm City"; a menu that's "broader than the usual sushi spot's", plus "friendly service", makes it a "weekly hangout" for many, but thirsty types clamor "they need a liquor license."

El Azteca S
24 | 12 | 20 | $18

Clarksville Shopping Ctr., 12210 Rte. 108 (Rte. 32), Clarksville, 410-531-3001
■ "Run by a Mexican family", this "surprisingly good hole-in-the-wall" in Clarksville cultivates many aficionados with "authentic", "homemade" renditions of "the real thing" (the "great margaritas by the pitcher" don't hurt either); the "location is out of the way" and it's "hard to find", but if you have a taste for "zesty" south-of-the-border dishes, you "can't afford not to eat here."

ELKRIDGE FURNACE INN S
23 | 26 | 23 | $36

5745 Furnace Ave. (bet. Main St. & Race Rd., east of Rte. 1), Elkridge, 410-379-9336
◪ "Celebrate anything romantic" at this "lovely", historic Elkridge estate where an intimate "getaway" ambiance encourages diners to "whisper" and the "mansion" quarters provide an "elegant" backdrop; while most laud its frequently "changing" French menu as "creative", others feel it's not up to the setting or the "prices"; still, furnace stokers advise "if you're not sure she'll say 'yes', propose here – it'll help."

Ellicott Mills Brewing Co. S   16 | 18 | 17 | $21
8308 Main St. (bet. Ellicott Mills Dr. & Old Columbia Pike),
Ellicott City, 410-313-8141
◪ "Large servings, great beer – what more is there?" ask
boosters of this Ellicott City brewpub, which may confirm
its image as a "guy's place"; while highbrows feel it needs
"more atmosphere and menu choices", anyone hankering
for a microbrew and "upscale" American bar grub in a
"lively, noisy" setting will feel welcome here.

ESPN Zone S   15 | 20 | 16 | $21
Power Plant, 601 E. Pratt St. (bet. Gay St. & Market Pl.),
410-685-3776
◪ The action never stops at this "noisy" multilevel dining/
entertainment complex in the Inner Harbor, a total "sports-
lovers" zone that redefines sensory overload with its
ubiquitous TVs and live jock sightings; while you "don't go
for the food", the "huge portions" of burgers, ribs and other
American eats can also be had at a new barge on the water.

Ethel & Ramone's S   – | – | – | M
1615 Sulgrave Ave. (Kelly Ave.), 410-664-2971
Edward Bloom, the chef-owner, has "greatly improved" the
menu at this "funky", "friendly" Mt. Washington spot with
his "daring, delicious" Creole- and Caribbean-accented,
seafood-slanted Eclectic cooking.

Eurasian Harbor S   – | – | – | E
Pier 5 Hotel, 711 Eastern Ave. (President St.), 410-230-9992
Ruth's Chris' Steve DiCastro hopes local regulars will join
Inner Harbor visitors in the former Chop House's dramatically
remade hotel dining room, or at the communal-table sushi
bar and new outdoor seating area, for International fusion
fare along the lines of 'East-meets-West crab cakes',
Indonesian chicken satay and desserts like caramelized
pineapple tart with coconut ice cream.

Faidley's   22 | 11 | 17 | $13
Lexington Mkt., 400 W. Lexington St. (Paca St.), 410-727-4898
■ "Bursting with Chesapeake flavor" – from among "the
best crab cakes in town" to the "funky, gritty" ambiance –
this Lexington Market stall located in a neglected part of
town is a "stand-up affair" where the "freshest clams,
oysters and fish sandwiches" make it a seafood-lovers
"Shangri-la"and a "must-see" for "visitors."

Fazzini's Italian Kitchen S   20 | 7 | 18 | $15
Cranbrook Shopping Ctr., 578 Cranbrook Rd. (York Rd.),
Cockeysville, 410-667-6104
■ Though there's "no atmosphere" at this family-friendly
strip mall eatery in Cockeysville, partisans swear that you'll
get "as good an Italian meal as you'll get" in the area "at
a cheap price"; you'll have to "bring your own wine", but
pasta fiends promise that it's "worth" the effort.

Fleming's [S] | – | – | – | E

720 Aliceanna St. (President St.), 410-332-1666
A West Coast fancy beef chain seeks to win the steakhouse stakes with a no-cigar (or even cigaret) policy, 100 wines by the glass, lighter decor, a street-level Inner Harbor East location, and by snagging Ruth Chris' former executive chef, Eric Littlejohn, who is both chef and partner here.

Forest Diner [S] | – | – | – | I

10031 Baltimore Nat'l Pike (Enchanted Forest Dr.), Ellicott City, 410-465-5395
One of the "last of the authentic old-time diners" on historic Route 40 in Ellicott City is this '40s original, "not a chain imitation like its next-door wanna-be" (a Double T Diner outpost); appreciative loyalists and their progeny, as ever, dig into American road chow that hasn't much changed over the decades.

Friendly Farms [S] | 18 | 12 | 19 | $19

17434 Foreston Rd. (Mt. Carmel Rd.), Upperco, 410-239-7400
◪ An "old-fashioned" country dinner served "*en famille*" at this 200-acre Upperco farm is a multigenerational "outing that kids can enjoy" – while they "feed the ducks", grown-ups can zero in on "pig portions" of "all-American" eats in a setting that'll "take you back home"; city slickers, though, beef "enough food for two" but also "enough noise for earplugs" and there's "no liquor" to ease the "wait."

Fuji [S] | ▽ 28 | 18 | 22 | $23

10226 Baltimore Nat'l Pike (bet. Boone's Ln. & Frederick Rd.), Ellicott City, 410-750-2455
■ "Hidden" on Route 40 west of Ellicott City, this "unsung hero" is a local "treasure" for "consistently good" Japanese standards and "excellent sushi"; a "lovely staff" adds to this "gem's" luster, making it a "sentimental favorite" for many.

Fusion Grill [S] | – | – | – | E

2402 Pleasantville Rd. (Fallston Rd.), Fallston, 410-877-1550
"A must if you love to eat" say foodies about this casual Fallston venue, but the jury's still out on whether the adventurous Eclectic menu (with Asian and Cajun accents) will please or jar local palates; expect "creative" seafood combinations served in a bright room with intimate alcoves.

Gabler's [S] | ▽ 21 | 16 | 19 | $27

2200 Perryman Rd. (Old Philadelphia Rd.), Aberdeen, 410-272-0626
■ Blessed with a "magical setting", this vintage crab house on the Bush River near Aberdeen serves up steamed Maryland crabs "the old-fashioned way" and teams them with the "best fries" amid unpretentious comforts that make it feel like you're "in your neighbor's backyard"; this is "what eating crabs should be" all about; N.B. open seasonally, reservations required.

G & M Restaurant S
21 9 16 $22

804 N. Hammonds Ferry Rd. (Nursery Rd.), Linthicum, 410-636-1777

◪ "Obscenely large", "meaty and perfectly cooked" crab cakes are the "only reason" that outsiders seek out this "Linthicum institution", a "blue-collar" bar whose denizens don't seem to mind its "dumpy" appearance, "smoky" room or lack of service.

Garry's Grill S
22 16 21 $18

Severna Park Shopping Ctr., 533A Baltimore-Annapolis Blvd. (McKinsey Rd.), Severna Park, 410-544-0499

See review in Annapolis and the Eastern Shore Directory.

Gecko's ◐S
– – – M

2318 Fleet St. (bet. S. Bradford St. & S. Patterson Park Ave.), 410-732-1961

Jim Smith's "unique" Southwestern cooking attracts locals to this "friendly" Canton spot that sports "funky" decor; while the bar can be boisterous, the dining room is a quiet place to sample the Chesapeake-accented "creative" (think catfish with a jalapeño cream sauce), if uneven, menu.

Genevieve's S
21 18 19 $18

(fka Margaret's Cafe)
909 Fell St. (bet. Thames & Wolfe Sts.), 410-276-5605

■ Chef Peter Rasmussen and Allison Dryer bought out the place, so while there's a name change, much remains the same at this "warm and friendly Fells Point place" whose "healthy" menu, "funky" furnishings and "peaceful energy" nurture artsy types; aesthetes praise the "high level of craftsmanship" evident in the home cooking.

Germano's Trattoria S
21 18 20 $32

300 S. High St. (Fawn St.), 410-752-4515

■ "Not flashy" yet "better than most" of the other Little Italy options, this "warm" and "cozy" trattoria really "seems to care", with a staff that's "as nice to tourists in shorts as to the well-dressed" locals who frequent here; it's "quiet enough for conversation" and the "creative" Tuscan-style menu is "worthy", but some caution that it's at its best when the eponymous owner is present.

Gertrude's S
19 23 18 $29

Baltimore Museum of Art, 10 Art Museum Dr. (N. Charles St.), 410-889-3399

■ Amid the "lovely surroundings" of the Baltimore Museum of Art and its "wonderful" sculpture garden, area native John Shields' "showcase" restaurant takes on a "unique effort" in resurrecting the "endangered vernacular cuisine" of the Chesapeake Bay; but despite some "interesting and flavorful" renditions of regional Maryland classics (paired with "compelling" wines), a few feel that the "food got lost in the translation" from his TV shows.

Gibby's [S] — | — | — | M
22 W. Padonia Rd. (York Rd.), Timonium, 410-560-0703
"They do wonderful things with crabs" at this "popular, noisy" Timonium seafooder that outgrew its original space and so added an atrium and patio; "more upscale than most" crab joints, it serves "some of the best fish north of the Beltway", which results in "long waits."

Giovanni's [S] ▽ 19 | 17 | 20 | $26
2101 Pulaski Hwy. (Mountain Rd.), Edgewood, 410-676-8100
◪ "Average Joes dine and dance to Sinatra-style" tunes (on weekends) and go for "great salads and bread" and lots of homey, if "not outstanding", food at this Edgewood Italian enclave; but while it's intimate and "charming", some feel it's a tad pricey for its far-out location.

Golden West Cafe [S] 22 | 15 | 18 | $13
842 W. 36th St. (bet. Chestnut & Elm Aves.), 410-889-8891
■ On Hampden's main thoroughfare, this "quirky", "dinky" Southwestern "cafe of love" is a bit of a throwback to the hippie '70s but with a "*nuevo*" twist, "hon"; groupies swear by the "terrific" breakfast burritos and the "Frito pie and grandma's bread pudding" add up to a "creative, high-quality" lunch or dinner; N.B. hours vary so call ahead.

Grille 700 [S] — | — | — | E
Marriott Waterfront Hotel, 700 Aliceanna St. (President St.), 410-385-3000
Baltimoreans hope a panoramic skyline view through 25-foot windows, a raw bar and career servers will add up to more than just typical hotel dining at this dramatic space in the deluxe new Inner Harbor East Marriott Waterfront high-rise; Contemporary American dishes like salt-crusted red snapper, pancetta-wrapped tenderloin and banana bread pudding may entice locals to join the visitors.

Gunning's Crab House [S] 18 | 10 | 16 | $24
3901 S. Hanover St. (Jeffrey St.), 410-354-0085
◪ While this "old-fashioned" South Baltimore marine haven "looks like someone's basement", it offers a "classic" "steamed crab" "experience", along with fried seafood, "corn dripping in milky butter" and for dessert, "great éclairs"; diehards complain that "only the name and location are the same" (the Gunning family is no longer involved), but others don't detect much difference.

Gunning's Seafood [S] ▽ 20 | 12 | 16 | $25
7304 Parkway Dr. (Dorsey Rd./Rte. 176), Hanover, 410-712-9404
◪ "Convenient to BWI" airport, this "famous" seafood stop set in a "bland" strip mall proves that "great crabs can wear anything"; the Gunnings, who "somehow always manage to get big", big crustaceans, also cook up the "crab cake of crab cakes" and a variety of seafood.

Hamilton's 🖪   24 | 22 | 22 | $39
Admiral Fell Inn, 888 S. Broadway (Thames St.), 410-522-2195
■ The "inventive" New American cuisine seems an apt fit for this "intimate, innovative" Fells Point fine-dining spot that's "great for dinner parties", thanks to its "good wine values", clubby coziness and "meticulous" manners; but critics cite some "ups and downs" in the food and service.

HAMPTON'S 🖪   28 | 29 | 27 | $58
Harbor Court Hotel, 550 Light St. (bet. Conway & Lee Sts.), 410-347-9744
■ "Never less than excellent", Baltimore's "best" hotel dining establishment is rated No. 1 for Service and ranks among the top three vote-getters for Food and Decor; "world-class" treatment, a "gorgeous" room and "beautiful harbor views" complement the "top-notch" seasonal New American fare, making this Charm City's foremost site for "special occasions"; in sum, it's "almost perfect."

Hard Rock Cafe 🖪   13 | 19 | 15 | $20
Power Plant, 601 E. Pratt St. (Market Pl.), 410-347-7625
See review in Washington, DC Directory.

Hard Times Cafe 🖪   19 | 14 | 17 | $14
8865 Stanford Blvd. (Dobbin Rd.), Columbia, 410-312-0700
See review in Washington, DC Directory.

Harryman House 🖪   20 | 20 | 19 | $30
340 Main St. (1¼ mi. north of Franklin Blvd.), Reisterstown, 410-833-8850
■ Housed in an 18th-century log cabin with a "rustic", "well-appointed" dining room and an adjoining tavern room, this "historic" Reisterstown American charmer works as both a "special-event" place and a "hangout for the horsey set"; even though it can be "uneven", locals rate it a "treasure."

Helen's Garden 🖪   22 | 20 | 21 | $21
2908 O'Donnell St. (Linwood Ave.), 410-276-2233
■ "Don't walk, run", to this "cute" "nook" urge Canton "comfort" seekers; while its "innovative", "varied" American menu (including many "healthy dishes") and "low-key" yet "stimulating" ambiance make it an "excellent value" already, the "hospitable" folks "keep making it better", and have recently added a new kitchen and roof deck.

HELMAND, THE 🖪   26 | 21 | 23 | $23
806 N. Charles St. (Madison St.), 410-752-0311
■ Combine a "wonderful" adventure for "bored taste buds", intriguing "ambiance", a "helpful staff" and "reasonable prices" and you'll usually wind up with a "full house", like at this popular Mount Vernon Afghan; it "wins over" most anyone who wants to break timid friends into "exotic" dining, "delight" a date or dig into the "best rack of lamb"; N.B. they've opened a sib, Tapas Teatro, further up the street.

Henninger's Tavern
24 | 22 | 22 | $28

1812 Bank St. (bet. Ann & Wolfe Sts.), 410-342-2172

■ Not only is this picturesque Fells Point tavern a "great local hideout" with some imported beers, but it also boasts "delicious", "original" New American fare, including "excellent" desserts; its "low-key", "arty" intimacy equally suits hip daters and "timid out-of-town" relations, but with less than a dozen tables and a "no-reservations" policy (except for large parties), going early is a cool idea for all.

Hoang's Seafood Grill & Sushi Bar S
20 | 15 | 17 | $22

Canton Cove Marina, 2748 Boston St. (Lakewood Ave.), 410-534-8888
1619 Sulgrave Ave. (Kelly Ave.), 410-466-1000

◪ "Affordably delicious" sushi, grilled seafood and other "authentic" dishes await at these Pan-Asian twins set in "pleasant" locations – a small, "cutesy" Mt. Washington site and a modern Canton venue near the water; champions cheer "anything grilled is great", the "seafood soup is addictive" and the "vegetarian selections" are "good for you", but dissenters retort that it's "inconsistent" and "slow" because they "try to do too many things."

Holy Frijoles S
21 | 15 | 17 | $13

908 W. 36th St. (bet. Elm & Roland Aves.), 410-235-2326

■ "Don't bother dressing up" for this funky, "crowded" Tex-Mex "hole-in-the-wall" in Hampden, where the eats are cheap and "they certainly don't skimp" on "serious" burritos and enchiladas (the vegetarian options "deserve credit" too); but "sporadic" service and long "waits" leave a handful of heretics wholly "uninspired."

House of Asia S
– | – | – | I

Lotte Plaza Ctr., 8815 Baltimore National Pike/Rte. 40 (Rte. 29), Ellicott City, 410-480-5100

Businesswoman Nina Song and her Hopkins researcher husband Paul Pham add to Ellicott City's new Asian dining destination status with their combo Thai (coconut curry duck) and Vietnamese (grilled lemon chicken) strip mall spot, attracting a crowd of students, worldly fans and expatriates hungry for an authentic taste of home.

Hull Street Blues Cafe S
20 | 16 | 19 | $23

1222 Hull St. (Fort Ave.), Locust Point, 410-727-7476

■ "A hidden treasure" near Ft. McHenry, this "real" slice of Baltimore set in a "renovated brick tavern" serves good "basic pub food", but it's best-known as a "fun place for a long brunch with lots of hungry friends"; its popularity, however, often spells a long wait for a table, though fans say it's "worth" it.

Hunan Manor [S] 23 | 21 | 21 | $20

7091 Deepage Dr. (Carved Stone Rd. & Snowden River Pkwy.), Columbia, 410-381-1134

◪ Known for its "consistently high-quality" multiregional fare and "gracious" handling of "large groups", this "best-value" Columbia Sino stalwart now sports a modish look accented by "gorgeous fish tanks"; foes who feel that it's "slipped lately" yawn "ho hum" over "average" eats, but they're drowned out by the many who pronounce this the "best Chinese in the area."

Hunters' Lodge ◐ [S] 22 | 19 | 19 | $34

9445 Baltimore Nat'l Pike/Rte. 40 (1 mi. west of Rte. 29), Ellicott City, 410-461-4990

◪ "Beautifully presented food in an unlikely location" amidst strip malls makes this young New American–Mediterranean much appreciated in Ellicott City, where its fancy rusticity provides a needed fine-dining "destination"; despite kudos for "interesting dishes", some find it "disappointing", which is perhaps why a menu change to a seafood-steak orientation is planned.

Ikaros [S] 20 | 15 | 20 | $22

4805 Eastern Ave. (Ponca St.), 410-633-3750

◪ "If you like Greek food and you're hungry", you "can't beat the prices" or the portions at this "quintessentially Baltimore" Greektown standby; you might "sink to the bottom of the Aegean after eating" some of its "heavy" fare (which isn't everyone's "idea of Greek"), but the fried calamari is "always tender" and so is the service – "these people make everyone feel at home."

India Palace [S] ▽ 21 | 16 | 19 | $19

Yorktowne Plaza, 35 Cranbrook Rd. (York Rd.), Cockeysville, 410-628-6800

■ Cockeysvilleans dub this BYO spot "the ultimate in a dependable neighborhood joint" for serving up some of Baltimore's "best Indian food" in their backyard; cynics may knock the "disorganized" service, but most diners are too busy enjoying the "authentically prepared" dishes to notice, plus on weekends, the strains of live sitar music help to smooth over any rough spots.

Jeannier's 24 | 19 | 22 | $33

Broadview Apts., 105 W. 39th St. (University Pkwy.), 410-889-3303

◪ Sure, it could be "more hip" (some wags dub it "Cafe d'Ancien"), but this "gracious" dowager near Johns Hopkins U features "excellent" French eating; "Baltimore's blue bloods" enjoy "profoundly good" classics and "fabulous" desserts in "serene" (or "drab") surroundings, but those who find it "stuffy" may prefer the "mellow" bar/cafe that transports one to a "Paris bistro."

Jennings Cafe ◐ ▽ 20 | 15 | 20 | $20
808 Frederick Rd. (Mellor Ave.), Catonsville, 410-744-3824
■ "Family-run", this "good neighborhood bar" on old Catonsville's main street is undeniably "quirky" with quite a "funky interior" (the knotty pine paneling, for example, runs sideways), but the "natives are friendly", the service is "always good" and you can chow down on a "really nice burger, homemade cucumber salad", "the best oyster stew ever" and a number of other American favorites.

Jilly's [S] – | – | – | I
1012 Reisterstown Rd. (E. Sudbrook Ln.), Pikesville, 410-653-0610
10030 Baltimore National Pike (Bethany Ln.), Ellicott City, 410-461-3093
"All walks of Pikesville life" mingle at this "pleasing, convenient" neighborhood spot for a "variety" of "great bar food", from "excellent steaks" to the "best shrimp salad in town"; though it's "always mobbed and rightly so", "quick" service keeps 'em happy; N.B. the spiffy neon-and-glass Ellicott City sib offers outdoor seating and breakfast.

Jimmy's [S] 16 | 11 | 18 | $12
801 S. Broadway (Lancaster St.), 410-327-3273
■ "You never know who you'll see" at this legendary Fells Point "tradition" – perhaps Julia Child, a "former governor" or the "Hopkins ER" team; a "must for *Homicide* TV fans", it's a weekend breakfast scene yet still a down-to-earth resource for a "cheap meal."

J.J.'s Everyday [S] ▽ 22 | 12 | 18 | $18
2141 York Rd. (Timonium Rd.), Timonium, 410-308-2700
■ "You really can go everyday" to this casual but "creative" Timonium American BYO, an "unexpected oasis" in a suburban strip mall; "great seafood and pastas", salads and other dishes amount to "gourmet food at diner prices", but the experience, while "friendly", can be "slow."

Johansson's Dining House [S] ▽ 20 | 18 | 18 | $27
4 W. Main St. (Rte. 27), Westminster, 410-876-0101
◪ At the hub of Westminster's 'Downtown', with a "view of the railroad tracks", is this "nice local place" with "eclectic decor" (ersatz British colonial empire trappings) and "enjoyable", "good-value" American food; be forewarned, however, that the "service needs improvement."

Johnny Dee's [S] – | – | – | I
1704 Joan Ave. (Loch Raven Blvd.), Parkville, 410-665-7000
Hidden underneath an old Parkville shopping center, "your grandfather's '50s basement den" is the same as it ever was, right down to the original vinyl lounge chairs, coffee tables and diehard '59 Colts fans; regulars mark their favorite sofas with little brass plaques and order shrimp salad, fresh-cut fries and other tasty bar nibbles.

John Steven, Ltd. ◐ [S] 20 | 17 | 16 | $21

1800 Thames St. (Ann St.), 410-327-5561

■ It's fun to "take out-of-town guests" to this "smoky", atmospheric former seamen's saloon on Fells Point's waterfront for "fab" "steamed mussels and shrimp" or "Americanized" sushi in the "interesting" bar area; more sedate seafood-centered American-Eclectic dining takes place in the dining room and in the courtyard.

Josef's Country Inn [S] 25 | 22 | 23 | $36

2410 Pleasantville Rd. (Rte. 152), Fallston, 410-877-7800

■ One of the better reasons for a "little drive" to the "country" in Harford County is this "off-the-path" spot, the kind of "place you want to think you discovered"; look forward to "solid", "top-quality" Continental fare with a German accent (that's "heavy" to some) and Maryland-style seafood served by a "hospitable" staff in a "pleasant" setting; N.B. reservations are a must.

Joy America Cafe [S] 23 | 24 | 20 | $36

American Visionary Art Museum, 800 Key Hwy. (Covington St.), 410-244-6500

◪ Now operated by Spike & Charlie's, this New American in the wacky Visionary Art Museum at the foot of Federal Hill offers a harbor view from the dining room and outdoor terrace (adjacent to a huge, funky spinning whirligig) to match the provocative seafood inventions spiked with sauces and salsas; an eager young staff entertains the urban clientele – the savvy go when the museum is open.

J. Paul's [S] 18 | 18 | 17 | $23

Harborplace, 301 Light St. Pavilion (Pratt St.), 410-659-1889

See review in Washington, DC Directory.

Jumbo Seafood [S] 20 | 14 | 18 | $21

48 E. Sudbrook Ln. (Old Court Rd.), Pikesville, 410-602-1441

■ Indeed, "the seafood is jumbo" and so is the crowd, but, alas, not the room at Pikesville's "great neighborhood Chinese", making the "cheap and fast" carryout the "only way to go" if you don't "love thy neighbor" "sharing [thy] table" (it's hard to go wrong with the "excellent soups" or "delicious orange beef").

Kali's Court [S] 23 | 24 | 21 | $39

1606 Thames St. (bet. Bond St. & Broadway), 410-276-4700

◪ One of several "trendy" Greek-Med seafood houses in Fells Point and among the "prettiest", this "noisy" haunt's "exquisite" grilled fish has suburbanites coming in droves ("everyone's here") and swooning over "such good food" (the courtyard and valet parking also earn kudos); but it's "not quite there yet" dissenters demur, citing "ordinary" fare, "inconsistent service" and an "ostentatious" air.

Kaufman's Tavern [S] ⊘ ▽ 18 | 16 | 19 | $20

329 Gambrills Rd. (Rte. 32), Gambrills, 410-923-2005

■ "A seafood stalwart in an area that needs one", this "family-oriented" institution (circa 1937) in Gambrills knows how to prepare crabs, fish and even "great prime rib"; its "nautically themed" premises function as a party place as well as a "neighborhood tavern", so be prepared for occasional waits.

Kawasaki 24 | 18 | 22 | $25

413 N. Charles St. (bet. Franklin & Mulberry Sts.), 410-659-7600
907 S. Ann St. (Thames St.), 410-327-9400 [S]

■ Knowing fans of these "trendy, popular" Japanese twins prefer sitting in the tatami room at the Charles Street original or at the sushi bar at the "cute" Fells Point branch to dine on just about the "best" raw fish around, as well as "great" traditional cooked dishes; while cold fish carp it's "not as good as its rep", most agree that the "fresh", "expertly prepared" fare and "impeccable" service keep this duo cuts "above the sushi-McDonald's."

Kelly's ◐ [S] ▽ 19 | 10 | 16 | $18

2108 Eastern Ave. (bet. Chester & Duncan Sts.), 410-327-2312

■ Kelly and Mary Sheridan's "great" "watering hole" in Southeast Baltimore is a classic "neighborhood bar"; folks flock here for the "best [steamed] crabs and camaraderie in town", "home-cooked American meals", "cheap" tabs and loud "fun" once the karaoke starts.

King's Contrivance [S] 24 | 25 | 23 | $40

10150 Shaker Dr. (Rtes. 29 & 32), Columbia, 410-995-0500

◪ This "beautiful historic" property in Columbia provides an "inviting", stately "country-house" backdrop for a "special party", "business meeting or tryst", and showcases "superior" American cuisine focusing on fresh ingredients; but knaves who knock the "dated" menu ask "why bother?"; N.B. the $19.95 early-bird is worth a try.

La Madeleine French Bakery [S] 18 | 17 | 14 | $16

6211 Columbia Crossing (Dobbin Rd.), Columbia, 410-872-4900

See review in Washington, DC Directory.

La Scala [S] ▽ 21 | 17 | 20 | $32

1012 Eastern Ave. (Central Ave.), 410-783-9209

■ "Extremely personable" chef-owner Nino Germano's Little Italy "neighborhood Italian" "where food is king" relocated a while back to a larger space, where he still prepares his famous "grilled Caesar salad" (and "don't forget mama's cannoli", a legend in its own right); N.B. the move outdates the above decor score.

La Tavola [S] 21 | 19 | 18 | $30

248 Albemarle St. (Fawn St.), 410-685-1859

■ "Creative", "modern, light" Italian cooking enlivened by "fresh seasonings" distinguishes this "spacious" spot from many of its Little Italy neighbors; the "comfortable" digs have a more subdued look, and while Miss Manners types feel the service also "needs to improve", most are beguiled by the "charming, outgoing" staff.

La Tesso Tana [S] 20 | 19 | 18 | $33

58 W. Biddle St. (Cathedral St.), 410-837-3630

■ "Wonderful" before a performance at the Meyerhoff Symphony Hall nearby, this "upscale" Italian does a "great job under difficult circumstances" on "concert nights"; its basement "hideaway" digs are too "cramped" for some, but can be "ideal for intimate moments."

Legal Sea Foods [S] 20 | 17 | 18 | $31

100 E. Pratt St. (Calvert St.), 410-332-7360

See review in Washington, DC Directory.

Liberatore's Bistro [S] 20 | 20 | 20 | $32

Freedom Village Shopping Ctr., 6300 Georgetown Blvd. (Liberty Rd.), Eldersburg, 410-781-4114

New Town Village Ctr., 9712 Groffs Mills Dr. (Lakeside Blvd.), Owings Mills, 410-356-3100

Timonium Corporate Ctr., 9515 Deereco Rd. (Padonia Rd.), Timonium, 410-561-3300

■ Some of the "best Italian stops north of the Beltway", these "consistent crowd-pleasers" combine "fine" "old-fashioned" Italian fare with a "try-hard" attitude in "elegant surroundings" suitable for "families" but "romantic enough for couples"; foes are frosty about cooking that "runs hot and cold", but sociable types warm to the "hot bar action."

LINWOOD'S [S] 26 | 26 | 25 | $43

McDonough Crossroads, 25 Crossroads Dr. (McDonough & Reisterstown Rds.), Owings Mills, 410-356-3030

■ Linwood Dame "gets it all right" at his "prestigious" Owings Mills New American, with a "creative" menu and an "accommodating" staff in a "clubby, cozy" setting that works equally well for casual bar dining or "special occasions" when elegant "ambiance and service count"; though it's too "pricey" and "stuffy" to some, the "worldly" set lauds it as a "class act" with "city sophistication."

Lista's [S] 15 | 18 | 15 | $22

Brown's Wharf, 1637 Thames St. (Broadway), 410-327-0040

◩ A "fine view of the harbor" from a "festive" patio attracts "groups" who come to "visit Mr. Cuervo" at this waterside Fells Point Mexican, much more so than the "expensive" "Americanized" fare that may be "ok for tourists" or the service that can be "arrogant"; still, after a "monster margarita and a water taxi ride", who can complain?

Loco Hombre 🅂 | 17 | 15 | 15 | $19 |

413 W. Cold Spring Ln. (Keswick Rd.), 410-889-2233

▪ "Crowded and loud", this Roland Park Tex-Mex pleases the "college crowd" with casual "fun" at a "good price"; don't expect authentic Mexican eating, but fans swear the "terrific specials" deserve notice, even if others wish management would pay more attention to a staff that sometimes "doesn't seem to care."

Lotte Plaza Market 🅂 | ▽ 18 | 8 | 11 | $12 |

Lotte Plaza Ctr., 8801 Baltimore National Pike/Rte. 40 (Rte. 29), Ellicott City, 410-750-9650
See review in Washington, DC Directory.

Louisiana 🅂 | – | – | – | E |

1708 Aliceanna St. (Broadway), 410-327-2610
An opulent setting evocative of New Orleans, accomplished with salvaged treasures, taste and imagination, is the backdrop for the sophisticated Creole-inspired cuisine presented at this Fells Point yearling; it's fast cultivated a clientele that knows how to use the room's flattering lighting and stylish appointments to its own best advantage.

LP Steamers 🅂 | – | – | – | M |

1100 E. Fort Ave. (Woodall St.), 410-576-9294
In the South Baltimore row houses marching up to Ft. McHenry, Bud Gardner fries and steams crabs, shrimp, clams and oysters for a mix of neighborhood regulars and newcomers who quickly become friends; new seating upstairs and a backyard deck provide needed breathing room for this very casual, slightly smoky, corner eatery.

Luigi Petti ◗🅂 | 17 | 16 | 17 | $26 |

1002 Eastern Ave. (Exeter St.), 410-685-0055
▪ Its "secret" clam sauce recipe (the "best in town") and the "nicest patio in Little Italy" are this "typical" Italian's notable features, even if the blasé shrug that there's little else "to write home about"; but regulars who go for a "cozy dinner near the fireplace" are seldom disappointed; N.B. the house salad and gnocchi are other good bets.

Maggie's 🅂 | 19 | 16 | 18 | $26 |

310 E. Green St. (Washington Rd.), Westminster, 410-848-1441
■ Off by itself on the edge of Westminster, this "small, cozy" "well-kept secret" "tries hard to please" with American fare (including "good crab cakes") and "decent bar food"; while it's a "nice neighborhood place", a few regulars insist it'd be even better if the dining area were a bit less "cramped" and not so "close to the bar scene."

Malibu Grill
Brazilian Steakhouse 🅂 | 18 | 15 | 17 | $22 |

10215 Wincopin Circle (Rte. 175), Columbia, 410-964-5566
See review in Washington, DC Directory.

Mamie's 🅂   – | – | – | I

911 W. 36th St. (Roland Ave.), 410-366-2996
Hopkins types and mill-town neighbors gather at this
BYO American for "excellent, homemade" "Old Baltimore
comfort food" in the "basement" of a former theater with
a "great Hampden look and feel"; regulars hail its quiet,
relaxed nature, Wednesday "lobster night" special and
"fresh vegetable choices", but nitpickers knock the
"unappealing" setting and "slow" pace.

Mangia Mangia 🅂   16 | 16 | 17 | $21

834 S. Luzerne Ave. (Hudson St.), 410-534-8999
☑ Adventurous customers "play with the menu" at this
"cute" Canton Italian by mixing and matching pastas and
sauces or designing their own brick-oven pizzas, while
the more cautious order "comfort"-food entrees; it's an
"interesting concept" that's "priced right", but "no value,
hon" to cynics who swipe at uneven "execution" and a
noisy "forced-fun environment", and dub the giant exterior
pasta mural its best creation.

Manley's Bistro 🅂   – | – | – | E

9065 Frederick Rd. (St. John's Ln.), Ellicott City,
410-480-2020
An Ellicott City commercial setting doesn't prevent instant
passage to Paris at this cozy spot where Keith Manley's
Contemporary French dishes like cassoulet Normandy are
paired with exotic desserts from Matthew Milani (ex White
House part-time pastry chef); N.B. hours and seating are
limited and the location is hard to find, so call ahead.

Manor Tavern 🅂   18 | 20 | 18 | $31

15819 Old York Rd. (Manor Rd.), Monkton,
410-771-8155
☑ "The horsey set" trots out to this tavern "deep in MD's
hunt country" to enjoy American-Continental classics in the
"romantic" "formal dining room" or to munch on "upscale
bar food by the fire" in the restaurant's casual, lower-priced
area; critics, however, complain that this "standby" is
"inconsistent" – while "occasionally excellent", it's more
often "not thoroughbred fare."

Marconi's   22 | 18 | 23 | $34

(aka Maison Marconi's)
106 W. Saratoga St. (bet. Cathedral St. & Park Ave.),
410-727-9522
☑ Baltimore's "grande dame of dining" upholds the "great
old standards" with classic Chesapeake and Continental
recipes that have been around since H. L. Mencken's time;
despite wisecracks about "embalming", it remains a
"uniquely Baltimorean" "landmark" Downtown replete with
"tuxedoed" waiters and a freshened up, "bright" setting.

Martick's 22 | 19 | 18 | $30

214 W. Mulberry St. (bet. Howard St. & Park Ave.), 410-752-5155

◪ While it's not "Old Paris", but rather Old Baltimore, this "quirky" French Bistro north of Downtown does have an air of Montmartre to it; lodged in a former speakeasy in a "tatty" part of town, it reflects the "incomparable" Morris Martick's "wonderful eccentricity in food and decor."

Matsuri [S] 25 | 18 | 21 | $22

1105 S. Charles St. (Cross St.), 410-752-8561

■ "Casual, friendly and hip", this South Baltimore Japanese packs a lot of "terrific" eating (some of "the best and freshest sushi", "great noodles", "tasty" combination plates and bento boxes) into one small space; on weekends, even its "quick and competent" crew can't always keep up with the crowds, but at least customers can kill time while they wait by checking out the "sumo wrestling on the tube."

McCabe's [S] 20 | 12 | 19 | $22

3845 Falls Rd. (41st St.), 410-467-1000

■ "Thick, juicy" burgers, "the best crab cakes" and "divine bread pudding" are among the "great home-cooked comfort foods" served up at this "cozy" "drop-in" pub in Hampden that attracts a real "cross-section" of the population; but shh! – locals "hate to praise" their "perfect tavern" as "it's crowded enough" already.

McCafferty's [S] 21 | 20 | 20 | $35

1501 Sulgrave Ave. (Newbury St.), 410-664-2200

■ "Beef is king" at this "manly steakhouse for sports fans" in Mount Washington that guys and dating couples alike "love" for the strong drinks, "prime beef" and "outstanding burgers"; but while most are drawn to its "dark, warm and comfortable" surroundings, fine bar and "collection of memorabilia", a few detractors can't get beyond the "noise" and "uneven" service.

MCCORMICK & SCHMICK'S [S] 22 | 21 | 21 | $35

Pier 5 Hotel, 711 Eastern Ave. (President St.), 410-234-1300

See review in Washington, DC Directory.

Mezzanotte [S] 21 | 18 | 20 | $26

4844 Butler Rd. (bet. Central & Railroad Aves.), Glyndon, 410-526-5711

Cafe Mezzanotte [S]

760 Ritchie Hwy. (south of W. McKinsey Rd.), Severna Park, 410-647-1100

■ Outer Baltimore dwellers are delighted to find these outlets for "creative", "yummy" Italian food in their own backyards: in Glyndon, the "very fresh" fare makes this "neighborhood restaurant" one of the "best of its kind", while in Severna Park the "great recipes" and "lovely decor" have diners wanting to "go back again" and again.

Michael's Cafe [S] 17 | 15 | 17 | $26

2119 York Rd. (Timonium Rd.), Timonium, 410-252-2022

◪ A "gathering place that's cheaper than a dating service", this sprawling Timonium sports bar is where thirtysomething singles crowd in for the "noisy" "happy-hour scene"; while it's "not gourmet dining", some claim this "local hangout" has "great crab cakes", though many find it too "smoky" to tell; N.B. they've added a patio.

Milltowne Tavern [S] 19 | 17 | 19 | $27

3733 Old Columbia Pike (Main St.), Ellicott City, 410-480-0894

◪ Housed in an 1860s-era building, this stone-walled American grill located on Ellicott City's historic Taylor's Row offers "fine, if not sublime", food and a "nice atmosphere", making it a "good" spot to order some crab cakes while hunting for antiques nearby.

MILTON INN [S] 25 | 27 | 24 | $48

14833 York Rd. (3 mi. north of Shawan Rd.), Sparks, 410-771-4366

■ "Class and character" plus "excellent" regional American fare with Continental touches proffered in an 18th-century "*Masterpiece Theatre*" manor setting sum up this "special-occasion" mecca in North Baltimore County; though it's "expensive", few places anywhere can match its "romantic" ambiance and most laud the owners (of the Brass Elephant and King's Contrivance renown) for "improving" its "quality"; P.S. the $30 dinner prix fixe Sundays–Fridays makes it possible to dine here without taking out a "bank loan."

Minato [S] 20 | 17 | 17 | $22

800 N. Charles St. (Madison St.), 410-332-0332

■ "We love this place" rave fans of this subterranean Japanese in Mount Vernon that serves some of the "best sushi in town", as well as numerous Vietnamese dishes; however, proving the adage that you can't please 'em all, a few complain that the menu provides "too many options" and service can be uneven.

Morning Edition Cafe [S] 23 | 18 | 15 | $17

153 N. Patterson Park Ave. (Fayette St.), 410-732-5133

■ "Bring a friend, a snack and a book" to occupy you during the long "wait" to get seated at this too popular, "fantastic brunch" spot north of Highlandtown that serves "homemade breads", muffins like "you can't make at home" and "great omelets"; fans enjoy the laid-back, "funky" ambiance (inside, that is – the neighborhood's not much to speak of) and cheer that this "Vermontesque" "find" is "such a cool place to eat."

MORTON'S OF CHICAGO [S] 25 | 22 | 23 | $51

Sheraton Inner Harbor Hotel, 300 S. Charles St. (Conway St.), 410-547-8255

See review in Washington, DC Directory.

Mt. Washington Tavern S   14 | 16 | 14 | $24
5700 Newbury St. (Sulgrave Ave.), 410-367-6903
◪ Perennially packed, this "local watering hole" offers a "good burger" and "raw bar fun"; detractors, though, say "it's better for spirits than for food" and complain vocally about the noise level ("loud, loud, loud!") and "drunken yuppie" clientele (the "J. Crew alumni club").

Mughal Garden S   22 | 17 | 20 | $20
920 N. Charles St. (bet. Eager & Read Sts.), 410-547-0001
◼ "You get your money's worth" at this Downtown Indian, whether you go for the "wonderful lunch buffet" and its cornucopia of choices or bring a "large group" of hungry friends for a "big-scale" feast; furthermore, the "attentive" treatment in surroundings "so velvety they're over the top" make dining here a "stress-reducer."

Nacho Mama's ●S   20 | 18 | 16 | $18
2907 O'Donnell St. (Linwood Ave.), 410-675-0898
◼ An "Elvis shrine" (literally), this "funky" Canton Mexican offers "rockin'" good times and "awesome", "cheap" chow (in "huge portions"), with "zany" touches like "chips in a hubcap"; while the place "has fun written all over it" for twentysomethings who "expect to wait for a precious table", some of their elders opt against eating amid the "kids and noise"; P.S. check out the collection of National Bohemian "paraphernalia" as you "drink a Natty Boh."

New No Da Ji S   17 | 12 | 16 | $17
2501 N. Charles St. (25th St.), 410-235-4846
◪ Starving students reach "all-you- can-stuff-in heaven" at this Korean-Japanese on North Charles Street that offers a "sushi smorgasbord" and Seoul food specialties; the "acid-flashback" decor and "interesting people-watching" are side benefits, especially on karaoke night.

New Towne Diner ●S   15 | 13 | 16 | $14
11316 Reisterstown Rd. (High Falcon Rd.), Owings Mills, 410-654-0066
◪ It's like a "*Diner* [the movie] reunion" at this "authentic-looking" Owings Mills retro spot where much of Northwest Baltimore brings their kids for chocolate milk shakes or "inexpensive" meals; critics, however, complain about "blah" food and add that the "staff has a bad attitude."

Nichi Bei Kai S   20 | 17 | 19 | $28
1524 York Rd. (Seminary Ave.), Lutherville, 410-321-7090
Columbia Mktpl., 9400 Snowden River Pkwy. (Oakland Mills Rd.), Columbia, 410-381-5800
◪ "Watching" "the chefs in action" at these separately owned suburban Japanese steakhouses is "half the fun (but watch out for the flying knives)"; but even though the "hibachi grill" "entertainment" can be "good theater", the more discriminating yawn "same old, same old."

Nick's Inner Harbor Seafood S   22 | 15 | 18 | $17
Cross St. Mkt., 1065 S. Charles St. (Cross St.),
410-685-2020
■ "All walks of Baltimore mix" at this Cross Street Market seafood stall for oysters, "great sushi" and steamed shrimp; a "gem" – *the* "place to be in Federal Hill" on Saturday afternoons – free of decor and amenities, it nevertheless possesses loads of atmosphere and always retains its "down-home feel."

Noodles Corner S   23 | 18 | 21 | $15
Lakeside Shopping Ctr., 8865 Stanford Blvd. (Dobbin Rd.),
Columbia, 410-312-0088
■ This "urban noodle house in a suburban strip mall" in Columbia pleases families and a laptop-and-briefcase-toting lunch crowd alike with an "amazing variety" of Asian-accented appetizers, soups and stir-fries that are "good, fast and cheap"; while one or two find some dishes "bland" and disparage the "spartan" interior, even critics end up "going often."

Obrycki's S   22 | 16 | 19 | $30
1727 E. Pratt St. (bet. Ann St. & Broadway),
410-732-6399
◪ Tie on a bib and dig into a pile of steamed crabs in season at this East Baltimore "standard-bearer" where the natives say nix to the "strange" "black-pepper spice" on their crustaceans ("leave that for the tourists") but concede that it serves "good crab cakes and shrimp", "fresh fish" and can't-miss chowder; even so, critics crab about the rather "expensive" tabs and the "busy, loud" "Colonial Williamsburg" setting; N.B. closed in winter.

Ocean Pride S   17 | 10 | 16 | $23
1534 York Rd. (Seminary Ave.), Lutherville, 410-321-7744
◪ "Convenient for a neighborhood crab fix" in Lutherville, this "plain seafood" house is "consistent" ("no better, no worse every year"), if not inspired; with vinyl seats and waterproof floors, it's "a great place for kids", but naysayers complain the kitchen "deep-fries everything" and advise "go for the steamed crabs only."

Olive & Sesame S   22 | 15 | 17 | $23
1500 Reisterstown Rd. (Old Court Rd.), Pikesville,
410-484-7787
■ Pikesville's "outstanding" (though "nondescript") choice for "delicious and healthy" Chinese, sushi and Japanese grilled items is this "neighborhood" newcomer that also offers a few Mediterranean dishes (hence the Olive in its name); but the popularity of this "little shopping center place" has a downside: on "busy nights" customers are often "jammed cheek by jowl" and the service can suffer.

Olive Grove [S] — | — | — | I

705 N. Hammonds Ferry Rd. (Nursery Rd.), Linthicum, 410-636-1385

"Fabulous" "unlimited salads", "huge crab cakes" and Italian-Greek specialties offered at "reasonable prices" keep this Linthicum roadhouse located near a Beltway warehouse park hopping; plus, it's expanded so much (they've recently remodeled the banquet room) that it can now "hold large parties" without feeling "mobbed."

One World Cafe [S] 17 | 17 | 14 | $13

904 S. Charles St. (Henrietta St.), 410-234-0235
100 W. University Pkwy. (N. Charles St.), 410-235-5777

■ Gen X-ers "hang, make new friends and eat well" at this pair of "inviting" coffeehouses with a "veggie outlook" that cooks up "cheap, tasty, healthy" food and "sinful desserts"; the South Baltimore flagship is counter-service only and tends toward the "funky", while the newer Homewood branch across from the Johns Hopkins campus is housed in a mod, "great space" tended to by a "disorganized but willing" staff; N.B. both venues have pool tables.

OPA! [S] 19 | 16 | 19 | $26

1911 Aliceanna St. (Wolfe St.), 410-522-4466

◪ The Hellenic tradition of hospitality can be found on the east side of "trendy" Fells Point at this "authentic" spot where the "owners welcome each table like family" and serve "good, fresh fish" and the "best lamb chops in town"; but the hard-to-please rate it "an also-ran in the Greek sweepstakes", citing "nothing special."

Orchard Market Cafe [S] 25 | 19 | 22 | $23

8815 Orchard Tree Ln. (E. Joppa Rd.), Towson, 410-339-7700

■ "Excellent Persian food" blossoms in an "unpretentious" setting at this east of Towson Middle Eastern where "lovely, unusual taste sensations", the "gracious" hospitality of a "wonderful family" and "attractive", "exotic" surroundings come together to give diners the "experience" of Iran; but "don't let the name fool you" – the "strip mall" in which this "find" is located "is no orchard"; P.S. its BYO policy means you can get a "terrific meal for a few $$."

OREGON GRILLE [S] 25 | 26 | 23 | $48

1201 Shawan Rd. (Beaver Dam Rd.), Hunt Valley, 410-771-0505

◪ In a tony, "clublike" Hunt Valley setting, chef Mark Henry "wows" "Baltimore bigwigs" and "hardcore yuppies" with some of the area's "best steaks", as well as "top-notch", "creative" regional American cuisine, all enhanced by "exceptional" wines and "pampering" service; though most "welcome" its "jacket-required" "formality", "magnificent bar" and "beautiful" terrace dining, dissenters find it too "upper-crusty" and balk at the "obscene" prices.

Orient 🅂
18 | 14 | 18 | $21

319 York Rd. (Chesapeake Ave.), Towson, 410-296-9000
■ A Towson "standby" with "above-average Chinese food" and a "great sushi bar", this "family-friendly" spot offers "big portions" of "predictable" standards (including "very nice lunch specials") in "plain", "casual" surroundings.

OUTBACK STEAKHOUSE 🅂
19 | 15 | 18 | $24

Perry Hall Sq., 4215 Ebenezer Rd. (Belair Rd.), 410-529-7200
Tollgate Plaza, 615 Belair Rd. (Rte. 24), Bel Air, 410-893-0110
Target Shopping Ctr., 4420 Long Gate Pkwy. (St. John's Ln.), Ellicott City, 410-480-0472
134 Shawan Rd. (McCormick Rd.), Hunt Valley, 410-527-1540
See review in Washington, DC Directory.

Owl Bar ●🅂
16 | 22 | 17 | $24

The Belvedere, 1 E. Chase St. (N. Charles St.), 410-347-0888
☑ "The atmosphere is palpable" at Baltimore's "most beautiful bar", a "not-to-be-missed" "landmark" in Mount Vernon's old Belvedere hotel that's now a "loud" "yuppie hangout"; go for its legendary "yard of beer" and a sense of history, but if you're hungry "stick to the brick-oven pizzas", as the rest of the casual, mostly American eats are merely "mediocre."

Panera Bread 🅂
22 | 17 | 17 | $12

The Mall in Columbia, 10300 Little Patuxent Pkwy. (Broken Land Pkwy.), Columbia, 410-730-9666
Woodholme Sq., 1852 Reisterstown Rd. (Mt. Wilson Ln.), Owings Mills, 410-602-5125
Towson Mktpl., 1238 Putty Hill Ave. (Goucher Blvd.), Towson, 410-821-9111
See review in Washington, DC Directory.

Paolo's 🅂
19 | 19 | 18 | $26

Harborplace, 301 Light St. Pavilion (Pratt St.), 410-539-7060
1 W. Pennsylvania Ave. (York Rd.), Towson, 410-321-7000
See review in Washington, DC Directory.

Papermoon Diner ●🅂
17 | 21 | 16 | $15

227 W. 29th St. (Remington Ave.), 410-889-4444
☑ "John Waters' Baltimore meets Roland Park" at this "24/7" "replica of what used to be", all awash with "kitschy" "weirdness"; the mix of American comfort foods and healthy fare "varies" (the service is equally "unpredictable"), but it continues to draw "tongue-studded, dreadlocked, neo-hippie" types despite reports that it's gone "yuppie."

Paradiso 🅂
▽ 21 | 19 | 21 | $23

20 Distillery Dr. (Locust St.), Westminster, 410-876-1421
■ Though it may not actually be paradise, it's awfully "nice" to find a serious Southern Italian establishment in "out-of-the-way" Westminster; regulars who "stuff themselves" at this "affordable", "kid-friendly" wood-and-brass spot consider it one of the "best around."

Patrick's of Cockeysville 19 | 16 | 19 | $26
Cranbrook Shopping Ctr., 550 Cranbrook Rd. (1 mi. east of York Rd.), Cockeysville, 410-683-0604
◪ Chef Tomas Sanz (ex Tio Pepe) lends an occasional Iberian accent during special 'Spanish weeks' at this "nice neighborhood" seafood and steakhouse "geared for the suburban crowd" in Cockeysville; but critics find the "quality sporadic" and dismiss the "uninspiring" Chesapeake eats as mostly "diner food in a dining-room disguise."

Pazza Luna 23 | 22 | 19 | $37
1401 E. Clement St. (bet. Decatur & Hubert Sts.), 410-727-1212
◪ So many "garlic lovers" are over the moon about this "out-of-the-way" Locust Point Northern Italian that its "cutesy", lunar-themed quarters are usually "packed"; the appeal is obvious, with "Sinatra serenading" martini sippers at the bar and devotees devouring the "best osso buco" under the "stars" ("on the ceiling", that is) upstairs, but dissenters claim it has "suffered from its popularity."

Peppermill [S] – | – | – | M
1301 York Rd. (Greenridge Rd.), Lutherville, 410-583-1107
Surprisingly good American "standards" "pack in the seniors" (the "60-year-olds are the kids" quips one whippersnapper) for dinner at this office tower north of Towson; by day, lawyers, business folks and ladies-who-lunch flock here as well for the "value"-priced food.

Perring Place [S] 19 | 12 | 19 | $21
2305 Cleanleigh Dr. (bet. McClean Blvd. & Perring Pkwy.), 410-661-0630
■ "The Eveready battery" of "good", casual" local dining, this North Baltimore old-timer is still "going strong" after more than three decades; get ready for "wonderful crab cakes" and other Traditional American eats, dished up in a "warm, comfy joint" that feels like "someone's house."

PETER'S INN ⊘ 26 | 17 | 20 | $19
504 S. Ann St. (Eastern Ave.), 410-675-7313
■ "Arrive early" or "wait" at this idiosyncratic "little hole-in-the-wall" in Fells Point with just a handful of tables; its short, "ever-changing" Eclectic bill of fare includes "imaginative", "scrumptious" "pub, comfort and gourmet food" at "reasonable prices"; a few gripe that this hip "find" is "too smoky", but that suits the regulars just fine.

Petit Louis [S] – | – | – | E
4800 Roland Ave. (Upland Ave.), 410-366-9393
A worldly uptown crowd fills Charleston's boisterous young sibling in the restored former Morgan-Millard in Roland Park for hearty Parisian bistro fare, matched by Tony Foreman's wine picks and delivered by suave servers; it's settling down to a smooth (but energetic) stride, with phone reservations and lunch (Tuesday–Friday).

P.F. Chang's China Bistro [S] | 21 | 21 | 18 | $25

Columbia Mall, 10300 Little Patuxent Pkwy. (Wincopin Circle), Columbia, 410-730-5344

See review in Washington, DC Directory.

Phillips [S] | 15 | 15 | 15 | $28

Harborplace, 301 Light St. Pavilion (Pratt St.), 410-685-6600

See review in Washington, DC Directory.

Pierpoint [S] | 24 | 16 | 20 | $37

1822 Aliceanna St. (bet. Ann & Wolfe Sts.), 410-675-2080

■ "Fells Point at its best" rave fans of chef-owner Nancy Longo's "hip, sophisticated" "small bistro with big seafood" flavor; expect "innovative", reinterpreted Maryland classics like smoked crab cakes and a "relaxing atmosphere", though some critics object to the "close" seating.

Pisces [S] | 25 | 25 | 22 | $37

Hyatt Regency Hotel, 300 Light St. (bet. Conway & Pratt Sts.), 410-605-2835

■ Take a "million-dollar" Inner Harbor vista and add "striking" decor, "consistently excellent" seafood and desserts, and a "personable" staff that makes diners feel like they're "on a cruise" and the result is a real "gem"; while admirers praise the "great fish, view and bar" at this largely "undiscovered" spot, cynics say they just can't escape the fact that they're "in a hotel."

Planet Hollywood [S] | 12 | 18 | 14 | $21

Harborplace, 201 E. Pratt St. (Light St.), 410-685-7827

See review in Washington, DC Directory.

POLO GRILL [S] | 26 | 25 | 24 | $47

Doubletree Inn at the Colonnade, 4 W. University Pkwy. (bet. Canterbury Rd. & N. Charles St.), 410-235-8200

■ "Baltimore's 'who's who'" and "new money" go to this "handsome" Homewood "public club" "to be seen", as well as to enjoy the "wonderful" American-Continental cooking ("great fried lobster tail") and "veteran" staff; some note the "serious $$" and "noise", but most would agree "if someone else is buying, I'm there!"; N.B. Michael Rork of Michael Rork's Town Dock in St. Michaels, will now be cooking here often.

Porter's [S] | – | – | – | M

1032 Riverside Ave. (E. Cross St.), 410-539-1999

The completely rebuilt Ransome's is now a buzzing but grown-up spot amidst quiet South Baltimore row houses focusing on ocean fare direct from co-owner Tom Fore's North Carolina seafood company; dishes like fresh shrimp in garlic sauce and roasted barbecue-sauced salmon draw outside-the-Beltway types as well as city dwellers, who fill up both the snug, clubby, art-filled dining room and the darker, more casual bar side.

Preston's 500 S   – | – | – | E
500 W. University Pkwy. (41st St.), 410-662-6030
"Excellent" New American creations mark this Roland
Park spot where the "interesting dishes" are served in an
"elegant but relaxing" ambiance; most find the "tasty" fare,
"nicely appointed" setting and "well-trained" staff make
for a "lovely dining experience."

PRIME RIB ● S   28 | 26 | 27 | $51
Horizon House, 1101 N. Calvert St. (Chase St.),
410-539-1804
■ Voted the Most Popular restaurant in the *Baltimore
Survey* (and ranked No. 2 among steakhouses), this
Downtown retro supper club with a "swank", big-city feel
proves that dressing up for a great evening of martinis, fine
wines and red meat has enduring appeal; while setting
"the standard" for beef and seafood (its crab dishes are as
notable as the signature prime rib), its "superior" service
and "'50s-era" "glamour" make any occasion truly "special."

Purim Oak S   ▽ 20 | 12 | 19 | $19
321 York Rd. (Chesapeake Ave.), Towson, 410-583-7770
■ "Do the buffet" at this Towson Asian, a "cheap", "tasty"
way to "learn about" the "healthy", varied cuisine of Korea
(but watch out – some dishes are "very hot"); the menu
highlights well-known Korean "favorites" that are so
"authentic" and interesting (like *bibimbop*) that you'll
barely notice the dark, plain surroundings; P.S. the buffet
also includes "lots of sushi" offerings.

Rallo's S   17 | 10 | 18 | $13
838 E. Fort Ave. (Lawrence St.), 410-727-7067
■ "A real South Baltimore dining experience" can be had
at this "'50s time warp" near Ft. McHenry, which serves
up "basic diner-style" "comfort foods" (including "lots of
fried stuff"); while the standout dishes include crab soup and
shrimp salad, it's also "fine for a fast sandwich at lunch."

Regi's S   17 | 18 | 17 | $23
1002 Light St. (Hamburg St.), 410-539-7344
◪ "Great for a pre–baseball game" meal in a "charming
Federal Hill" spot within walking distance of Camden
Yards (there's also a shuttle bus), this "neighborhood" bar
serves up "typical" American-Eclectic pub grub; though
regulars say it "always satisfies", critics complain that
"it's gone too upscale for its own good" and now suffers
from a "confused identity."

Ricciuti's S   ▽ 17 | 12 | 17 | $17
Hickory Ridge Ctr., 6420 Freetown Rd. (Cedar Ln., off Rte. 32),
Columbia, 410-531-0250
See review in Washington, DC Directory.

River Watch [S] 17 | 16 | 17 | $25
207 Nanticoke Rd. (Middleborough Rd.), Essex, 410-687-1422
■ "Summertime fun" beckons at this "neighborhood seafood place" "right on the water" in Essex, where the crowds come to eat steamed crabs, drink beer and watch the boats from the outdoor deck, as well as to listen to live bands; thanks to its "fresh", "reasonably priced" fare and active bar scene, it keeps hoppin' year-round.

Rothwell's [S] 20 | 16 | 19 | $30
106 W. Padonia Rd. (York Rd.), Timonium, 410-252-0600
◪ Some of the "best steaks in the suburbs" are cooked up at this "hidden jewel" located in a Timonium strip mall gush "meat-loving" fans who find it a "consistently pleasant" "local spot" for regional American fare; others sigh they "just can't get excited about this place."

Ruby Lounge 22 | 21 | 20 | $28
Park Plaza Bldg., 802 N. Charles St. (Madison St.), 410-539-8051
■ "Dress up" and "sip a martini" at this "Hollywood-mod" supper club featuring a "creative" Eclectic menu that "surfs trends" and is "nice for the price"; given the "artsy" "paintings" on its walls, this "hip space" is right at home in Mount Vernon's "cultural district", while the occasional rudeness make "NYC guests" feel right at home.

RUDYS' 2900 [S] 27 | 22 | 25 | $42
2900 Baltimore Blvd. (Rte. 91), Finksburg, 410-833-5777
■ "Way, way out" in Finksburg, this Continental-American has cultivated a discriminating coterie that's willing to make the trip to enjoy the "consistent" excellence of the "Rudy and Rudi twosome" (chef-owner Rudy Speckamp cooks up "inspired" "gourmet and regional favorites" that please both "steak-and-potato guys" and lovers of haute cuisine, while co-owner Rudi Paul provides "great personal attention"); though it has a "nice country ambiance", it could possibly use a third Rudy to do some "redecorating."

Rusty Scupper [S] 15 | 20 | 16 | $29
402 Key Hwy. (Covington St.), 410-727-3678
◪ Boasting a "spectacular" view across the harbor to Downtown Baltimore, this "attractive" maritime site near Federal Hill is a major tourist draw; locals favor its "sunny terrace" for drinks or brunch, since with few exceptions the American seafood dishes are "just average"; P.S. optimists hope that the chef's addition of trend-smart dishes to the family-friendly menu is a sign that the food will "improve."

RUTH'S CHRIS STEAK HOUSE [S] 25 | 23 | 23 | $47
1777 Reisterstown Rd. (Hooks Ln.), Pikesville, 410-837-0033
600 Water St. (bet. Gay St. & Market Pl.), 410-783-0033
See review in Washington, DC Directory.

Sabatino's ◐ [S] | 18 | 15 | 20 | $27 |

901 Fawn St. (S. High St.), 410-727-9414

◪ "We love Sabs!" cheer fans of "one of Little Italy's most popular Italians", where the staff "can handle anything", including the "vivid late-night characters" who (together with its famed Bookmaker's salad and garlic bread) are its major attraction; but while admirers of this "cornerstone" rave about the "best eggplant parmigiana", detractors retort it's a "tourist trap" that's a "Teflon all the way."

Saigon [S] ▽ | 24 | 7 | 21 | $15 |

3345 Belair Rd. (Erdman Ave.), 410-276-0055

■ The place for "phenomenal" *pho* is this plain Vietnamese in Northeast Baltimore, where a "warm family" serves patrons a "wide variety" of its native dishes; it's a "real" experience and a "great value", though a few feel they've "watered down" the flavors "to suit American tastes."

Samos ⊄ | 25 | 9 | 19 | $15 |

600 S. Oldham St. (Fleet St.), 410-675-5292

■ Voted the top Greek restaurant in this *Survey*, this corner eatery serves an "enormous variety" of "authentic" dishes (plus some American eats) at prices that make it "value-driven eating"; good news: owner Nick Georgales and his "friendly" crew gained "some breathing room" with a recent expansion and renovation (not yet reflected in the above decor rating).

Sander's Corner [S] | 15 | 16 | 17 | $17 |

2260 Cromwell Bridge Rd. (Loch Raven Dr.), Glen Arm, 410-825-5187

◪ "Go for breakfast" on the "lovely" outdoor deck of this old-fashioned Glen Arm American and get treated to an "eye-opening view" of Loch Raven woods; even though the cooking (and interior) "never quite lives up to expectations", it can provide a "nice" dessert break while biking or hiking.

San Sushi [S] | 22 | 14 | 19 | $22 |

9832 York Rd. (Padonia Rd.), Timonium, 410-453-0140

San Sushi Too [S]

10 W. Pennsylvania Ave. (York Rd.), Towson, 410-825-0908

◪ While the Towson branch "fulfills either a sushi or Thai mood" with "good" fish and rice creations, as well as "fiery", "fabulous" Siamese fare, the newly expanded Timonium spot focuses on Japanese fare, sushi and Sam Sesum's treatment of the day's fresh seafood.

Sascha's 527 | – | – | – | M |

527 N. Charles St. (Centre St.), 410-539-8880

Veteran Baltimore caterer Sascha Wolhandler's swank, historic Mount Vernon ex-beauty salon (it served as a movie set for the film *Diner*) with dimly lit, romantic tables has found a following for the Eclectic kitchen's wide-ranging dishes, from portobello fries to seafood bisque.

Scotto's Cafe 🅂   ▽ 24 | 20 | 21 | $26
5 Bel Air S. Pkwy. (Rte. 24), Bel Air, 410-515-2233
■ "Fine [Northern] Italian cooked by the owner shines amid the malls and chains" on the fast-growing Route 24 corridor in Bel Air; the kitchen's consistently "excellent", "great-value" dishes earn "three cheers" from locals, who find the understated ambiance "kind of sexy", even if "looking over a shopping center" can be "a downer."

Shogun 🅂   24 | 16 | 21 | $26
316 N. Charles St. (Saratoga St.), 410-962-1130
◪ Pioneering the local sushi craze, this "stark" Downtown Japanese slices some of the "freshest", most "authentic" raw fish rolls, while also preparing "great" *shabu-shabu, shu mai* and other "varied" dishes that attract "students and poor academics"; admirers "love" the "little" tatami room and the "reasonable" prices.

Shula's Steak House 🅂   20 | 17 | 19 | $40
Wyndham Baltimore Inner Harbor Hotel, 101 W. Fayette St. (bet. Charles & Liberty Sts.), 410-385-6601
◪ At Don Shula's "clubby" Downtown "carnivore cavern", the "personable" waiters pass around the "menu on a football", contributing to a convivial atmosphere that's "extra-special for sports fans" and "great for groups"; brace yourself for the "amazing girth of the steaks", but also note that detractors beef it's too "expensive" and that "taste is secondary to size" here.

Silver Dinner ●🅂   13 | 14 | 14 | $15
Towson Towne Ctr., 825 Dulaney Rd. (Fairmount Ave.), Towson, 410-823-5566
See review in Washington, DC Directory.

Simon's Pub   ▽ 23 | 19 | 21 | $19
2031 E. Fairmount Ave. (Chester St.), 410-522-4477
■ "Hard to find" in a "rough" part of Butchers Hill near Hopkins Hospital is one of Baltimore's most "inviting" little "neighborhood pubs", featuring "cool bartenders" who'll quench your thirst with a "great beer selection" and a truly "creative" kitchen that turns out carefully crafted American bar eats, along with "imaginative specials", for a "few" lucky tables.

Sisson's 🅂   – | – | – | M
36 E. Cross St. (bet. Charles & Light Sts.), 410-539-2093
The new owners have kept the name and microbrews, but this old marketplace South Baltimore bar is all grown-up now, with a calm, exposed-brick dining room where couples linger over seafood dishes, steaks and prime ribs at direct-from-the-ranch prices that undersell their national beefery competitors.

Sly Horse Tavern [S] ▽ 22 | 22 | 22 | $26

1678 Village Green (Clubhouse Gate Rd.), Crofton, 410-721-4550

■ Crofton dwellers are proud of this "local hideaway" reminiscent of "a Civil War tavern" and insist it's "worth" the trip despite its "off-the-beaten-path" location between Baltimore and Annapolis; a "rare find", it serves Traditional American fare in such comfortable surroundings that it's "like dining in your own living room with a private chef."

SoBo Cafe [S] 20 | 17 | 16 | $16

6 W. Cross St. (S. Charles St.), 410-752-1518

■ "Hip" art on the walls and "hipsters" at the tables form quite a contrast with the kitchen's updated American comfort cooking (don't miss "Baltimore's best" chicken pot pie) at this "funky", "cheap" South Baltimore haunt; even if it's "easy to be ignored" by the laid-back servers, the eats and the vibes are so "good" that they're "reasons" alone to "live in the neighborhood."

Sotto Sopra [S] 23 | 23 | 21 | $38

405 N. Charles St. (Mulberry St.), 410-625-0534

■ This fashionably dark Charles Street Italian has settled down to serve "wonderful pastas" and "osso buco to die for" in a quiet, "sophisticated" setting evocative of the street's grand days.

Spike & Charlie's [S] 22 | 20 | 19 | $36

1225 Cathedral St. (Preston St.), 410-752-8144

■ Where would the "symphony and opera set" be without this "arty, tasteful" and "creative" New American?; with its "stylish" menu and "great" wines, it's just the place for pre- or post-show dining; as the "mother ship" of a convoy of modern eateries in the area (Atlantic, Joy America Cafe, Vespa), it's hanging in there, even if a few find it a bit "cold."

Sunset ◐ [S] 18 | 19 | 19 | $26

625 Greenway Ave. (Aquahart Rd.), Glen Burnie, 410-768-1417

■ "A throwback to '50s- and '60s-style eating", this Glen Burnie American "longtimer" still draws crowds that come for everything "from business lunches to anniversary" celebrations; the "jaded" may think the decor's "tiresome", but loyalists like that it's "wonderfully old-fashioned."

Sushi Hana [S] 24 | 18 | 22 | $23

6 E. Pennsylvania Ave. (York Rd.), Towson, 410-823-0372

■ "Uniquely Japanese", this "wonderful little place" in Towson is renowned for "excellent everything" (especially the "outstanding sushi", of course), "delicately" prepared and "prettily" presented by "very kind and patient" servers; a "relaxing" spot to dine in, it also offers "great carryout."

Sushi-Ya [S] 21 | 15 | 20 | $21
Valley Ctr., 9616 Reisterstown Rd. (Greenspring Valley Rd.), Owings Mills, 410-356-9995
■ Ideally located in Owings Mills' 'pink mall' for those seeking a respite after shopping or a movie is this "serene" Japanese offering "high-quality" sushi; the "friendly" and "accommodating" staff further helps make it an eatery that's "unusually good for a mall."

Suzie's Soba [S] 20 | 17 | 18 | $18
1009 W. 36th St. (Roland Ave.), 410-243-0051
◪ At her "creative" noodle nook, Suzie adds an "interesting" Japanese-Korean twist to Hampden's dining possibilities, offering soups, stir-fries, sushi and other "good stuff"; yet while her followers consider it a "fun" option, dissenters find the chow "bland" and the service "snail-paced."

Szechuan 21 | 13 | 20 | $18
1125 S. Charles St. (Cross St.), 410-752-8409
■ "Always fresh, good and spicy", this South Baltimore Chinese "never disappoints" because the "energetic folks" who run it consistently produce "incredible" egg rolls, "great" *moo shu* pork and "the best" *kung pao* chicken; it's "cheap and quick" and you can carry out – enough said.

Szechuan Best [S] 23 | 12 | 19 | $18
8625 Liberty Rd. (Old Court Rd.), Randallstown, 410-521-0020
■ While the multiregional Chinese menu at this "homey" Randallstown staple is "broad" enough to "suit everyone", the dishes that really draw in an "Asian clientele" are the Cantonese and Beijing-style specialties (notably "delicious" Peking duck), as well as the "terrific" weekend dim sum; ask the "friendly" waiters about these "authentic" options or "just point" at what looks good – it's all a "great value."

Szechuan House [S] 22 | 15 | 21 | $19
Galleria Towers, 1427 York Rd. (Seminary Ave.), Lutherville, 410-825-8181
■ "They try hard" at this "plain room" in Lutherville (north of Towson) by serving some of the area's "freshest, best Chinese cooking" and by providing nice touches like "hot towels", which help elevate it above many other spots; other pluses: the "fast kitchen and friendly servers"; N.B. a new expansion should ease the prime-time crunch.

Tapas Teatro ◑ [S] – | – | – | M
1711 N. Charles St. (Lanvale St.), 410-332-0110
The popular Helmand's new sibling just above the train station is a cool pre- or post-cinema scene tucked into the Charles Theater and spilling out to relaxed sidewalk tables (until the bridge re-opens); it's a great date spot for sampling Med dishes like paellas, hot and cold tapas, and cardamom vanilla ice cream with mango, figs and dates; N.B. it's best to park in the garage across the street.

Ten-O-Six [S] | 22 | 15 | 18 | $30

1006 Light St. (E. Hamburg St.), 410-528-2146

■ "Chef-owner Thomas Chungsakoon scores big" in South Baltimore with his menu mix of fancy country-club Continental classics and "excellent" Thai renditions, pulling in an equally diverse clientele; what's lacking in decor (and space) is compensated by "wonderful" dishes that are a "feast for the eye", but a couple of doubters warn about the "erratic" service.

TERSIGUEL'S [S] | 26 | 24 | 24 | $43

8293 Main St. (Old Columbia Pike), Ellicott City, 410-465-4004

■ In a "charming old Ellicott City" townhouse, Fernand Tersiguel and his family run the top-rated Gallic in the Baltimore area, serving Country French classics like Châteaubriand ("one of the best around"), seasonal specials and well-chosen wines in an "inviting, warm" setting evocative of a "fine inn" in France; but despite the proprietor's "watchful" eye, some say it's "inconsistent."

Thai [S] | 25 | 15 | 21 | $19

3316-18 Greenmount Ave. (33rd St.), 410-889-6002

■ Though many wish Baltimore's "best Thai" was in a "better location", they willingly "brave" the pilgrimage to this recently renovated Waverly storefront (now with new owners) for the "smooth curries", "fabulous lamb and squid" and other tongue-tinglers from its extensive menu; it's not much to look at, but the people are "pleasant" and you can "eat well for a moderate price."

Thai Landing | 23 | 16 | 21 | $21

1207 N. Charles St. (Biddle St.), 410-727-1234

■ "Convenient to the symphony" and galleries, this Mount Vernon Thai has its many fans disputing whether "the service is the best thing" about it or if it's the kitchen's "excellent" "turn-on-the-heat" cooking (decor clearly lags third); Charlie, the ever-popular waiter, and the rest of the staff "really want you to enjoy" your meal and though it's "always packed", it somehow never feels too crowded.

Thai Orient [S] | 17 | 16 | 17 | $22

Valley Ctr., 9616-I Reisterstown Rd. (Greenspring Valley Rd.), Owings Mills, 410-363-3488

■ Extensively decorated and housed in a "pleasant setting" "in suburbia", this Asian alternative is "a good place to take the parents", as it "tries to please" "many different palates" with a nice "combination of Thai and Chinese"; located in Owings Mills' 'pink mall', it's a "great" stop "before or after the movies."

That's Amore [S] | 18 | 16 | 18 | $25

720 Kenilworth Dr. (Bosley Ave.), Towson, 410-825-5255

See review in Washington, DC Directory.

Timber Creek Tavern 🗢 ▽ 19 | 15 | 18 | $22
10092 Belair Rd./Rte. 1 (Miller Rd.), Kingsville,
410-529-7999
■ Tucked away in Kingsville on US Route 1, this "outdoorsy-looking" turn-of-the-century "roadhouse next to the forest" at Gunpowder State Park's trail entrance is handy "after a hike"; a "comfy" local bar, it serves up "good", Traditional American eats, but it can get "too smoky" and "noisy."

Timbuktu 🗢 – | – | – | M
1726 Dorsey Rd. (Rte. 100), Hanover, 410-796-0733
Its exotic name notwithstanding, this Greek-American steak and seafooder, a "between-planes treat" near BWI Airport, is an "old-fashioned" spot where "all types of people" come for lunch or after church for the "excellent crab cakes" and other simple crowd-pleasers; N.B. it's very tricky to find, so call ahead for directions.

TIO PEPE 🗢 25 | 22 | 23 | $42
10 E. Franklin St. (bet. Charles & St. Paul Sts.),
410-539-4675
☑ Perennially popular, this Downtown Spanish-Continental with an "underground mystique" (it's housed in a "noisy cellar") is a "happy-occasion" fiesta for many aficionados, who "go back" (and back) for "excellent" paella, suckling pig and other "rich", "decadent" dishes (not to mention "don't-miss sangria"); but despite the atmospherics and the "professional service", lots of complaints surface about the "ridiculous" "waits, even with reservations", as well as the feeling that "rudeness rules" if you're not a regular.

Tomato Palace 🗢 17 | 16 | 17 | $19
10221 Wincopin Circle (Rte. 175), Columbia,
410-715-0211
■ Whimsically decorated and kid-friendly, this tongue-in-cheek Columbia Italian packs in the crowds with its "really good" brick-oven pizzas, plus pastas, panini and salads – all "hearty", "fast" and "cheap" affairs that come with a "great" lakeside view from the patio; it may be "noisy", but regulars rely on it as a "tried-and-true haven."

Towne Hall ●🗢 – | – | – | E
Greenspring Station, 2360 W. Joppa Rd. (Falls Rd.),
Brooklandville, 410-339-6300
At the rebuilt ex-Harvey's at Greenspring Station, Cal Ripken teams with other investors to produce an affordable New American with a menu ranging from the sophisticated (horseradish-crusted salmon) to bar bites (burgers, steamed shrimp); toss in a jazz brunch and courtyard dining and it's clear they hope this county crossroads will serve as all things to all locals.

Towson Diner ●S   15 | 15 | 16 | $16

718 York Rd. (Bosley Ave.), Towson, 410-321-0407

■ "By diner standards", this recently rebuilt Towson landmark "does its job well", providing "great breakfasts", "mom's fast food", "mile-high pies" and "interesting" characters around the clock; but a few purists gripe that it's too clean, "shiny" and "comfy" to be the real thing.

TRATTORIA ALBERTO   26 | 18 | 23 | $47

1660 Crain Hwy. S. (Underpass Rte. 100), Glen Burnie, 410-761-0922

☑ Stuck in an "old strip mall" in Glen Burnie, this "special-occasion" Northern Italian staffed by "tuxedoed waiters" delivers "inspired cooking" (the "homemade gnocchi" is "superb"), but many warn that the "ridiculous prices" may "make you expire" (particularly the "too $$$ specials"); whether it's "worth it" will have to be your call.

Velleggia's S   18 | 17 | 19 | $28

829 E. Pratt St. (Albemarle St.), 410-685-2620

☑ Expect "red sauce on everything" at this "longtime Little Italy establishment", which the faithful insist still dishes up "satisfactory Neapolitan dishes" suitable for "familiar family dining"; those less sentimental, however, say "beware" – the "glory days" of this "tourist trap" are over.

Vespa   23 | 19 | 20 | $25

1117-21 S. Charles St. (Cross St.), 410-385-0355

■ "Not your mama's Italian", this "happening" South Baltimore neighborhood bistro is where the young and hungry go for "creative" cooking, "fantastic vino" and a "lively atmosphere"; plus, there's "ambiance galore" in the "sleek" room, adding up to "dollar for dollar" one of "the best dining values" around.

Viccino Bistro S   23 | 18 | 20 | $34

1317 N. Charles St. (Mt. Royal Ave.), 410-347-0349

■ Applauded by "symphony and opera" ticket-holders as a "delicious yet underrated" "find" north of Mount Vernon, this Eclectic bistro shines the spotlight on "interesting" fusion cuisine, delivered in a citified setting by an "energetic young staff"; it's sure to be busy "before a show" (when "service slows" down), but at other times it'll "always have an open table for you."

Vito's Cafe S   19 | 15 | 18 | $24

Scott's Corner Shopping Ctr., 10249 York Rd. (Warren Rd.), Cockeysville, 410-666-3100

■ "Good family fare" ("excellent brick-oven pizza") is the "simple" draw of this "neighborhood Italian" in Cockeysville; although foes deride the "predictable" menu, strip mall location, and "cranky"service, it's "priced right" and it's BYO.

Williamsburg Inn [S] | 20 | 19 | 20 | $29 |

11131 Pulaski Hwy. (Ebenezer Rd.), White Marsh, 410-335-3172

■ "My mother's favorite place to go on Mother's Day" is this "comfortable family restaurant", a "classic Old Baltimore" way station in White Marsh between Baltimore and Bel Air; its early-bird special of American standards attracts a seasoned crowd, but probably its biggest claim to fame is mixing "the best" "huge drinks" "in town for the money."

Windows [S] | 22 | 25 | 21 | $32 |

Renaissance Harborplace Hotel, 202 E. Pratt St. (bet. Calvert & South Sts.), 410-685-8439

■ "Remarkably good" New American cuisine, along with a "beautiful view of the Inner Harbor", makes this "lovely" hotel dining room a "Downtown power lunch scene" and since the staff "does a good job accommodating a diverse clientele", it's also an "elegant" choice for cocktails and soft music, "a quiet dinner" or a pleasant Sunday "brunch with weekend visitors."

Windows on the Bay [S] | – | – | – | M |

1402 Colony Rd. (Ft. Smallwood Rd.), Pasadena, 410-255-1413

For an "informal, friendly" respite, "people go out of their way" to this American seafood house set in a wooded Pasadena marina, where chef-owners Mark Morgan and Dennis Walz serve up their "fresh" cooking; P.S. the screened-in patio offers a "nice view" of the Patapsco River and sunsets over Rock Creek.

Woman's Industrial Exchange | 18 | 16 | 21 | $13 |

333 N. Charles St. (Pleasant St.), 410-685-4388

■ Perhaps "the last of the 19th-century crafts and baked-good shops", this "endangered" Downtown institution remains a genteel "haven for a quiet lunch" or breakfast at an "excellent" price; perhaps even more important than its "wholesome" American home cooking (think "chicken salad with tomato aspic and homemade pies") is its "nostalgic value", exemplified by waitresses who are older than your grandma ("be patient"), leading many loyalists to "hope it'll go on forever."

Woodfire [S] | – | – | – | M |

Park Plaza, 580P Ritchie Hwy. (McKinsey Rd.), Severna Park, 410-315-8100

"Despite its shopping center location", this slick Severna Park offshoot of Garry's Grill serves "large" portions of surprisingly delicious meats and fish cooked over its glowing namesake in an open kitchen, which makes the room "too smoky" for some, but the "great" service makes everyone breathe a little easier; cozy, dark booths foster quiet conversations, while the back bar hops with live music.

Ze Mean Bean Cafe 🅂   20 | 20 | 20 | $19 |
1739 Fleet St. (S. Ann St.), 410-675-5999
◼ Known for its Slavic "charm" and "cozy", cuddle-up comforts, this "quaint" Fells Point coffeehouse has blossomed into a real restaurant, turning out "delectable", "eclectic Eastern European–American" dishes that reflect "real care in preparation"; at nighttime, the ambiance is further enlivened by varied live music and the "kindness" of its young crew (and full liquor service).

Zorba's Bar & Grill ◗🅂   18 | 12 | 16 | $21 |
4710 Eastern Ave. (Oldham St.), 410-276-4484
◪ "Great" salads, "fresh" grilled fish and spit-roasted lamb or pork make it "worth the trip" to Greektown to join in on the fellowship and zesty eating found in a traditional "village" restaurant; a meal is "cheap" and filling, but note that there's not much ambiance.

Annapolis and the Eastern Shore

	F	D	S	C
Adam's Ribs [S]	20	12	18	$19

Eastport Shopping Ctr., 921C Chesapeake Ave. (Bay Ridge Ave.), Annapolis, 410-267-0064
169 Mayo Rd. (Old Solomon Rd.), Edgewater, 410-956-2995
■ BBQ fans give the thumbs up to the sweet, "excellent" slow-smoked ribs at this "unpretentious", "tasty but messy" duo; it's "casual and easy with kids" and offers meals that are like "home cooking – but someone else cleans up."

	F	D	S	C
Annie's Paramount Steak House [S] ▽	20	19	20	$30

500 Kent Narrows Way/Rte. 18 (Rte. 50, exit 42), Grasonville, 410-827-7103
◪ Surveyors are split over the wisdom of going out for "beef in the heart of seafood country", but many "locals" praise the "good"-value meals at this big Kent Narrows steakhouse ("if you can get in"); critics say "ok but no home run"; at least everyone agrees that the view is "pretty."

	F	D	S	C
Baines Southern Cuisine [S]	–	–	–	M

306 N. Talbot St. (Dodson Ave.), St. Michaels, 410-745-0783
Linwood Baines' novel idea – a down-home Southern eatery right on the main drag of ritzy St. Michaels – is sure to be a hit, with crowd-pleasing comfort foods that are hard to find anywhere: catfish, fried chicken, sweet potato pie and ribs grilled out back; his brother Harold's Orioles memorabilia decorates the walls.

	F	D	S	C
Bay Hundred [S]	–	–	–	M

6178 Tilghman Island Rd. (bridge over Knapps Narrows), Tilghman Island, 410-886-2126
By the drawbridge in Tilghman Island, outdoor tables on the dock afford a close eye on workboats unloading rockfish, crabs and oysters; some find their way into the Continental-Chesapeake dishes or show up as steamed crabs or fried oyster sandwiches; N.B. it's best to call ahead.

	F	D	S	C
Bistro St. Michaels [S] ▽	27	22	24	$37

403 S. Talbot St. (Mulberry St.), St. Michaels, 410-745-9111
■ Well-heeled visitors on an Eastern Shore retreat "love coming" to this "hip" St. Michaels bistro for seasonal fare like "perfectly cooked soft-shell crabs" and "wonderful", modern Continental dishes (with a seafood emphasis); make no mistake about it – this kitchen is serious, though that "dedication" has made it "one of the best" in town.

Blue Heron
– | – | – | E

236 Cannon St. (Cross St.), Chestertown, 410-778-0188
College profs, B&Bers and upscale locals flock to this
casual, bright dining room and patio located on a leafy
residential street in historic Chestertown for new twists
on traditional Eastern Shore–style fin fare; wallet-watchers,
though, find it a "little pricey" for their liking.

Cafe Normandie S
21 | 20 | 19 | $28

185 Main St. (Church Circle), Annapolis, 410-263-3382
☑ Appointed with a warming fireplace, this "comfy" Country
French alternative to Annapolis' "dockside lairs" is a "cozy"
bistro whose "interesting" crêpes, "home cooking" and
bon marché "early-bird deals" make for interesting Gallic
dining; but some report "variable" food and service.

Cantler's Riverside Inn S
22 | 16 | 19 | $23

458 Forest Beach Rd. (Brown's Wood Rd.), Annapolis,
410-757-1311
■ "Take a boat" to this "classic" waterfront seafood house
near Annapolis (it's hard to find by car and "parking's a
pain") for a "must"-try steamed crab experience in a
"beautiful" setting overlooking a wooded creek; opt to
dine out on the "wonderful" deck (kids never fail to be
entertained by the "crab shedding tanks") and you'll be
treated to a messy but "super" meal.

Carrol's Creek Cafe S
21 | 22 | 21 | $30

410 Severn Ave. (4th St.), Annapolis, 410-263-8102
■ Boasting a "marvelous view" of Annapolis harbor from
its waterside deck and window tables, this "festive" (or
"hectic") Eastport New American is a popular destination
for an alfresco brunch, cocktails at "sunset" or a dinner
composed of "great fish" and "terrific bread pudding";
though it attempts to be "accommodating", a few post
storm warnings about getting "stuck in the back room."

Chick & Ruth's Delly S
17 | 14 | 17 | $12

165 Main St. (Conduit St.), Annapolis, 410-269-6737
■ "Milk shakes with middies and magic tricks by the owner"
(Ted Levitt, son of the late Chick and Ruth), make this "old-
fashioned deli/diner" near the State House "a must"; with
a "ma-and-pa fast food" menu of breakfast goodies and
"decent sandwiches", it's "tacky, bustling" and truly "fun."

Columbia
– | – | – | E

28 S. Washington St. (Glenwood Ave.), Easton, 410-770-5172
Foodies come from afar for "excellent" dinners in Stephen
Mangasarian's one-man show: an art-filled 1795 grand
townhouse in Downtown Easton (he lives upstairs), where
the New American cooking with Yankee twists (Maine
lobster cakes) showcases his garden's herbs and local
farm and bay harvests in dishes such as roast lamb with
pistachio and raspberry sauce and Maryland crab cakes.

Corinthian S
22 | 23 | 20 | $36 |

Loews Annapolis Hotel, 126 West St. (Lafayette Ave.), Annapolis, 410-263-1299

☑ Candlelit "elegance" distinguishes this "upscale" New American hotel dining room as one of Annapolis' prime "special-occasion" spots, while during the "legislative season" it buzzes from breakfast onwards; but though its "stunning plates" strike many admirers as "very good", others "expected more", especially in the way of service (it "needs better management" and "more staffers").

Crab Claw S⌿
20 | 19 | 19 | $26 |

156 Mill St. (Talbot St.), St. Michaels, 410-745-2900

☑ Crabs and boats – the "quintessential" Eastern Shore pairing – make this waterside seafood house in St. Michaels a casual summertime "paradise" if you're in the mood to "join the crowds and crack crabs", "picnic-style" (there's more formal dining upstairs); "cheerful" service is included in "the package" too, though realists squawk about "too many tourists" and "screaming kids."

Davis' Pub S
▽ 18 | 14 | 18 | $16 |

400 Chester Ave. (4th St.), Annapolis, 410-268-7432

■ The "smoky" "little secret" of the Maritime Republic of Eastport is this wooden house bursting with "local sailor color" ("the people are the decor"); it's a "comfortable place to hang" with American seafood and "comfort" fare, but it's already "too small", so the gang hopes that the joint doesn't turn into a "tourist trap"; outdoor seating is available.

Double T Diner ◑S
15 | 13 | 17 | $14 |

12 Defense St. (West St.), Annapolis, 410-571-9070
See review in Baltimore Directory.

Fisherman's Inn S
20 | 20 | 21 | $26 |

3116 Main St. (Rte. 50), Grasonville, 410-827-8807

Crab Deck S
3116 Main St. (Rte. 50), Grasonville, 410-827-6666

☑ Even if some warn "don't go out of your way" to this "tourist place" in Grasonville, others think it's "a perfect stop on the way to Ocean City"; the inn "doesn't look like much fun from the outside", but inside it's filled with "interesting" nautical decor and it dishes up "old-fashioned" "Eastern Shore food" ("lots of fried" stuff); next door is the "great" Crab Deck, a famed "local watering hole."

Galway Bay ◑S
21 | 21 | 22 | $22 |

61-63 Maryland Ave. (State Circle), Annapolis, 410-263-8333

■ "A locals' hangout" in Annapolis, this "dark pub" is a "home away from home" for many, offering an "upscale taste of old" Ireland with "very good" renditions – Irish whiskey soup, "great shepherd's pie" and "the best corned beef and cabbage"; it's all served in a "nicely renovated space" and, of course, they pour "perfect pints of Guinness."

Garry's Grill [S] 22 | 16 | 21 | $18

914 Bay Ridge Rd. (Georgetown Rd.), Annapolis, 410-626-0388

■ If you "love food", especially "great" "down-home" American breakfasts, head to this casual eatery, which also offers lots of tempting baked goods and "interesting", "healthy" dishes; what's more, the fare is "attractively served" and value-priced, which means that it fills up early.

General Tanuki's [S] – | – | – | M

25 Goldsborough St. (Washington St.), Easton, 410-819-0707

Staid Downtown Easton has quickly taken to the gregarious charms of the ex-naval aviator dad/California kid team of Matt and John General and their young Pacific Rim spot with sushi bar, 120 wines, 12 sakes, Philippine spring rolls, red curry calamari and curry fried oysters; 'aloha Sundays' feature mai tais, hula dancers, mellow Hawaiian music and plenty of flowered shirts.

Governor's Grille [S] ▽ 21 | 24 | 23 | $39

177 Main St. (Conduit St.), Annapolis, 410-263-6555

◪ "Another upscale steakhouse" is now competing in Annapolis' prime beef sweepstakes, featuring "great food" (including daily surf 'n' turf combinations) in a "classy", high-ceilinged room; but to the budget-minded, it seems "kind of out of place" among the more popularly priced restaurants on Main Street near the State House; N.B. call ahead to check hours.

Harbour Lights [S] – | – | – | E

Harbour Inn, 101 N. Harbor Rd. (Chew St.), St. Michaels, 410-745-5102

This dressy hotel dining room with a view of St. Michaels harbor shines on under new owner Bob Pascal and chef Randolph Sprinkle, whose New American takes on regional fare like orange chipotle rockfish join standards like crab soup; there's a more casual bar downstairs by the pool.

Harris Crab House [S] 21 | 16 | 19 | $26

433 Kent Narrows Way N. (Rte. 50, exit 42), Grasonville, 410-827-9500

■ "Wonderful crabs" and a "fabulous" sunset are a time-honored "way to end an Eastern Shore vacation" and this "sizable" American seafood "shanty" on Kent Narrows is loaded with shore traditions, including its own steamed-crab spicing and "homemade" Nutty Buddy ice cream "treats."

Harrison's [S] 20 | 15 | 20 | $27

21551 Chesapeake House Dr. (Rte. 33), Tilghman Island, 410-886-2121

■ Loyalists would drive to the "ends of the earth" for the sense of Eastern Shore "history" at this Tilghman Island inn, not to mention its "down-home", "family-style" meals; whether it's winter oysters or summer seafood, this century-old operation cooks it up "not fancy but good."

Harry Browne's S
24 | 22 | 24 | $34

66 State Circle (bet. East St. & Maryland Ave.), Annapolis, 410-269-5124

■ "Location, location, location" isn't the only reason this "sophisticated", clubby Continental "by the State House" is a "lobbyist's watering hole"; it also boasts "imaginative" food, a "good wine cellar" and "terrific" service, along with a "relaxing" atmosphere that's suitable for either a "romantic" dinner or an easy evening out with friends.

Hemingway's S
– | – | – | M

Pier 1 Marina, 357 Pier 1 Rd. (Rte. 50), Stevensville, 410-643-2722

Visitors to Kent Island can't miss this "great waterside bar" and dining room "at the foot of the Bay Bridge" where Bill Kelly's good seafood dishes support one of the "best water views of the Chesapeake" from the porch and outdoor bar.

Holly's S
▽ 16 | 10 | 18 | $15

108 Jackson Creek Rd. (Rte. 50), Grasonville, 410-827-8711

◪ Housed in a motel in the Kent Narrows area, this diner is a veritable "locals' retreat" and "an important Shore fixture for businesspeople and tourists"; even if some shrug "ordinary", plenty of fans dub it "chicken salad heaven"; N.B. check out the table of vintage cowboy trading cards.

Imperial Hotel S
– | – | – | E

208 High St. (bet. Cross & Queen Sts.), Chestertown, 410-778-5000

In Chestertown, a charming 18th-century Chesapeake port, this "lovely old" hotel's dining rooms provide "beautiful" backdrops for the "excellent" kitchen's seasonally changing, regional American cuisine; sure it's pricey, but it's a "special" "hideaway" destination that's "worth the trip."

Inn at Easton S
– | – | – | VE

28 S. Harrison St. (South Ln.), Easton, 410-822-4910

Elizabeth and Andrew Evans offer sophisticated Med, New French and Pacific Rim fare with some local touches (Peking roast duck, oysters poached in white truffle cream, sweet-and-spicy soft shell crabs) in the small, high-ceilinged drawing room of their grand Downtown Easton 1790 B&B, which opened to a well-heeled mix of locals and visitors.

INN AT PERRY CABIN S
27 | 29 | 26 | $60

308 Watkins Ln. (Talbot St.), St. Michaels, 410-745-2200

■ Rated No. 1 for Decor, this luxurious Eastern Shore retreat is "an elegant experience from start to finish"; everyone's treated like a "celeb" and a meal in its modern Continental restaurant is "one that you won't forget"; though a few quibble about "pretentious" pampering, most just wish they lived "closer" so they could "visit more", especially for the "wonderful" formal tea served on the patio, which boasts a spectacular view of the water; N.B new owner Orient Express plans big changes.

Jalapeño S   ∇ 22 | 16 | 23 | $26
*Forest Plaza Shopping Ctr., 85 Forest Plaza (Riva Rd.),
Annapolis, 410-266-7580*

■ "An excellent" addition to the Annapolis restaurant scene,
this entry brings uncommon traffic to an "out-of-the-way"
Parole shopping center with its "agreeable" combo of "good
food, value and service"; look for a "spicy, interesting mix
of Spanish and Mexican favorites", including "great" tapas,
all washed down with "perfect" sangria and margaritas.

JOSS CAFE & SUSHI BAR S   26 | 18 | 21 | $23
195 Main St. (Church Circle), Annapolis, 410-263-4688

■ Ranked as the top Japanese in the *Baltimore/Annapolis
Survey,* this "tight and cozy" bento box of a sushi bar
near the State House is always "filled with happy diners"
enjoying "unbelievably" "fine and unusual" raw "treats" and
"other good menu items"; what's more, the staff is "generally
attentive" and "accommodating", and the atmosphere
"welcoming", even "festive."

Kennedyville Inn S   – | – | – | M
*11986 Rte. 213 (5 mi. north of Chestertown), Kennedyville,
410-348-2400*

At this "intimate and casually dressy" country crossroads
house a few miles north of Chestertown, chef-owner Kevin
McKinney reinvents regional American dishes (think crab
ravioli with shiitake mushrooms and Old Bay cream sauce)
and pit-smokes succulent meats, "pleasing sophisticated,
relaxed diners" who promise that it's "worth the drive" for
such a "great surprise in the middle of nowhere."

Latitude 38 S   ∇ 22 | 18 | 21 | $35
*26342 Oxford Rd. (Bonfield Ave.), Oxford,
410-226-5303*

■ Small wonder that Oxford "locals" (both full- and part-
time) set their compasses toward this casual yet stylish
American whose bar is a popular "relax-after-boating"
berth and whose "great", creative cooking covers "a lot
of latitude"; furthermore, it's "usually very even", "honors
reservations" and the staff thankfully has "no attitude."

Les Folies S   ∇ 24 | 23 | 25 | $36
*2552 Riva Rd. (bet. Aris Allen Blvd. & Rte. 50), Annapolis,
410-573-0970*

■ Though it's located in Parole and its setting evokes a
Mediterranean villa, "the food is like a Paris brasserie's"
at this young bistro whose classic renditions (notably
"fabulous steak and lobster" dishes and "excellent crème
brûlée") have Francophiles whistling 'La Marseillaise';
owned and run by pros Alain Matrat and chef Jean-Claude
Galan, their experience shows in the "interesting menu"
and "nice" ambiance, causing devotees to cheer "keep
up the good work."

LEWNES' STEAKHOUSE [S] 28 | 23 | 26 | $45

401 Fourth St. (Severn Ave.), Annapolis, 410-263-1617

■ Proving beyond any doubt that diners still love to go out for "prime steaks" and "great wines", this "locally owned" "gentlemen's club" in Eastport is ranked No. 1 for Food in the *Baltimore/Annapolis Survey*; well-hooved carnivores gather here for hefty portions of "really outstanding beef", accompanied by traditional sides; yes it's "pricey", but it's well "worth it" as it's "excellent on all fronts."

Le Zinc [S] – | – | – | E

101 Mill St. (Tilghman St.), Oxford, 410-226-5776

"Very European", this "quirky" French bistro is one of Oxford's "best" restaurants, dazzling diners with an ever-changing roster of "innovative" dishes (often focusing on seafood), accompanied by offbeat, well-priced wines; it's all very casual and "fun" yet the cooking is serious.

Maria's Italian Ristorante ◐ [S] 21 | 18 | 22 | $29

12 Market Space (Green St.), Annapolis, 410-268-2112

◪ Dig into a slice of "Little Italy in Little Annapolis" at this "warm, cozy and crowded" family spot that residents have been going to since high school; "they'll please you or die trying", dishing up "nicely cooked food", but the hard-to-impress shrug "just ok."

Mason's – | – | – | E

22 S. Harrison St. (South Ln.), Easton, 410-822-3204

In Downtown Easton, Mary and Matthew Mason's gourmet shop has expanded next door to the family's grand 1860 Victorian home, and offers shrimp salad and burgers at lunch and French Bistro (veal paillard with hollandaise) and Mediterranean dinners accented with Bay ingredients (capellini with backfin crabmeat); tables on the porch and a pretty garden are pluses.

Matapeake Restaurant & Deli [S] – | – | – | M

401 Love Point Rd. (Cockey Ln.), Stevensville, 410-643-5330

Old-time shore specialties (oyster fritters, fried chicken and pan-fried rockfish) draw regulars from as far as Annapolis to tiny Stevensville, hidden a quarter-mile off Route 50 near the Bay Bridge, where Chris Pettit left advertising to buy a deli and serve serious dinners next door with his wife Krista (who's also an author of children's books); the outside tables offer a nice breakfast and lunch respite.

McGarvey's [S] – | – | – | M

8 Market Space (Main St.), Annapolis, 410-263-5700

A youthful crowd gathers at this old-style American saloon near the Annapolis city dock for "sometimes-loud" good times and some of the "best bar fare" around; belly up to the extensive raw bar inside the dark room or enjoy steamed mussels and shrimp (along with more ambitious specials like crab-stuffed salmon) at a sunny table outside.

Michael Rork's Town Dock [S] 23 | 18 | 20 | $33

125 Mulberry St. (Talbot St.), St. Michaels, 410-745-5577

◪ Devoted followers of Michael Rork (ex Hampton's) head to his "bustling" waterside restaurant in St. Michaels for updated Eastern Shore classics and American favorites; it's all served amid "casual" comforts inside and out on the "memorable deck", but "disappointed" gastronomes lament it's "not as good as touted."

Middleton Tavern ◐ [S] – | – | – | M

2 Market Space (Main St.), Annapolis, 410-263-3323

Fans of this colonial-era Annapolis American tout the "atmosphere and history" evoked by the "stone interior and fireplaces", as well as the porch that's "great for brunch"; but foes cite "sloppy" service and "overpriced" fare – "they make you pay for the fact that George Washington ate here."

Morsels [S] – | – | – | M

205 N. Talbot St. (Mill St.), St. Michaels, 410-745-2911

"Don't tell about this one (it's our special secret)" plead enthusiasts of this "real find" on the main drag of St. Michaels, a tiny, "funky and fun" spot that presents a "surprisingly innovative" seafood-focused Italian-Med menu; fans only hope that it won't become another "tourist trap"; N.B. call ahead for hours, which are limited.

Narrows [S] 24 | 21 | 23 | $33

3023 Kent Narrows Way S. (Rte. 50, exit 41), Grasonville, 410-827-8113

■ "Seafood at sunset" – "wonderful crab cakes and cream of crab soup" – out on a screened-in porch extending over the water or inside a "somewhat elegant" (in a "folksy" way) room earns this Kent Narrows American many "best of Shore" nominations; P.S. to max out on the local color, join the neighbors who gather to watch the "Christmas boat parade" (at dusk on the Saturday after Thanksgiving).

NORTHWOODS [S] 26 | 21 | 24 | $37

609 Melvin Ave. (Ridgely Ave.), Annapolis, 410-268-2609

■ A "great-value" prix fixe meal at this Continental in Annapolis makes "dressy" dining affordable, while its candlelit residential setting and "refined" manners add romance (when it's not too "cramped"); especially popular during the legislative session (those bill-watchers can sure spot a good "deal"), it remains "reliable and steady" year-round, making it one of the area's best options.

O'Learys [S] 24 | 20 | 22 | $35

310 Severn Ave. (Third St.), Annapolis, 410-263-0884

■ "The freshest fish in town, cooked to order", is the lure of this attractive Eastport seafood house where diners mix-and-match their finny pick with a cooking method of their choice, or choose from well-conceived menu dishes and specials, all teamed with interesting wines; dinner only.

OUTBACK STEAKHOUSE [S] 19 | 15 | 18 | $24
Hechinger Plaza, 2207 Forest Dr. (Rte. 2), Annapolis, 410-266-7229
See review in Washington, DC Directory.

Out of the Fire – | – | – | E
22 Goldsborough St. (Washington St.), Easton, 410-770-4777
Sophisticated Eastonites of all ages descend on this former McCrory's five-and-dime store where Tuscan-yellow walls display local art; when it's booked up on weekends, pros sit at the wine bar or the kitchen bar and watch Dave Sarfaty make his wood-burning hearth sing, turning local seafood and produce into smoky Eclectic-Mediterranean dishes and pizzas; N.B. the chef loves to watch you too.

Piccola Roma Ristorante [S] 24 | 22 | 24 | $33
200 Main St. (Church Circle), Annapolis, 410-268-7898
■ "Romantic and intimate" (read "tight" seating), this historic Annapolis ristorante feels "like Italy", with servers who "go the extra mile" and bring to table a "wonderful choice of antipasti, good wines and fresh fish" (the "whole grilled rockfish is to die for"); no wonder so many of the "state's elected officials" and savvy foodies have made this "top-drawer" Italian one of their favorites.

Ram's Head Tavern [S] 19 | 20 | 19 | $23
33 West St. (bet. Calvert St. & Church Circle), Annapolis, 410-268-4545
◪ "Sit on the patio and try the beers" (more than 125 "great" selections) at this "up-to-date brewpub" in Annapolis, a "noisy place good for a group of friends" where the live "music is a draw"; despite its "average" "tavern-level" American grub, many regulars also depend upon it for a "welcome lunch break."

Red Hot & Blue [S] 20 | 15 | 17 | $19
200 Old Mill Bottom Rd. S. (Rte. 50), Annapolis, 410-626-7427
See review in Washington, DC Directory.

Robert Morris Inn [S] 22 | 25 | 23 | $36
314 N. Morris St. (Tredavon Rd.), Oxford, 410-226-5111
■ The "ancient charm" of this "lovely and quiet" historic inn right near the Oxford-Bellevue ferry is its "great atmosphere of yesteryear", which offers Shore travelers "a step back in time"; relax and linger over "traditional Maryland dishes", beginning with "the best cream of crab" soup, and like most surveyors you'll find it a "delightful dining experience."

RUTH'S CHRIS STEAK HOUSE [S] 25 | 23 | 23 | $47
301 Severn Ave. (3rd St.), Annapolis, 410-990-0033
See review in Washington, DC Directory.

Sean Donlon Irish Pub S   ▽ 19 | 18 | 21 | $26

37 West St. (Calvert St.), Annapolis, 410-263-1993
■ Many a lad nominates this upscale "neighborhood" watering hole as one of the "best" Irish pubs in Annapolis thanks to its "excellent beers" and a "good", if "limited", menu of basic stick-to-the-ribs fare; some frugal types mope that "it's too pricey to be authentic", but plenty of others are happy to hang here; N.B. there's live traditional music Tuesdays–Saturdays.

Tilghman Island Inn S   ▽ 20 | 17 | 21 | $31

21834 Coopertown Rd. (Rte. 33), Tilghman Island, 410-886-2141
☑ Granted, the "beautiful view" of the Bay (as well as a wildfowl marsh) is the primary lure of this contemporary inn perched on Tilghman Island, but its New American kitchen also gets some polite applause for its "lovely fresh seafood", served fireside in the wintertime and out on the waterside deck come summer; critics, though, carp "used to be better", finding the cooking now merely "average."

Treaty of Paris S   22 | 24 | 20 | $37

Maryland Inn, 16 Church Circle (Main St.), Annapolis, 410-216-6340
☑ Housed in a "lovely" 1772 building, this historic Annapolis landmark is a "longtime favorite" thanks to its colonial-era atmosphere that makes it "great for celebrating an affair" (or a legislative coup), as well as for its "well-prepared" Maryland seafood dishes and Continental classics, "fine jazz" and "sumptuous" Sunday brunch; detractors, however, lament that the food is "dowdy" and warn "go early if you don't want "cozy" to turn into "cramped."

Tsunami S   ▽ 24 | 20 | 19 | $27

51 West St. (Church Circle), Annapolis, 410-990-9868
■ Get caught up in "a tour de force of sushi delights" at this highly hip, "eclectic" Japanese "bistro experience" in Annapolis, which also appeals with an "interesting" menu of Asian "fusion" cuisine; lauded as a "great place" with a "friendly", "welcoming" vibe, it's regarded by boosters as one of the "best dining" options in town.

208 TALBOT S   26 | 23 | 24 | $45

208 N. Talbot St. (bet. Dodson Ave. & North St.), St. Michaels, 410-745-3838
■ Join the Shore's "upper crust" at this "romantic" New American "hideaway" in St. Michaels, where the "beautiful presentations" of "innovative" dishes (based on local seafood and produce) amount to "art on your plate"; "extremely well-run", it's definitely a "worthy" "destination" in this charming maritime town.

Waterman's Crab House S   ▽ 20 | 17 | 20 | $28 |
Rock Hall Harbor, 21055 Sharp St. (Chesapeake Ave. &
Sharp St. Wharf), Rock Hall, 410-639-2261
■ Take in an "unbeatable" "sunset view from the crab deck
on the water" at this Rock Hall seafood house, a "fun"
"little gem" that's "worth the trip" for "a real Maryland
experience"; a couple of grouches find it merely "routine",
but most laud the namesake crustaceans as "excellent",
including the "huge and perfect crab cakes."

Wild Orchid Cafe S   - | - | - | E |
909 Bay Ridge Ave. (Chesapeake Ave.), Annapolis, 410-268-8009
Everyone from couples out for "romantic dining" to Naval
Academy middies and their families are discovering this
"well-hidden secret" located southwest of Downtown
Annapolis, thanks to chef-owner Jim Wilder's "unique",
"interesting" New American menu, served in a "charming
old house" with a terrace and garden fountain; N.B. it's
hard to find, so call ahead for directions.

Baltimore
Indexes

CUISINES
LOCATIONS
SPECIAL FEATURES

CUISINES*

Afghan

Helmand

American (New)

Antrim 1844
Baldwin's Station
Brass Elephant
Brighton's
Carrol's Creek/A
Charleston
Columbia/A
Corinthian/A
Corks
Grille 700
Hamilton's
Hampton's
Harbour Lights/A
Helen's Garden
Henninger's Tavern
Hunters' Lodge
J.J.'s Everyday
John Steven
Joy America
Latitude 38/A
Linwood's
Preston's 500
Spike & Charlie's
Tilghman Island Inn/A
Towne Hall
208 Talbot/A
Wild Orchid Cafe/A
Windows

American (Regional)

Angelina's
Barn Rest.
Bay Hundred/A
Bayou Blues
Charleston
Imperial Hotel/A
Maggie's
Matapeake/A
Milton Inn

Oregon Grille
Polo Grill
Rothwell's

American (Traditional)

Alonso's
Artful Palate
Barn Rest.
Baugher's
Bay Cafe
Blue Moon
Cafe Hon
Candle Light Inn
Capitol City Brewing
Captain Harvey's
Cheesecake Factory
Clyde's
Corner Stable
Crazy Lil's
Davis' Pub/A
DuClaw Brewing
Duda's Tavern
Ellicott Mills Brewing
ESPN Zone
Friendly Farms
G & M Rest.
Garry's Grill
Hard Rock Cafe
Hard Times Cafe
Harrison's/A
Harryman House
Hull St. Blues
Jennings Cafe
Jilly's
Jimmy's
Johansson's
Johnny Dee's
J. Paul's
Kaufman's Tavern
Kelly's
King's Contrivance
Mamie's
Manor Tavern

* A=Annapolis/Eastern Shore

McCabe's
McGarvey's/A
Michael Rork's/A
Michael's Cafe
Middleton Tavern/A
Milltowne Tavern
Morning Edition
Mt. Washington Tavern
Narrows/A
Owl Bar
Peppermill
Perring Place
Planet Hollywood
Rallo's
Ram's Head Tavern/A
Regi's
Rusty Scupper
Samos
Sander's Corner
Simon's Pub
Sisson's
Sly Horse Tavern
SoBo Cafe
Sunset
Timber Creek Tavern
Timbuktu
Williamsburg Inn
Windows on the Bay
Woman's Ind. Exch.
Woodfire

Asian

Asean Bistro
General Tanuki's/A
Hoang's
Inn at Easton/A
Lotte Plaza Mkt.
Noodles Corner
Olive & Sesame
Purim Oak
San Sushi
Tsunami/A

Bakery

La Madeleine
Panera Bread

Barbecue

Adam's Ribs/A
Bare Bones
Corner Stable
Red Hot & Blue/A
Sisson's

Brazilian

Malibu Grill

Cajun/Creole

Bayou Blues
Louisiana
Sisson's

Californian

California Pizza Kit.
Paolo's

Chesapeake Regional

Blue Heron/A
Columbia/A
Faidley's
Fisherman's Inn/A
Gecko's
Gertrude's
Josef's
Kennedyville Inn/A
Marconi's
Michael Rork's/A
Pierpoint
Robert Morris Inn/A
Treaty of Paris/A
208 Talbot/A

Chinese

Asean Bistro
Bamboo House
Cafe Zen
Ding How
Hunan Manor
Joey Chiu's
Jumbo Seafood
Olive & Sesame
Orient
P.F. Chang's
Szechuan

Szechuan Best
Szechuan House
Thai Orient

Coffeehouse

City Cafe
Desert Cafe
Donna's
One World Cafe
Ze Mean Bean

Coffee Shop/Diner

Chick & Ruth's/A
Double T Diner
Double T Diner/A
Forest Diner
Holly's/A
Jimmy's
New Towne Diner
Papermoon Diner
Silver Dinner
Towson Diner

Continental

Bay Hundred/A
Bistro St. Michaels/A
Brass Elephant
Cafe Bretton
Candle Light Inn
Captain Harvey's
Harry Browne's/A
Inn at Perry Cabin/A
Josef's
Manor Tavern
Marconi's
Milton Inn
Northwoods/A
Polo Grill
Rudys' 2900
Ten-O-Six
Tio Pepe
Treaty of Paris/A

Crab House

Bo Brooks
Cantler's/A
Captain Harvey's
Crab Claw/A

Crab Shanty
Fisherman's Inn/A
Gabler's
Gibby's
Gunning's Crab
Harris Crab House/A
Obrycki's
River Watch
Waterman's/A

Deli/Sandwich Shop

Attman's Deli
Chick & Ruth's/A
DiPasquale's
Panera Bread

Dim Sum

Szechuan Best

Eastern European

Ze Mean Bean

Eclectic/International

Bandaloops
Bicycle
Brewer's Art
City Cafe
Coburn's
Donna's
Elkridge Furnace Inn
Ethel & Ramone's
Eurasian Harbor
Fusion Grill
Genevieve's
John Steven
One World Cafe
Out of the Fire/A
Peter's Inn
Regi's
Ruby Lounge
Sascha's 527
Viccino Bistro
Ze Mean Bean

French

Cafe Bretton
Cafe Normandie/A
Elkridge Furnace Inn
Jeannier's

La Madeleine
Les Folies/A
Le Zinc/A
Martick's
Petit Louis
Tersiguel's

French (Bistro)

Crepe du Jour
Mason's/A

French (New)

Inn at Easton/A
Manley's Bistro

German

Josef's

Greek

Acropolis
Black Olive
Ikaros
Kali's Court
Olive Grove
OPA!
Samos
Timbuktu
Zorba's B&G

Hamburgers

Alonso's
Capitol City Brewing
Crazy Lil's
ESPN Zone
Hard Rock Cafe
Jennings Cafe
J. Paul's
McCabe's
McCafferty's
Simon's Pub
Towne Hall

Indian

Akbar
Ambassador Din. Rm.
Banjara
Bombay Grill
India Palace
Mughal Garden

Irish

An Poitin Stil
Claddagh Pub
Galway Bay/A
Sean Donlon/A

Italian

(N=Northern; S=Southern;
N&S=Includes both)

Aldo's (S)
Alonso's (N&S)
Amicci's (N&S)
Angelina's (N&S)
Bertucci's (N&S)
Boccaccio (N)
Caesar's Den (N&S)
Cafe Troia (N&S)
California Pizza Kit. (N&S)
Chiapparelli's (N&S)
Ciao Bella (N&S)
Cosmopolitan B&G (N&S)
Dalesio's (N&S)
Da Mimmo (N&S)
Della Notte (N&S)
DiPasquale's (N&S)
Due (N)
Fazzini's (N&S)
Germano's (N)
Giovanni's (N&S)
La Scala (N&S)
La Tavola (N&S)
La Tesso Tana (N&S)
Liberatore's Bistro (N&S)
Luigi Petti (N&S)
Mangia Mangia (N&S)
Maria's Italian/A (N)
Mezzanotte (N&S)
Morsels/A (N&S)
Olive Grove (N&S)
Paolo's (N&S)
Paradiso (S)
Pazza Luna (N)
Piccola Roma/A (N&S)
Ricciuti's (N&S)
Sabatino's (N&S)
Scotto's Cafe (N)

Sotto Sopra (N&S)
That's Amore (N&S)
Tomato Palace (N&S)
Trattoria Alberto (N)
Velleggia's (S)
Vespa (N&S)
Vito's Cafe (N&S)

Japanese

Bamboo House
Cafe Zen
Edo Sushi
Fuji
Hoang's
Joss Cafe/A
Kawasaki
Matsuri
Minato
New No Da Ji
Nichi Bei Kai
Olive & Sesame
San Sushi
Shogun
Sushi Hana
Sushi-Ya
Suzie's Soba
Tsunami/A

Korean

New No Da Ji
Purim Oak
Suzie's Soba

Mediterranean

Hunters' Lodge
Inn at Easton/A
Kali's Court
Mason's/A
Morsels/A
Olive & Sesame
Out of the Fire/A
Tapas Teatro

Mexican/Tex-Mex

Austin Grill
El Azteca
Holy Frijoles
Jalapeño/A

Lista's
Loco Hombre
Nacho Mama's

Middle Eastern

Desert Cafe
Orchard Mkt. Cafe

Noodle Shop

Noodles Corner
Saigon

Persian

Orchard Mkt. Cafe

Pizza

Bertucci's
California Pizza Kit.
Mangia Mangia
Out of the Fire/A
Owl Bar
Paolo's
Ricciuti's
Tomato Palace
Vito's Cafe

Seafood

Angelina's
Atlantic
Backfin
Barn Rest.
Bay Hundred/A
Bertha's
Black Olive
Blue Heron/A
Bo Brooks
Cantler's/A
Captain Harvey's
Carrol's Creek/A
Crab Claw/A
Crab Shanty
Davis' Pub/A
Duda's Tavern
Faidley's
Fisherman's Inn/A
Gabler's
G & M Rest.
Gibby's
Governor's Grille/A

Gunning's Crab
Gunning's Seafood
Harris Crab House/A
Harrison's/A
Hemingway's/A
Hoang's
John Steven
Josef's
Kali's Court
Kaufman's Tavern
Legal Sea Foods
LP Steamers
Mamie's
Matapeake/A
McCormick & Schmick's
McGarvey's/A
Michael Rork's/A
Narrows/A
Nick's
Obrycki's
Ocean Pride
O'Learys/A
Patrick's/Cockeysville
Phillips
Pierpoint
Pisces
Porter's
Prime Rib
River Watch
Robert Morris Inn/A
Rusty Scupper
Sisson's
Tilghman Island Inn/A
Timbuktu
Treaty of Paris/A
Waterman's/A
Windows on the Bay

Southern/Soul
Baines Southern/A

Southwestern
Austin Grill
Blue Agave
Gecko's
Golden West

Spanish
Cafe Madrid
Jalapeño/A
Patrick's/Cockeysville
Tio Pepe

Steakhouse
Annie's Paramount/A
Fleming's
Governor's Grille/A
Lewnes' Steakhse./A
Malibu Grill
McCafferty's
Morton's of Chicago
Nichi Bei Kai
Oregon Grille
Outback Steakhse.
Outback Steakhse./A
Patrick's/Cockeysville
Prime Rib
Ruth's Chris
Ruth's Chris/A
Shula's Steak House

Thai
Ban Thai
House of Asia
San Sushi
Ten-O-Six
Thai
Thai Landing
Thai Orient

Vegetarian
(Most Chinese, Indian and
Thai restaurants usually offer
vegetarian dishes)
Cafe Zen
Genevieve's
Golden West
Helen's Garden
Hoang's
Holy Frijoles
One World Cafe

Vietnamese
House of Asia
Minato
Saigon

LOCATIONS

BALTIMORE

Business District/ Downtown/ Convention Center/ Camden Yards/ Inner Harbor

Brighton's
Cafe Bombay
California Pizza Kit.
Capitol City Brewing
Cheesecake Factory
Donna's
ESPN Zone
Faidley's
Hampton's
Hard Rock Cafe
Joy America
J. Paul's
Legal Sea Foods
Marconi's
Martick's
McCormick & Schmick's
Morton's of Chicago
Paolo's
Phillips
Pisces
Planet Hollywood
Rusty Scupper
Ruth's Chris
Shula's Steak House
Tio Pepe
Windows

Canton

Atlantic
Austin Grill
Bay Cafe
Bo Brooks
Claddagh Pub
Coburn's
Cosmopolitan B&G
Gecko's
Helen's Garden
Hoang's

Mangia Mangia
Nacho Mama's

Downtown/Charles St./ Mt. Vernon

Akbar
Ban Thai
Bombay Grill
Brass Elephant
Brewer's Art
City Cafe
Donna's
Helmand
Kawasaki
La Tesso Tana
Minato
Mughal Garden
New No Da Ji
Owl Bar
Prime Rib
Ruby Lounge
Sascha's 527
Shogun
Sotto Sopra
Spike & Charlie's
Thai Landing
Viccino Bistro
Woman's Ind. Exch.

East Baltimore

Attman's Deli
Kelly's
Obrycki's
Simon's Pub

Federal Hill/ South Baltimore

Bandaloops
Banjara
Bicycle
Blue Agave
Corks
Crazy Lil's

Gunning's Crab
Hull St. Blues
LP Steamers
Matsuri
Nick's
One World Cafe
Pazza Luna
Porter's
Rallo's
Regi's
Sisson's
SoBo Cafe
Szechuan
Ten-O-Six
Vespa

Fells Point

Bertha's
Black Olive
Blue Moon
Cafe Madrid
Ding How
Duda's Tavern
Genevieve's
Hamilton's
Henninger's Tavern
Jimmy's
John Steven
Kali's Court
Kawasaki
Lista's
Louisiana
OPA!
Peter's Inn
Pierpoint
Ze Mean Bean

Hampden/Roland Park/ Homewood/ Charles Village

Alonso's
Ambassador Din. Rm.
Cafe Hon
Donna's
Gertrude's
Golden West
Holy Frijoles
Jeannier's

Loco Hombre
Mamie's
McCabe's
One World Cafe
Papermoon Diner
Petit Louis
Polo Grill
Preston's 500
Suzie's Soba
Tapas Teatro

Harbor East/Little Italy

Aldo's
Amicci's
Boccaccio
Caesar's Den
Charleston
Chiapparelli's
Ciao Bella
Dalesio's
Da Mimmo
Della Notte
Eurasian Harbor
Fleming's
Germano's
Grille 700
La Scala
La Tavola
Luigi Petti
Sabatino's
Velleggia's

Highlandtown/Greektown

Acropolis
Ikaros
Morning Edition
Samos
Zorba's B&G

Mt. Washington/ Lake Roland

Crepe du Jour
Desert Cafe
Donna's
Ethel & Ramone's
Hoang's
McCafferty's
Mt. Washington Tavern

OUTER BALTIMORE

Brooklandville

Joey Chiu's
Towne Hall

BWI/Linthicum/Elkridge

Elkridge Furnace Inn
G & M Rest.
Gunning's Seafood
Olive Grove
Timbuktu

Columbia

Akbar
Asean Bistro
Bertucci's
Bombay Grill
Clyde's
El Azteca
Hard Times Cafe
Hunan Manor
King's Contrivance
La Madeleine
Malibu Grill
Nichi Bei Kai
Noodles Corner
Panera Bread
P.F. Chang's
Ricciuti's
Tomato Palace

Ellicott City/Catonsville

Bare Bones
Candle Light Inn
Crab Shanty
Double T Diner
Ellicott Mills Brewing
Forest Diner
Fuji
House of Asia
Hunters' Lodge
Jennings Cafe
Jilly's
Lotte Plaza Mkt.
Manley's Bistro
Milltowne Tavern

Outback Steakhse.
Tersiguel's

Essex/Dundalk

River Watch

Glen Burnie/Severna Park/Pasadena

Adam's Ribs
Cafe Bretton
Cafe Mezzanotte
Double T Diner
Garry's Grill
Kaufman's Tavern
Sly Horse Tavern
Sunset
Trattoria Alberto
Windows on the Bay
Woodfire

Hunt Valley/North Baltimore Co.

Friendly Farms
Manor Tavern
Milton Inn
Oregon Grille
Outback Steakhse.

Lutherville/Timonium/Cockeysville

An Poitin Stil
Artful Palate
Bamboo House
Bare Bones
Bertucci's
Corner Stable
Ding How
Donna's
Edo Sushi
Fazzini's
Gibby's
India Palace
J.J.'s Everyday
Liberatore's Bistro
Michael's Cafe
Nichi Bei Kai

ANNAPOLIS/EASTERN SHORE

Annapolis

Adam's Ribs
Cafe Normandie
Cantler's
Carrol's Creek
Chick & Ruth's
Corinthian
Davis' Pub
Double T Diner
Galway Bay
Garry's Grill
Governor's Grille
Harry Browne's
Jalapeño
Joss Cafe
Les Folies
Lewnes' Steakhse.
Maria's Italian
McGarvey's
Middleton Tavern
Northwoods
O'Learys
Outback Steakhse.
Piccola Roma
Ram's Head Tavern
Red Hot & Blue
Ruth's Chris
Sean Donlon
Treaty of Paris
Tsunami
Wild Orchid Cafe

Kent Narrows/ Near Eastern Shore/ St. Michaels/Chestertown

Adam's Ribs
Annie's Paramount
Baines Southern
Bay Hundred
Bistro St. Michaels
Blue Heron
Columbia
Crab Claw
Crab Deck
Fisherman's Inn
General Tanuki's
Harbour Lights
Harris Crab House
Harrison's
Hemingway's
Holly's
Imperial Hotel
Inn at Easton
Inn at Perry Cabin
Kennedyville Inn
Latitude 38
Le Zinc
Mason's
Matapeake
Michael Rork's
Morsels
Narrows
Out of the Fire
Robert Morris Inn
Tilghman Island Inn
208 Talbot
Waterman's

SPECIAL FEATURES

Additions

Baines Southern/A
Barn Rest.
Bay Hundred/A
Blue Agave
Coburn's
Crazy Lil's
Crepe du Jour
Eurasian Harbor
Fleming's
General Tanuki's/A
Grille 700
Harbour Lights/A
House of Asia
Inn at Easton/A
LP Steamers
Manley's Bistro
Mason's/A
Matapeake/A
Out of the Fire/A
Porter's
Tapas Teatro
Towne Hall

Breakfast

(Best of many;
see also Hotel Dining)

Blue Moon
Cafe Hon
Chick & Ruth's/A
Donna's
Double T Diner
Holly's/A
Jimmy's
Mamie's
Morning Edition
New Towne Diner
Woman's Ind. Exch.

Brunch

(Best of many)

Carrol's Creek/A
Gertrude's
Hampton's

Harryman House
Helen's Garden
Hull St. Blues
Joy America
Morning Edition
Morsels/A
Polo Grill
Preston's 500
Treaty of Paris/A
Windows
Ze Mean Bean

Buffet Served

(Check prices, days
and times)

Akbar
Ambassador Din. Rm.
Banjara
Bombay Grill
Galway Bay/A
India Palace
Morning Edition
Mughal Garden
New No Da Ji
Phillips
Purim Oak
Saigon
Szechuan Best
Windows

Business Dining

(Best of many)

Atlantic
Bamboo House
Barn Rest.
Boccaccio
Bombay Grill
Brass Elephant
Brighton's
Charleston
Corinthian/A
Due
Fleming's
Governor's Grille/A
Hampton's

Fisherman's Inn/A*
Garry's Grill*
Garry's Grill/A*
Hard Rock Cafe
Outback Steakhse.
Outback Steakhse./A
Planet Hollywood
Tomato Palace

Delivery/Takeout
(Best of many; D=delivery, T=takeout)

Artful Palate (T)
Baines Southern/A (T)
Barn Rest. (T)
Bay Hundred/A (T)
Blue Agave (T)
Blue Moon (T)
City Cafe (T)
Coburn's (T)
Crab Shanty (T)
Crazy Lil's (T)
Crepe du Jour (T)
Della Notte (T)
Due (T)
Eurasian Harbor (T)
Faidley's (T)
Fisherman's Inn/A (T)
Garry's Grill (T)
General Tanuki's/A (T)
Grille 700 (T)
Harbour Lights/A (T)
Holly's/A (T)
Linwood's (T)
Mamie's (D,T)
Manley's Bistro (T)
Mason's/A (D,T)
Ocean Pride (D)
One World Cafe (T)
Porter's (D,T)
Sabatino's (T)
Samos (D,T)
Sascha's 527 (T)
Scotto's Cafe (T)
Tapas Teatro (T)

Dessert
Baugher's
Blue Moon
Charleston
Cheesecake Factory
City Cafe
Desert Cafe
Donna's
Due
Helen's Garden
Holly's/A
Hull St. Blues
Linwood's
New Towne Diner
Pierpoint
Sander's Corner
Sascha's 527
SoBo Cafe
Spike & Charlie's
Vespa
Woman's Ind. Exch.

Entertainment
(Call for days and times of performances; best of many)

Angelina's (guitar)
Baldwin's (bluegrass/country)
Bare Bones (bands)
Bay Cafe (varies)
Bayou Blues (blues/jazz)
Bertha's (jazz)
Bombay Grill (sitar)
Da Mimmo (piano/vocals)
Fisherman's Inn/A (bands)
Harryman House (DJ)
India Palace (sitar music)
Kaufman's Tavern (varies)
Kelly's (karaoke)
McCafferty's (cellist/piano)
Michael Rork's/A (jazz/light rock)
Out of the Fire/A (guitar)
Prime Rib (bass/piano)
Ram's Head/A (blues/folk/jazz)
River Watch (bands)
Sean Donlon/A (Irish)
Tilghman Island Inn/A (piano)

Towne Hall (jazz)
Treaty of Paris/A (blues/jazz)
Windows (band)
Ze Mean Bean (folk/jazz/Slavic)

Family Style

Friendly Farms
Harrison's/A
That's Amore

Fireplace

Antrim 1844
Brewer's Art
Elkridge Furnace Inn
Hull St. Blues
Johansson's
John Steven
Luigi Petti
Mason's/A
Milton Inn
Petit Louis
Robert Morris Inn/A
Sander's Corner
Tilghman Island Inn/A
Ze Mean Bean

Game in Season

Blue Agave
Corks
General Tanuki's/A
Grille 700
Hampton's
Harbour Lights/A
Inn at Easton/A
Josef's
King's Contrivance
Louisiana
Preston's 500

Historic Interest

(Year opened; *building)
1710 Robert Morris Inn/A*
1740 Milton Inn*
1740 Ram's Head Tavern/A*
1744 Elkridge Furnace Inn*
1772 Treaty of Paris/A*
1791 Harryman House*

1832 John Steven
1850 Martick's*
1860 Woman's Ind. Exch.*
1860s Milltowne Tavern*
1870 208 Talbot/A*
1880 Henninger's Tavern
1880 Manor Tavern*
1883 Baldwin's Station*
1886 Sander's Corner*
1890 Tersiguel's*
1900 King's Contrivance*
1900 Timber Creek Tavern*
1902 Imperial Hotel/A*
1904 Ellicott Mills Brewing*
1904 Sotto Sopra*
1905 Hunters' Lodge
1913 Johansson's*
1920 Marconi's
1938 Gabler's*

Hotel Dining

Admiral Fell Inn
  Hamilton's
Doubletree Inn/Colonnade
  Polo Grill
Harbor Court Hotel
  Brighton's
  Hampton's
Harbour Inn
  Harbour Lights/A
Hyatt Regency
  Pisces
Imperial Hotel
  Imperial Hotel/A
Inn at Perry Cabin
  Inn at Perry Cabin/A
Loews Annapolis Hotel
  Corinthian/A
Marriott Waterfront
  Grille 700
Maryland Inn
  Treaty of Paris/A
Pier 5 Hotel
  Eurasian Harbor
  McCormick & Schmick's
Renaissance Harborplace
  Windows

Sheraton Inner Harbor
   Morton's of Chicago
Wyndham Inner Harbor
   Shula's Steak House

Late Late – After 12:30

(All hours are AM;
* check locations)

An Poitin Stil (2)
Bandaloops (2)
Brewer's Art (2)
Claddagh Pub (2)
Double T Diner (24 hrs.)*
Double T Diner/A (24 hrs.)*
DuClaw Brewing (2)
Duda's Tavern (1)
Ellicott Mills Brewing (2)
ESPN Zone (1)
Henninger's Tavern (1)
Hunters' Lodge (2)
John Steven (1:30)
Papermoon Diner (24 hrs.)
Planet Hollywood (2)
Sabatino's (3)
Towson Diner (24 hrs.)
Zorba's B&G (2)

Meet for a Drink

An Poitin Stil
Atlantic
Bay Cafe
Brass Elephant
Brewer's Art
Capitol City Brewing
Carrol's Creek/A
Claddagh Pub
Donna's
DuClaw Brewing
Ellicott Mills Brewing
Fleming's
Harryman House
Jeannier's
Johansson's
John Steven
J. Paul's
Kelly's
Manor Tavern

Michael's Cafe
Nick's
Paolo's
Phillips
Preston's 500
Ram's Head Tavern/A
Ruby Lounge
Sean Donlon/A

Offbeat

Barn Rest.
Brewer's Art
Chick & Ruth's/A
Faidley's
Genevieve's
Holly's/A
Holy Frijoles
John Steven
Kelly's
Maggie's
Martick's
Papermoon Diner
Peter's Inn

Outdoor Dining

(G=garden; P=patio;
S=sidewalk; T=terrace;
W=waterside; best of many)

Ambassador Din. Rm. (G)
Antrim 1844 (T)
Austin Grill (P)
Baines Southern/A (P)
Bay Cafe (P)
Bay Hundred/A (P,W)
Bicycle (P)
Black Olive (G)
Blue Heron/A (P)
Candle Light Inn (P)
Cantler's/A (P,W)
Carrol's Creek/A (T)
Cheesecake Factory (P,W)
City Cafe (S)
Crab Claw/A (T,W)
Desert Cafe (S)
Donna's (P,S)
Ethel & Ramone's (S)
Eurasian Harbor (P,W)

Fisherman's Inn/A (P,W)
Gertrude's (T)
Gibby's (P)
Golden West (P)
Gunning's Crab (G,P)
Harbour Lights/A (P,W)
Harris Crab House/A (P,W)
Harrison's/A (T,W)
Harry Browne's/A (P)
Harryman House (T)
Hemingway's/A (W)
Imperial Hotel/A (G)
Inn at Easton/A (P)
Inn at Perry Cabin/A (P,W)
Jilly's (P)
John Steven (P)
Josef's (G,P)
Joy America (T)
Kali's Court (P)
Kaufman's Tavern (G)
Kawasaki (S,W)
La Tesso Tana (S)
Latitude 38/A (P)
Legal Sea Foods (P)
Le Zinc/A (T)
Liberatore's Bistro (S)
Lista's (P,W)
LP Steamers (P)
Luigi Petti (P)
Manley's Bistro (S)
Manor Tavern (P)
Maria's Italian/A (S)
Mason's/A (G)
Matapeake/A (P,S)
McCormick & Schmick's (P,W)
McGarvey's/A (S)
Michael Rork's/A (P,W)
Middleton Tavern/A (T)
Narrows/A (P,W)
Northwoods/A (P)
O'Learys/A (W)
One World Cafe (P)
Oregon Grille (P,T)
Paolo's (T,W)
Planet Hollywood (P)
Ram's Head Tavern/A (P)

Regi's (S)
River Watch (P,W)
Robert Morris Inn/A (W)
Rothwell's (P)
Rusty Scupper (P,W)
Sander's Corner (T)
Sean Donlon/A (S)
Sly Horse Tavern (P)
Tapas Teatro (S)
Tilghman Island Inn/A (P,W)
Tomato Palace (P,W)
Towne Hall (P)
Vespa (S)
Vito's Cafe (S)
Waterman's/A (W)
Wild Orchid Cafe/A (G,P)
Windows on the Bay (P,W)

Parking
(L=parking lot;
V=valet parking;
*=validated parking)
Aldo's (V)
Ambassador Din. Rm. (V)
Atlantic (L)
Austin Grill (L)
Bay Hundred/A (L)
Black Olive*
Boccaccio (V)
Bombay Grill (L)
Brass Elephant (L)
Caesar's Den (V)
Cafe Normandie/A*
Cantler's/A (L)
Carrol's Creek/A (L)
Charleston (V)
Chiapparelli's (V)
Corinthian/A (L,V)
Da Mimmo (V)
Fisherman's Inn/A (L)
Fleming's (V)*
General Tanuki's/A (L)
Germano's (V)
Gertrude's (L)
Grille 700 (L,V)
Hamilton's (V)
Hampton's (V)

Harbour Lights/A (L)
House of Asia (L)
India Palace (L)
Kali's Court (V)
King's Contrivance (L)
Lotte Plaza Mkt. (L)
Louisiana (V)
Luigi Petti (V)
Manley's Bistro (L)
Matapeake/A (L)
McCormick & Schmick's*
Perring Place (L)
Piccola Roma/A (V)
Pisces (V)
Polo Grill (V)
Porter's (L)
Preston's 500 (V)
Prime Rib (L,V)*
Ram's Head Tavern/A*
Ruth's Chris (V)
Ruth's Chris/A (V)
Shogun*
Shula's Steak House*
Sotto Sopra (V)
Towne Hall (L)
Treaty of Paris/A (V)
Viccino Bistro (V)
Windows*

Parties & Private Rooms

(Any nightclub or restaurant charges less at off-times; * indicates private rooms available; best of many)
Antrim 1844
Baldwin's Station*
Barn Rest.*
Black Olive
Bombay Grill*
Brass Elephant*
Caesar's Den*
Cafe Madrid*
Candle Light Inn
Carrol's Creek/A*
Charleston
Chiapparelli's*
Corks*
Crazy Lil's*
ESPN Zone*

Eurasian Harbor*
Fisherman's Inn/A*
Fleming's*
Friendly Farms
General Tanuki's/A*
Grille 700*
Hamilton's*
Harbour Lights/A*
Hunters' Lodge*
Ikaros*
Imperial Hotel/A*
Inn at Perry Cabin/A*
King's Contrivance
Liberatore's Bistro*
LP Steamers*
Luigi Petti
Manor Tavern
Mason's/A*
McCormick & Schmick's*
Michael Rork's/A
Milltowne Tavern*
Milton Inn
OPA!*
Oregon Grille*
Rothwell's
Rudys' 2900
Tapas Teatro
Tersiguel's
Towne Hall
Treaty of Paris/A*

People-Watching

Atlantic
Barn Rest.
Brewer's Art
Chick & Ruth's/A
Donna's
Double T Diner
Holy Frijoles
Michael Rork's/A
Paolo's
Polo Grill
Shula's Steak House
208 Talbot/A

Power Scenes

Bistro St. Michaels/A
Charleston
Chick & Ruth's/A
Linwood's
McCormick & Schmick's
Milton Inn

Oregon Grille
Polo Grill
Prime Rib
Ruth's Chris/A
208 Talbot/A
Windows

Prix Fixe Menus
(Call to check prices,
days and times)
Antrim 1844
Brass Elephant
Hampton's
Inn at Perry Cabin/A
King's Contrivance
Northwoods/A
Preston's 500
Tersiguel's
Treaty of Paris/A
208 Talbot/A

Pub/Bar/Microbrewery
Angelina's
An Poitin Stil
Bare Bones
Bertha's
Claddagh Pub
Davis' Pub/A
Duda's Tavern
Galway Bay/A
Johansson's
John Steven
Kelly's
McCabe's
Ram's Head Tavern/A
Regi's
Sean Donlon/A
Simon's Pub
Sisson's
Timber Creek Tavern
Treaty of Paris/A

Quiet Conversation
Desert Cafe
Fleming's
Hampton's
La Tesso Tana
Trattoria Alberto
Ze Mean Bean

Raw Bar
Barn Rest.
Bertha's
Faidley's
Grille 700
LP Steamers
McCormick & Schmick's
McGarvey's/A
Michael's Cafe
Middleton Tavern/A
Mt. Washington Tavern
Nick's
Ocean Pride
Owl Bar
Phillips
Porter's
Waterman's/A
Windows

Reservations Advised
Antrim 1844
Black Olive
Charleston
Gabler's
Hampton's
Inn at Easton/A
Inn at Perry Cabin/A
Kelly's
Lewnes' Steakhse./A
Linwood's
Milton Inn
Oregon Grille
Polo Grill
Preston's 500
Prime Rib
Ruth's Chris
Tersiguel's
208 Talbot/A

Romantic
Antrim 1844
Charleston
Corinthian/A
Desert Cafe
Harry Browne's/A
Harryman House
Joss Cafe/A
Les Folies/A
Louisiana
Milton Inn
Northwoods/A

Prime Rib
Treaty of Paris/A

Senior Appeal
Baugher's
Candle Light Inn
Chiapparelli's
Crab Shanty
Friendly Farms
Liberatore's Bistro
Narrows/A
Northwoods/A
Peppermill
Perring Place
Prime Rib
Robert Morris Inn/A
Rudys' 2900
Velleggia's
Woman's Ind. Exch.

Singles Scenes
Austin Grill
Bay Cafe
Brewer's Art
Capitol City Brewing
DuClaw Brewing
Ellicott Mills Brewing
Johansson's
John Steven
J. Paul's
McCafferty's
Michael's Cafe
Mt. Washington Tavern
Nacho Mama's
Nick's
Ram's Head Tavern/A
River Watch

Sleepers
(Good to excellent food,
but little known)
Artful Palate
Bistro St. Michaels/A
Corinthian/A
Fuji
Gabler's
India Palace
Jalapeño/A

Jennings Cafe
J.J.'s Everyday
Johnny Dee's
Joss Cafe/A
Latitude 38/A
Les Folies/A
Le Zinc/A
Saigon
Scotto's Cafe
Sly Horse Tavern

Tea
(Check days & times)
Bertha's
Brighton's
Inn at Perry Cabin/A

Teflons
(Get lots of business, despite
so-so food, i.e. they have
other attractions that prevent
criticism from sticking)
Alonso's
Bay Cafe
Bayou Blues
Capitol City Brewing
Double T Diner
Double T Diner/A
ESPN Zone
Hard Rock Cafe
Lista's
Mt. Washington Tavern
New Towne Diner
Phillips
Planet Hollywood

View
Baldwin's Station
Bay Cafe
Cantler's/A
Carrol's Creek/A
Cheesecake Factory
Crab Claw/A
Fisherman's Inn/A
Gabler's
Gertrude's
Hampton's
Harris Crab House/A

Harrison's/A
Inn at Perry Cabin/A
Joy America
J. Paul's
Lista's
McCormick & Schmick's
Michael Rork's/A
Narrows/A
Paolo's
Phillips
Pisces
Rusty Scupper
Sander's Corner
Tilghman Island Inn/A
Tomato Palace
Windows

Visitors on Expense Accounts

Brass Elephant
Charleston
Corinthian/A
Da Mimmo
Fleming's
Hampton's
Inn at Perry Cabin/A
King's Contrivance
Lewnes' Steakhse./A
Linwood's
Louisiana
McCafferty's
Milton Inn
Morton's of Chicago
Oregon Grille
Preston's 500
Prime Rib
Robert Morris Inn/A
Rudys' 2900
Ruth's Chris
Ruth's Chris/A
Shula's Steak House
Tersiguel's
Tio Pepe
208 Talbot/A

Winning Wine Lists

An Poitin Stil
Boccaccio
Caesar's Den
Cafe Madrid
Charleston
Corks
Dalesio's
Fleming's
Hamilton's
Hampton's
Inn at Perry Cabin/A
Linwood's
Milton Inn
Morton's of Chicago
Oregon Grille
Preston's 500
Prime Rib
Rudys' 2900
Spike & Charlie's
Tersiguel's

Worth a Trip

Aberdeen
  Gabler's
Chestertown
  Imperial Hotel/A
Easton
  Columbia/A
Oxford
  Latitude 38/A
  Robert Morris Inn/A
Rock Hall
  Waterman's/A
St. Michaels
  Bistro St. Michaels/A
  Inn at Perry Cabin/A
  208 Talbot/A
Sykesville
  Baldwin's Station
Taneytown
  Antrim 1844
Tilghman Island
  Harrison's/A

Rating Sheets

To aid in your participation in our next *Survey*

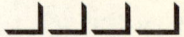

Restaurant Name _____
Phone _____
Comments _____
_____
_____

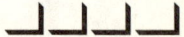

Restaurant Name _____
Phone _____
Comments _____
_____
_____

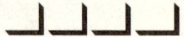

Restaurant Name _____
Phone _____
Comments _____
_____
_____

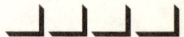

Restaurant Name _____
Phone _____
Comments _____
_____
_____

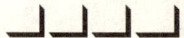

Restaurant Name _____
Phone _____
Comments _____
_____
_____

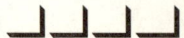

Restaurant Name _____
Phone _____
Comments _____
_____
_____

	F	D	S	C

⌐⌐⌐⌐

Restaurant Name _____
Phone _____
Comments _____
_____
_____

⌐⌐⌐⌐

Restaurant Name _____
Phone _____
Comments _____
_____
_____

⌐⌐⌐⌐

Restaurant Name _____
Phone _____
Comments _____
_____
_____

⌐⌐⌐⌐

Restaurant Name _____
Phone _____
Comments _____
_____
_____

⌐⌐⌐⌐

Restaurant Name _____
Phone _____
Comments _____
_____
_____

⌐⌐⌐⌐

Restaurant Name _____
Phone _____
Comments _____
_____
_____

F | D | S | C

⌐⌐⌐⌐

Restaurant Name _____
Phone _____
Comments _____
_____
_____

⌐⌐⌐⌐

Restaurant Name _____
Phone _____
Comments _____
_____
_____

⌐⌐⌐⌐

Restaurant Name _____
Phone _____
Comments _____
_____
_____

⌐⌐⌐⌐

Restaurant Name _____
Phone _____
Comments _____
_____
_____

⌐⌐⌐⌐

Restaurant Name _____
Phone _____
Comments _____
_____
_____

⌐⌐⌐⌐

Restaurant Name _____
Phone _____
Comments _____
_____
_____

F | D | S | C

⌐⌐⌐⌐

Restaurant Name _____
Phone _____
Comments _____
_____
_____

⌐⌐⌐⌐

Restaurant Name _____
Phone _____
Comments _____
_____
_____

⌐⌐⌐⌐

Restaurant Name _____
Phone _____
Comments _____
_____
_____

⌐⌐⌐⌐

Restaurant Name _____
Phone _____
Comments _____
_____
_____

⌐⌐⌐⌐

Restaurant Name _____
Phone _____
Comments _____
_____
_____

⌐⌐⌐⌐

Restaurant Name _____
Phone _____
Comments _____
_____
_____

Wine Vintage Chart 1985-1999

This chart is designed to help you select wine to go with your meal. It is based on the same 0 to 30 scale used throughout this *Survey.* The ratings (prepared by our friend **Howard Stravitz**, a law professor at the University of South Carolina) reflect both the quality of the vintage and the wine's readiness for present consumption. Thus, if a wine is not fully mature or is over the hill, its rating has been reduced. We do not include 1987, 1991 or 1993 vintages because they are not especially recommended for most areas.

	'85	'86	'88	'89	'90	'92	'94	'95	'96	'97	'98	'99
WHITES												
French:												
Alsace	24	19	22	28	28	23	27	25	22	23	25	22
Burgundy	23	24	19	25	21	23	22	26	28	25	24	25
Loire Valley	–	–	–	26	25	–	22	24	26	23	22	23
Champagne	28	25	24	26	29	–	–	24	27	24	24	–
Sauternes	22	28	29	25	27	–	–	22	23	24	23	–
California:												
Chardonnay	–	–	–	–	–	–	22	26	22	26	23	26
REDS												
French:												
Bordeaux	26	27	25	28	29	18	24	25	24	23	24	22
Burgundy	24	–	23	26	29	22	21	26	27	25	24	25
Rhône	25	19	25	28	27	15	23	25	22	24	27	25
Beaujolais	–	–	–	–	–	–	–	23	21	24	23	24
California:												
Cab./Merlot	26	26	–	21	28	25	27	26	25	26	23	25
Zinfandel	–	–	–	–	–	–	–	26	25	24	23	22	23
Italian:												
Tuscany	26	–	23	–	26	–	23	25	19	28	25	24
Piedmont	25	–	25	28	28	–	–	23	26	28	26	25

May We Quote You?

Be a part of
ZAGATSURVEY®

To join in any of our Surveys, please fill out and return this card.

☐ Mr.　☐ Mrs.　☐ Ms.
_____
Your Name

_____
Street Address   Apt. #

_____
City   State   Zip

_____
E-mail Address

_____
Occupation

I'd like to be a surveyor for the following city:

_____

or a surveyor for Hotels, Resorts & Spas ☐

To order our guides as gift copies or spares, go to zagat.com/shop.

More to say? Join our special squad of savvy consumers to share your opinions in all kinds of compelling polls. To sign up, check the box below.

☐ YES, I want to participate in special Zagat polls throughout the year.

*　　*　　*

☐ This book was a gift　　☐ Bought by me　　☐ Surveyor copy

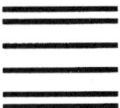

BUSINESS REPLY MAIL

FIRST-CLASS MAIL PERMIT NO 4064 NEW YORK, NY

POSTAGE WILL BE PAID BY ADDRESSEE

ZAGATSURVEY®
4 COLUMBUS CIRCLE FL 5
NEW YORK NY 10102-1374